BARsecrets:

An Essay Approach

for the Multistate Subjects

Dennis P. Saccuzzo

Nancy E. Johnson

Applications of Psychology to Law, Inc.
San Diego, California

All model answers, analyses and material other than fact patterns are the property of *Applications of Psychology to Law, Inc.* and may not be reproduced without permission.

Other books in the Bar Secrets® series:
   Hidden Issues – Beating the Bar at its own Game
   The Multistate Subjects
   The California-Specific Subjects
   Model Approach to Applying the Law
   The Essay Workbook
   An Essay Approach for the California-Specific Subjects
   The 1L Book
   The 2L Book

Federal Civil Procedure
Corporations - Federal Securities and the Common Law
Remedies
Professional Responsibility
Torts
Contracts & UCC Sales
Property
Criminal Law
Criminal Procedure
Constitutional Law
Evidence
California Community Property
California Wills & Trusts

FIRST EDITION, FIRST PRINTING.
Copyright © 2005 by Applications of Psychology to Law, Inc.

ISBN 1-933089-11-3

For further information, please contact *Applications of Psychology to Law, Inc.*
2341 Jefferson Street, Suite 101
San Diego, CA 92110

Telephone: 619.299.8525
FAX: 619.299.8527
E-mail: info@barsecrets.com

Contents

Acknowledgments

All fact patterns are from the California Bar's Committee of Bar Examiners. Pursuant to action taken on September 29, 2001, the California Bar waived all of its copyrights in its essay fact patterns beginning with the July 2001 Bar exam. The fact patterns and two selected answers for each question, written by Bar candidates who passed the Bar exam and wrote a good answer, are posted on the California Bar's web site (www.calbar.ca.gov).

We wish to express our gratitude to the California Bar's Committee of Bar Examiners, and particularly to Russell Carpenter, Dean Barbieri, and Gayle Murphy for their high degree of professionalism and for their prompt responsiveness to inquiries and requests for information.

We emphasize that we have no affiliation with the California Bar's Committee of Bar Examiners and that their waiver of copyright in no way indicates an endorsement of this work.

The California Bar's policy of posting its questions and selected answers reflects not only its openness and commitment to assisting Bar candidates, but also its commitment to free and equal access to examples and important study aids. The California Bar exam is known as one of the most difficult, if not the most difficult Bar exam in the country. Nevertheless, its processes and procedures are fair and for the most part open to public view. The California Bar's decision to make all parts of the written exam freely accessible to the public ensures that all candidates may have access to prior exam materials and levels the playing field insofar as every candidate has the opportunity to practice the format of the task. We believe this increases the validity of test results as a true indicator of competence and reduces the error in scores due to varying levels of opportunity to practice "examsmanship."

Memorizing the law is not enough: competence requires the ability to apply the law in specific formats, including essays, performance exams, and multiple choice items. Performance exams are also freely available through the California Bar's web site. The California Bar cannot release multiple-choice items from the Multistate Bar Exam (the MBE portion of the exam) because the National Conference of Bar Examiners (NCBE, a private corporation) copyrights those materials. NCBE sells the limited number of older MBE items they have chosen to release. For information, visit their web site at www.ncbex.org. Applications of Psychology to Law, Inc. has no affiliation with NCBE and does not endorse NCBE by providing this information.

Why You Must Learn to Apply the Law

The MBE, as well as the essays, emphasize application of the law, rather than rote memory of rules. By carefully studying these essays, you can learn how the law is applied to numerous everyday hypotheticals.

The Big Mistake Made by Law Students and Bar Candidates

One of the most common mistakes made by law students and Bar candidates is that they fail to learn how to apply the law. The reasoning goes something like this:

How can I answer an essay or multiple choice question unless I know the law? Because I don't know the law well enough, I must continue to memorize the rules.

Unfortunately, people who reason like this spend far too much time memorizing, and never really learn the law. Ironically, the reason they never learn the law is because they rarely, if ever, try to apply their knowledge. The truth is, the only way to learn the law is to apply it.

Why Memorizing Legal Principles Won't Work – It's Necessary but not Sufficient

Reading and re-reading, or memorizing and re-memorizing a rule of law is not the way to learn the law. If you want to learn the law, you must apply it to fact patterns. Indeed, law professors and Bar examiners do not ask students to regurgitate a rule of law or write a treatise in an area of law. Instead, they present you with a hypothetical fact pattern to evaluate how well you can apply your knowledge of the law to the given facts and analyze to a conclusion.

If this is what you're being tested on, then it makes no sense to spend most of your time memorizing legal principles. **You must practice for the type of problem you will be facing.** Taking thousands of MBEs and looking up the answer, while useful and necessary, is not the fastest way to learn how to apply the law to multiple choice and essay hypotheticals. By studying the models herein, you will greatly enhance the learning process.

Some Examples

Memorizing the law with little attention to its application would be like a baseball player spending 90% of his time lifting weights or doing pushups to become a better hitter, or a novice reading the rule book for the *Tour de France* to learn how to ride a bicycle. Although strength may be necessary to hit a long ball, the best way to learn to hit is to practice hitting. The best way to learn to ride a bicycle is to get on a bicycle and ride it. It is true that you might be awkard or even fall at first, but eventually you learn.

Consider another example. The rules of chess can be learned by just about anyone in less than an hour. Now who would make a better chess player – an enthusiast who studies and memorizes the rules again and again, perhaps even spending some time studying the history of chess, or the one who starts playing? In chess, as in law school and on the Bar exam, the best are those who are players. They practice applying their knowledge and, in so doing, learn the law much better and with much greater understanding than those who feel the need to go over the rules again and again at the expense of time applying them.

The Purpose of the Book

The purpose of *Bar Secrets: An Essay Approach for the Multistate Subjects* is to show you how the law is applied in a broad variety of contexts. The principles of law illustrated should prove invaluable for any law student or Bar candidate facing an essay or multiple choice exam. Careful study of these fact patterns and model answers will richly reward any law student or Bar candidate.

Why this Book is Essential Reading for Bar Candidates

For those taking any Bar exam, a careful study of these fact patterns, models, and commentaries is invaluable. Models that illustrate how to apply the major principles of law most commonly tested on Bar exams are provided and analyzed. Although most states, including California, recurrently test the same big issues again and again (for example, landlord/tenant, hearsay, subject matter jurisdiction, and defamation to name a few), the manner in which these topics are tested tends to change. Studying older fact patterns is not enough for most people.

What You Must Do to Succeed

Whether it's a law school exam or a Bar exam, to succeed on multiple choice as well as essay exams you must go back to the basics! Practice writing actual fact patterns in each subject, then check yourself by studying a well-written model. Augment this practice by issue-spotting several more fact patterns in each subject and again checking yourself by studying a well-written model. This book can and should be used for either or both of these purposes.

Two Approaches

One approach to using this book is to take the essays a subject at a time. Begin with a quick review of the subject, such as the combination outline/flow charts (schema) in the *Bar Secrets*® substantive law books. These law books present the rules of law as well as their exceptions, standards, elements and factors in a hierarchical format that mimics the way information is stored and retrieved by the human mind. It is a scientifically designed approach to law studies that will save you many long and frustrating hours.

With the overview in front of you to use as a reference, and as in an open-book test, read and answer the fact pattern. Then immediately check yourself to make sure you have identified the relevant issues and properly applied the relevant facts to them.

A second approach is to use the materials in your final study in the days just prior to the actual exam, after you've already written out at least two or three fact patterns as described above and made some effort to learn the relevant legal principles. In using this second approach, you should issue-spot the fact pattern closed-book. Read the fact pattern and on the right margin, jot down the issues as they appear. Then carefully study the model. Be sure to spend extra time reviewing any issue you missed or did not understand.

Source of Law for Models

Our sources of law for the models are the *Bar Secrets*® substantive law books, which reflect the majority rules in each subject area unless otherwise specified for a specific state. There are 4 substantive books: one covering the multi-state subjects (contracts, torts, property, evidence, constitutional law, criminal law, and criminal procedure), one covering the California-specific subjects [federal civil procedure, corporations (federal securities laws + common law), professional responsibility (ABA rules + California distinctions), remedies (majority rules), California community property, California wills, and trusts (majority rules)], a 1L book [covering contracts, torts, property, criminal law, and federal civil procedure], and a 2L book [covering evidence, constitutional law, criminal procedure, professional responsibility (ABA rules + California distinctions), California wills, and trusts (majority rules)]. For more information on these books, visit our website at http://www.barsecrets.com.

Our Approach to Multiple Choice Questions

Our approach to multiple choice questions involves a combination of studying the structure of the law, practicing and reviewing models, and taking actual released and simulated MBE questions. Actual released questions are available directly from the publisher, NCBE (www.ncbex.org). Many Multistate review companies also license these materials. Released questions and explanations can also be found in books such as *Strategies & Tactics for the MBE* (Walton & Emanuel – Aspen Law).

Step 1: <u>Begin with the structure of the law</u>.
The most systematic and efficient way to approach the MBE is to begin by learning the structure of the law, as presented in *Bar Secrets: The Multistate Subjects*. The structure of the law consists of rules, exceptions, definitions, standards, presumptions, elements, factors, and legal tests. *Bar Secrets: The Multistate Subjects* presents all of these for each of the 7 MBE subjects in an outline/flow chart. Please note that this outline/flow chart is the basic core you will need to have at your command. Once you master this basic core, you can then integrate any details or new learning into that core.

Step 2: Take practice MBE-type items.
Once you have a grip on the basic structure of the law, the next step is to take MBE-type questions. Initially you should read at a pace that is comfortable for you. With practice, you will get faster.

In the early stages, we recommend that you take each MBE-type question one at a time. Treat each of the 4 alternative answer choices as a separate true/false question. If you believe an answer choice is false, you should attempt to mentally articulate why the answer choice is incorrect (*e.g.,* misstates the law; assumes facts not in evidence; misstates the facts, etc.). With practice, you should improve in both speed and accuracy.

Step 3. Study *Bar Secrets: An Essay Approach for the Multistate Subjects*.
For best results, you should alternate between actual released or MBE-type questions and careful study of 2 or 3 of the model essay answers. The models will help you grasp the legal principles and their application at a much faster rate than if you relied only on unrelated and often esoteric multiple choice questions.

Remember, your studies and mastery are done in stages or "iterations." You go through all the subjects one at a time using the above 3 steps. You then repeat the process. Each time you will re-study the structure of the law, take additional essays, and study additional models. Quicken the pace as the exam date gets close.

Our Approach to Writing

The Multistate subjects are tested on the MBE and in many states on essays as well. Our approach to essay writing is straightforward, effective, and easy to learn. We begin with a very brief statement of the issue. Next, we discuss the relevant background law as extracted from the *Bar Secrets*® substantive books that contain combination outlines/flow charts in an organized manner. An outline contains the basic skeleton of the law, including definitions, rules, elements, factors, standards, and other important information. A flow chart is like a diagram or map. It illustrates the essential steps or basic decisions one might make in responding to an essay fact pattern. In our scientifically based approach to law studies we combine them by integrating flow charts into the outline, making the law more accessible than any other possible format.

These outlines/flow charts have many advantages. At a glance, they present the overall organization of the law and provide a tool into which you can integrate new knowledge. They function as excellent issue checklists to aid in spotting all issues raised by a fact pattern. They can also be used in the encoding (*i.e*, learning) and retrieval (*i.e.,* recall) process.

Background Law. From the background law comes the premise from which we begin. You should note the difference between presenting background law and the approach in a simple IRAC. In an IRAC format, one presents only the on-point rule of law, a tight-fitting premise from which to reason deductively based on the facts. The IRAC format, taught widely, gives the minimum law needed to analyze an issue. In our experience, the

IRAC approach, even when all the issues are covered, is not the best approach for achieving high scores on Bar or law exams.

In providing background law, we give more than the minimum on-point rule. Instead, we try to provide a broader context including any relevant standards, definitions, and factors where appropriate.

A definition tells what a term means. Generally, all legal terms of art should be defined. A standard tells us what is needed to prove a rule or element. For example, in defamation the standard for a defamatory statement is that it would tend to lower one's reputation in the community. Therefore, to show a statement is defamatory, it is necessary to use the facts to argue that the statement would tend to lower the plaintiff's reputation. Elements are the specifics that must be proven to make a prima facie case. Issues are triggered when there are facts that go to an element. Where there are elements, all must be proven to succeed on a cause of action.

Factors, by contrast, are the specific considerations a court will weigh in coming to a determination on an issue. It is not necessary to prove all the factors. Instead, they are evaluated in a balancing test.

In presenting background law, we attempt to provide relevant definitions, standards, elements, and factors. Then we identify exactly what is at issue in the fact pattern under consideration.

The Analysis. After presenting the background law, we skip a line (for good form and ease of reading) and give our analysis. A good analysis uses as many relevant facts as possible to argue a point. In basic terms, you must prove your case.

A common mistake is to be conclusory. A conclusory analysis begins with the law and then asserts, without proof or facts, that the case has been made. For example, one might give the definition of hearsay, followed by the conclusion that "here, we have hearsay." You must show why the statement is hearsay. If hearsay is an out of court statement offered to for its truth, you must show that you have an out of court statement, and that it is being offered for its truth. You do this by articulating in your answer where and/or when the statement was made, demonstrating that it was, in fact, made out of court. You then make a valid argument explaining why the statement is being offered for its truth.

In conducting your analysis, it is usually better to take a position and support it with facts and legal principles that to "ping pong" by arguing both sides. The vast majority of issues are clear one way or another. Coming up with strained counter arguments in such circumstances is counterproductive because it wastes time. It is only where an issue is arguable or unclear that both sides should be given. Even here, you must be decisive and come down on one side or the other.

Conclude with confidence. It is essential to articulate your conclusion, and with some confidence. For example, we have observed numerous selected answers from successful candidates on the California Bar's website that are just plain wrong, but are asserted with such confidence as to be convincing. By contrast, candidates who fail to conclude, or show uncertainty, are usually penalized with low scores.

Each of our models follows our suggested writing format. In consequence, the approach is illustrated repeatedly, making it easy to learn and adapt to your own personal style.

Strategies for Finishing

Needless to say, it is important to finish. Because of time constraints, it is not always possible or even desirable to routinely and mechanically follow the model approach. Instead, there are a number of good strategies that can be used in the middle of an answer to vary your style and finish.

First, you must realize the importance of **primacy effects**, or first impressions. Graders make up their minds quickly, and once made up, find it difficult to change. An answer that begins strongly, according to the suggested format with good, accurate background law, a strong analysis that uses the relevant facts to prove or disprove a point, and a confident conclusion is well on the way to a high score.

In the middle it is necessary to find a way to speed things up, because it is vitally important that you raise all colorable issues (*i.e.*, where some fact goes to at least one element of a prima facie case). This can be done in a number of ways. One is to enumerate the rule and elements, but rather than discuss each element, just go to the one that fails to show a particular case can be made. A second approach is to discuss the facts and merely imply, rather than articulate, the relevant law. There is even room for an occasional conclusory response for minor issues. Each of these approaches are illustrated, and you should try to note when they are used to get a better idea how to use these strategies to cover your bases in terms of issue-spotting, and also finish the essay.

Bar Exams

Bar exams vary in length from 1 ½ to 3 days. Time allowed for essays varies from ½ to 1 full hour for each essay. For more information on a specific state's exam format, you can visit their website. The California Bar is a 3-day test, with 6 one-hour essays, given from 9 – 12 on Tuesday and Thursday mornings. The format for the California Bar exam, and its scoring procedures, are discussed in detail in *Bar Secrets: The California-Specific Subjects.*

CONTRACTS

Pure Contracts (always with remedies issues):

Crossover Questions:

Contracts + Torts + Professional Responsibility:

FEBRUARY 2005 CALIFORNIA BAR EXAM -- QUESTION 2

1-HOUR ESSAY

PC manufactures computers. Mart operates electronics stores.

On August 1, after some preliminary discussions, PC sent a fax on PC letterhead to Mart stating:

> We agree to fill any orders during the next six months for our Model X computer (maximum of 4,000 units) at $1,500 each.

On August 10, Mart responded with a fax stating:

> We're pleased to accept your proposal. Our stores will conduct an advertising campaign to introduce the Model X computer to our customers.

On September 10, Mart mailed an order to PC for 1,000 Model X computers. PC subsequently delivered them. Mart arranged with local newspapers for advertisements touting the Model X. The advertising was effective, and the 1,000 units were sold by the end of October.

On November 2, Mart mailed a letter to PC stating:

> Business is excellent. Pursuant to our agreement, we order 2,000 more units.

On November 3, before receiving Mart's November 2 letter, PC sent the following fax to Mart:

> We have named Wholesaler as our exclusive distributor. All orders must now be negotiated through Wholesaler.

After Mart received the fax from PC, it contacted Wholesaler to determine the status of its order. Wholesaler responded that it would supply Mart with all the Model X computers that Mart wanted, but at a price of $1,700 each.

On November 15, Mart sent a fax to PC stating:

> We insist on delivery of our November 2 order for 2,000 units of Model X at the contract price of $1,500 each. We also hereby exercise our right to purchase the remaining 1,000 units of Model X at that contract price.

PC continues to insist that all orders must be negotiated through Wholesaler, which still refuses to sell the Model X computers for less than $1,700 each.

1. If Mart buys the 2,000 Model X computers ordered on November 2 from Wholesaler for $1,700 each, can it recover the $200 per unit price differential from PC?

2. Is Mart entitled to buy the 1,000 Model X computers ordered on November 15 for $1,500 each? Discuss.

Call 1. Can Mart Recover from PC?

For Mart to recover from PC, they must show that a valid contract was formed and the applicable law pertaining to that contract supports that claim.

Applicable Law

The UCC applies to the sale of goods. All other contracts are governed by the common law. Goods are things that are moveable at time of identification to the contract.

At issue is a purported contract between Mart and PC involving the sale of computers by PC to Mart. Because computers are moveable things, they are goods and the UCC will apply.

Special Merchant Rules

Where the UCC applies, there are special rules pertaining to merchants. Merchants are persons who deal in or have special knowledge of the kinds of goods involved in the transaction.

Facts stipulate that PC manufactures computers. As a manufacturer, PC would be a merchant because to manufacture a good would require specialized knowledge. Mart operates electronics stores and is in the business of selling computers. As such, they too would have specialized knowledge in the goods at issue and would be considered merchants. Therefore, the special merchant rules would apply.

Contract Validity

A valid contract requires offer, acceptance, and consideration.

Offer

An offer is a manifestation of present intent to enter into a bargain, communicated in definite and certain terms. Under the UCC, only the quantity term need be specific. An offer confers the power to create a contract by taking specific action.

PC sent a fax on PC letterhead to Mart agreeing to fill any order during the next 6 months for their Model X computer up to a maximum of 4,000 units at $1500 each. The terms were definite in that PC specified a particular model at a particular price for up to a specific number of units. The quantity term was not a fixed quantity, but rather up to a maximum of 4,000. This would be a type of requirements contract in which the quantity term is the buyer's requirement or need of some good. In a requirements contract, the quantity term is considered to be the buyer's requirements, and therefore such contracts are considered valid under the UCC. The language used by PC, "We agree to fill any order . . ." along with such specific and definite terms leaves no doubt that PC has invited acceptance by Mart. As such, the offer is valid.

Merchant Firm Offer

Under the UCC, a signed written offer by a merchant is irrevocable without consideration. On August 1 PC agreed to fill any orders for the next 6 months.

Although no facts indicate that the offer was signed, it was on PC letterhead and Mart would have a good argument that the firm offer rule should apply.

Acceptance

Under the UCC, acceptance may be made by any reasonable manner and any reasonable means under the circumstances. Mart responded with a fax, the same medium used by PC. They did so 9 days later with a clear, unequivocal statement "We're pleased to accept your proposal." The medium used, the timing, and the clarity of Mart's response are indicative of an unequivocal acceptance of PC's offer and terms. Therefore the acceptance is valid.

Acceptance with Different and Additional Terms

Mart's acceptance was followed by a statement that their stores would conduct an advertising campaign to introduce the Model X computer to their customers. Arguably this could be construed as an acceptance with an additional term. Under the UCC, an expression of acceptance is valid even though it states different or additional terms unless acceptance is made conditional upon them. Even if Mart's advertising campaign is considered an additional term, no facts indicate that Mart made its acceptance conditional upon Mart conducting an advertising campaign. Therefore the acceptance is valid.

Under the UCC, among merchants additional terms will become part of the contract unless the offer expressly limits acceptance to the terms of the offer, or the additional term materially alters it, or notice of objection is made within a reasonable time. No facts indicate an express limitation to the offer or notice of objection. Moreover, PC will still get its price of $1500 per unit, so the advertising campaign does not materially alter PC's bargain. Therefore, the advertising campaign may be considered part of the contract.

Consideration

Consideration is a promise or act in exchange for a promise or act in which there is legal detriment. The elements are bargained-for exchange and legal detriment.

When PC agreed to fill orders for their Model X computer, they bargained to sell up to 4,000 units at $1500 per unit. Mart's acceptance bargained to buy up to 4,000 units at $1500 per unit. Therefore there was bargained-for exchange. PC incurred the legal detriment of having to sell up to 4,000 units. Arguably, Mart incurred no legal detriment. However, under the UCC in a requirements contract consideration is found in the assumption that the parties will act in good faith. Moreover, assuming that Mart's advertising campaign is an additional term, Mart is incurring the legal detriment of paying to advertise PC's product. Indeed, Mart arranged with local newspapers for advertisements touting the Model X computer. Thus there was valid consideration based on the bargained-for exchange and Mart's legal detriment to either act in good faith or conduct the advertising campaign.

Conclusion. A valid contract was formed.

Statute of Frauds

Contracts for the sale of goods of $500 or more fall under the Statute of Frauds and are unenforceable absent a written agreement. This contract is for up to 4,000 units at $1500 apiece, well over the $500 requirement. Absent a written agreement, the contract is unenforceable. Facts indicate only 2 faxes, an offer faxed by PC on PC letterhead and an acceptance faxed by Mart. The agreement, however, was not reduced to writing. Absent an exception, the contract will be unenforceable.

Exception: Written Confirmation

Under the UCC, unless written objection is received within 10 days, a written confirmation between merchants sent within a reasonable time is an exception to the requirement of a writing imposed by the Statute of Frauds.

On August 10 Mart sent a fax to PC accepting their proposal. The fax was sent within 9 days, a reasonable time, and both PC and Mart are merchants. Mart's fax therefore qualifies as a written confirmation.

Exception: Sufficient Memo Signed by the Party to be Charged

A written offer signed by the party to be charged also suffices as a sufficient memo. Although no facts indicate PC actually signed its faxed offer, the offer was on PC letterhead. Moreover, modern fax machines generally print the identity of the sender. Therefore Mart has a very good argument that the identity of PC is very clear and equivalent to a signed memo, even if there isn't an actual signature on the fax.

Additional Evidence of a Contract

Under the UCC, conduct by the parties which recognizes the existence of a contract is sufficient to establish a contract. On Sept. 10, Mart mailed an order for 1,000 Model X computers and PC delivered them, so the conduct of both parties recognized and confirmed the existence of a contract between them.

Attempted Modification

Under the UCC, modifications of a contract require no consideration as long as the parties act in good faith (contrary to the common law, where modification requires new consideration). Where the original contract is covered by the Statute of Frauds, any modification must also be in writing.

On Nov. 3rd PC sent a fax to Mart stating that all orders must now be negotiated through Wholesaler. This requirement would modify the contract, under which PC agreed to fill any orders. This attempted modification would fail for 2 reasons. First, it does not comply with the Statute of Frauds because there is no subsequent agreement reduced to writing, and no facts indicate acceptance or written confirmation signed by Mart, the party to be charged. Second, the alteration does not appear to be commercially reasonable because it is not fair to insist that Mart would now have to negotiate with Wholesaler after it has already negotiated all terms with PC. It could be fair if Wholesaler would abide by the quantity and price terms in the negotiated agreement, but it would not be fair if Wholesaler changed the terms. Nor would it be reasonable or honest if PC turned over its control to Wholesaler after having agreed upon its terms with Mart, without ensuring that those terms would be honored by Wholesaler.

Anticipatory Repudiation

Anticipatory repudiation is definite and unequivocal language that a party intends not to perform. The aggrieved party can await performance or resort to breach remedies.

On Nov. 2nd following its successful advertising campaign, Mart mailed a letter to PC ordering 2,000 additional units pursuant to their agreement. However, after Mart received the fax from PC the next day, it contacted Wholesaler to determine the status of its order. Wholesaler demanded a price of $1700 per unit. This was a notification that Wholesaler did not intend to perform in the manner agreed upon in the MART-PC contract. Thus, in turning over distribution to Wholesaler, PC repudiated the contract. Mart did not resort to breach remedies but instead attempted to get adequate assurances from PC.

Breach

Breach is an unjustified failure to perform an absolute duty. A major or material breach is one that goes to the basis of the bargain. Such a breach occurs where the non-breaching party does not receive the substantial benefit of his bargain. It excuses the injured party's counter-performance and allows a right to damages.

On Nov. 15th Mart demanded adequate assurance by sending a fax to PC insisting that their Nov. 2nd order for 2,000 units be sold at the contract price of $1500 each. However, PC continued to insist that orders be negotiated through Wholesaler, which refuses to sell for less than $1700 per unit. PC had a duty to perform under the original terms and by insisting that Mart deal with Wholesaler under different terms, PC has unjustifiedly failed to perform. Because price of the Model X computer was the basis of Mart's negotiations and bargain with PC, this is a major breach. Therefore Mart will be entitled to contract remedies under the UCC.

Remedies

An aggrieved party under a contract is entitled to his expectation, or the benefit of his bargain. Where a seller breaches, the buyer is entitled to the cost to cover minus the contract price, plus incidentals and consequentials (damages that are reasonably foreseeable at the time of contract).

The contract price is $1500 per unit. To cover, Mart would be required to purchase the computers for $1700 each because Wholesaler is now the exclusive distributor. Therefore Mart would be entitled to the cover price of $1700 minus the contract price of $1500, or $200 per unit. If Mart purchases the 2,000 Model X computers ordered on Nov., 2nd for $1700 each, it can in fact recover the $200 per unit price differential from PC.

Call 2. Is Mart entitled to buy the 1000 Model X computers?

The PC-Mart agreement specified that Mart had the right to purchase a maximum of 4,000 Model X computers at $1500 each for the next 6 months, beginning on Aug. 1. Mart ordered 1000 on Sept. 10th and 2,000 more on Nov. 2nd. They were therefore entitled to order 1000 more within 6 months of Aug. 1.

On Nov. 15th, well within the 6-month time frame, Mart properly exercised its right to purchase the remaining 1,000 units of Model X at the contract price. PC refused, and Mart has at least 2 theories that would entitle them to purchase the remaining 1,000 – specific performance and replevin.

Specific Performance

Mart would be entitled to specifically enforce the contract if they can meet the following elements: inadequate legal remedy or other proper circumstances, definite and certain terms, feasibility of enforcement, mutuality, and no defenses.

Inadequate Legal Remedy

Wholesaler is the exclusive distributor. If they or PC refuse to sell the additional 1,000 Model X computers to Mart, then Mart would have no other way to get the Model X computers they advertised to their customers. If Mart is able to cover through Wholesaler at $1700 apiece, then they could sue for the difference and the legal remedy would be adequate. If, however, they cannot cover, then the legal remedy would be inadequate because the Model X computer would be considered unique chattel. Thus if Mart is to specifically enforce the contract both PC and Wholesaler must refuse to sell them to Mart. Assuming this was to happen, Mart must still meet the remaining elements.

Definite and Certain Terms

As discussed above, the terms were definite and certain.

Feasibility of Enforcement

The contract is not a personal services or employment contract. Enforcement would merely involve the transfer of previously-contracted-for goods that are apparently available. Therefore the court can enforce the contract using its power of contempt.

Mutuality

The modern rule is the security of performance test, which asks whether plaintiff's performance can be secured to the satisfaction of the court. Again, the court can use its power of contempt to order Mart to pay $1500 per unit if it orders PC to deliver the 1000 units to Mart.

Defenses

The only possible defense is the Statute of Frauds, discussed above. If for any reason PC has a valid defense, Mart can sue under a detrimental reliance theory. Under this theory, the courts will enforce a promise if reliance is reasonable, detrimental, and foreseeable, where enforcement is necessary to prevent injustice. PC made a promise, its offer. It was reasonable for Mart to rely on a written promise by a merchant; they relied to their detriment by conducting an advertising campaign; and the reliance was foreseeable given that PC is a merchant and was put on notice by Mart that it intended to rely by advertising. Enforcement would be necessary because it would not be just to allow PC to avoid its obligations.

Under a contract theory, if Mart cannot cover, they will be entitled to buy 1,000 Model X computers for $1500 each. Under a reliance theory, the court will fashion an equitable remedy, which may include specific performance or Mart's actual damages, at the court's discretion.

Replevin

A second theory that Mart could use is replevin. This theory requires goods identified to the contract and the buyer's inability to cover after reasonable effort. As discussed above, the computers were in fact identified to the contract. Therefore, if Mart cannot cover after reasonable efforts, they would be entitled to the 1,000 Model X computers under this legal theory as well.

1-Hour Essay

Travelco ran a promotional advertisement which included a contest, promising to fly the contest winner to Scotland for a one-week vacation. Travelco's advertisement stated: "The winner's name will be picked at random from the telephone book for this trip to 'Golfer's Heaven.' If you're in the book, you will be eligible for this dream vacation!"

After reading Travelco's advertisement, Polly had the telephone company change her unlisted number to a listed one just in time for it to appear in the telephone book that Travelco used to select the winner. Luckily for Polly, her name was picked, and Travelco notified her. That night Polly celebrated her good fortune by buying and drinking an expensive bottle of champagne.

The next day Polly bought new luggage and costly new golfing clothes for the trip. When her boss refused to give her a week's unpaid leave so she could take the trip, she quit, thinking that she could look for a new job when she returned from Scotland.

After it was too late for Polly to retract her job resignation, Travelco advised her that it was no longer financially able to award the free trip that it had promised.

Polly sues for breach of contract and seeks to recover damages for the following: (1) the cost of listing her telephone number; (2) the champagne; (3) the luggage and clothing; (4) loss of her job; and (5) the value of the trip to Scotland.

1. What defenses should Travelco assert on the merits of Polly's breach of contract claim, and what is the likely outcome? Discuss.

2. Which items of damages, if any, is Polly likely to recover? Discuss.

JULY 2002, QUESTION 4
CONTRACTS

-- Written by Dennis P. Saccuzzo & Nancy E. Johnson

Commentary:

As in all Bar questions, it is important to be responsive to the question. Notice that there are two calls. The first asks for defenses. A weak response to this question would be one that followed an outline and talked about offer, acceptance and consideration without framing these issues in terms of Travelco's defenses, e.g. the lack of an offer, lack of consideration, and so forth. Call 2 asks for damages for 5 different items. As always when the Bar gives multiple items or parties, it is essential to distinguish among the items to demonstrate knowledge of the subtleties of the law.

This was a difficult contracts question because there are at least two theories of offer and no clear facts giving rise to acceptance. The Bar looked favorably on answers that found an offer, and the key to offer was establishing that there were definite and certain terms. The model answer that follows considers 2 possible offers, the offer of a chance to win a trip (the advertisement) and the actual notification that P had won. However, both selected answers considered only one possible offer, which was sufficient for a high score.

The next big issue was whether there was consideration. Again, the analysis of consideration was not a simple matter because it was necessary to look at what Travelco was actually bargaining for. It was arguable whether Travelco was bargaining for P to put her name in the phone book, and they certainly did not bargain for her to make the various purchases that she did. Therefore Travelco's defense of lack of consideration is strong.

To get a high score on this question, it was necessary to thoroughly analyze the alternate theory of promissory estoppel. A strong answer would enumerate the elements of promissory estoppel and within a sub-headnote for each element, discuss the facts that go to it.

Finally, as indicated, it is essential to distinguish among the various items for which Polly sought damages. Notice that the main issues were reasonableness and foreseeability; the 5 items differed in terms of their reasonableness and foreseeability. Finally, it was possible to distinguish between damages as a result of breach of contract and those that would result based on reliance theory, as illustrated in the answer that follows.

goods = moveable personal property

Model Answer

Applicable Law

The common law applies to all contracts except those covered by the UCC. The UCC applies to contracts for the sale of goods, with goods defined as movable personal property. The contract at issue involves a prize of a trip to Scotland, which is not a good. Therefore, the common law applies.

Call 1. Travelco's Defenses to Breach of Contract

Travelco's main defense is that there was no contract. Valid contract formation requires offer, acceptance, and consideration.

Lack of Offer

An offer requires manifestation of present intent to enter a bargain, communicated in definite and certain terms. An offer confers the power to create a contract by taking specific action.

Normally, public advertisements are not considered offers, but rather invitations or proposals soliciting offers. Travelco will argue that their ad was not an offer, but merely a solicitation to attract customers who would then offer to buy their services. The problem for Travelco is that their terms were very definite and certain: the contest winner's name would be picked from the telephone book, there would be only one winner, the prize was a trip to Scotland, and anyone in the phone book was eligible. Under an objective theory, such definite terms usually indicate to an ordinary person that she would have the power to create a contract by taking specified action.

Because the terms were definite and certain and reasonably conferred on Polly the power to create a contract by acting to put her name in the phone book, Polly has a strong argument that there was a valid offer of a chance to win a trip to Scotland. Even if the ad itself was not an offer, when Travelco notified Polly that she had won, they again presented in definite and certain terms an offer of a trip. In either case, there is an offer and this defense will fail. *Even if Ad fails as offer, notification can provide evidence of an offer.*

Lack of Valid Acceptance

Under the common law, valid acceptance is an unconditional assent to be bound by the offer. Polly has a problem in that no facts indicate acceptance.

If the offer stems from the definite and certain terms of the ad, then she can argue that the Travelco ad was a unilateral contract in that it called for acceptance by performance rather than acceptance by a counter-promise, as in a bilateral contract. Where there is a unilateral contract, part performance creates an option contract so that the offer cannot be withdrawn. The issue is whether listing her number in the telephone book constituted performance. No clear facts indicate that Travelco actually solicited new telephone listings, so this is not Polly's best argument. *Unilateral K* *option K*

If the offer was the notification that she had won, Polly's argument that she validly accepted is stronger. Her subsequent conduct in purchasing champagne, luggage, and clothing indicate that she accepted the offer of the trip.

Lack of Consideration

Travelco's best argument is that there is no contract because there was no consideration. Consideration involves bargained-for exchange and legal detriment by both parties.

what were they bargaining for?

Travelco will argue that both their ad promising to fly the contest winner to Scotland and their notification that Polly had won were both nothing more than gratuitous promises in that they did not bargain for any legal detriment from Polly. Nor did Polly suffer any legal detriment. Again the issue is whether Travelco bargained for Polly to put her number in the phone book. If they did, then Polly's act of listing her number constituted both acceptance and consideration, because providing a telephone listing to the public leads to numerous unsolicited calls, including marketing calls from travel agencies such as Travelco.

gratitors promise

detriment to Polly

Polly can also argue that there was bargained-for exchange when she accepted the offer of a trip. Travelco was bargaining for publicity and received it when it publicly awarded a valuable prize. However, Travelco has a good argument that it was not bargaining for the detriment Polly incurred when she purchased the champagne, luggage, and clothing. Even if Polly loses on the consideration argument, she will prevail on the alternate theory of promissory estoppel.

Promissory Estoppel

-A promise which creates: reasonable, detrimental reliance that is foreseeable. -necessary to prevent injustice

When consideration is not found, the court will still enforce promises under a theory of promissory estoppel. It requires a promise and reliance that is reasonable, detrimental, and foreseeable. The court will enforce the promise as necessary to prevent injustice.

Promise: Travelco promised to award a trip to Scotland and then promised the trip to Polly when they notified her she had won.

Reliance: Polly had no reason to doubt Travelco, so her reliance was reasonable. She suffered detriment with all of her purchases and, as discussed below, at least some of the detriment she suffered was foreseeable.

Enforcement Necessary: As discussed below, Polly was damaged and enforcement will be necessary to redress the harm.

Because Polly can meet the elements of promissory estoppel, Travelco will be estopped from asserting the defense of lack of consideration. As discussed below, the court will award either contract/expectation damages or reliance damages.

Court may award breach of contract (expectation) damages or reliance damages.

Other Defenses

Travelco will also fail under other possible defenses. <u>Revocation of offer</u> <u>will not work because they had made the offer when they notified her that she had won, and she had accepted before Travelco had a chance to withdraw,</u> as discussed above.

<u>Unilateral mistake</u> is generally not a defense and the narrow range of exceptions that allow it to be a defense normally apply to mistakes by contractors and are not applicable here.

No facts indicate <u>impossibility</u>; <u>simply not being financially able to award a free trip</u> <u>would not make this objectively impossible for Travelco unless they were bankrupt.</u> Likewise, <u>commercial impracticability</u> is not indicated by the facts.

Finally, the Statute of Frauds is irrelevant here because the contract, if it exists, can be completed within one year.

Call 2: Polly's damages.

<u>Polly's damages will depend in part on whether a contract is found or whether her</u> <u>claim is based on promissory estoppel (reliance). If promissory estoppel is applied,</u> <u>Polly may get either her expectation or reliance damages, based on what best serves</u> <u>the interests of justice.</u>

1. Listing her number in the telephone directory

[margin note: Contract Theory:]

If a contract is found, then listing the number could be considered part of the consideration and Polly would not be entitled to recover the cost. Moreover, under a contract theory Polly would be awarded her expectation, the value of the trip. Because listing her number is an expense she would have incurred as part of the bargain, she would not be entitled to reimbursement.

[margin note: Promissory Estoppel Theory:]

On a promissory estoppel theory, the issue would be whether <u>the promise of a</u> <u>chance at winning a trip could reasonably and foreseeably have induced detrimental</u> <u>reliance, and whether justice would require that Polly be compensated.</u> Given the wording in the ad, "if you're in the book, you will be eligible for this dream vacation!" it is foreseeable that <u>some individuals would have their numbers listed in</u> <u>order to be eligible.</u> Making the listing is reasonable, given the value of the prize, and it is detrimental because it <u>incurs not only a fee for the change but also some loss of</u> <u>privacy.</u> Unless Polly is given the value of the trip she won, justice would require her being reimbursed for her reliance.

2. Expensive bottle of champagne

[margin note: consequential Damages:]

Under a <u>contract theory, the champagne was not part of the bargain and would not</u> <u>be awarded as expectation</u> damages. However, the champagne could be construed as a <u>consequential</u> damage (*i.e.*, reasonably foreseeable at the time of contract). It is reasonably foreseeable that if someone wins an expensive dream vacation, she might buy an expensive bottle of champagne to celebrate. Therefore, under a contract theory she would not only be awarded her expectation (the value of the trip), but she could also recover the cost of the champagne as a consequential damage because she lost money she would not otherwise have spent.

Under a reliance theory the analysis would again be similar in that the purchase of expensive champagne is reasonably foreseeable reaction and Polly suffered detriment. However, if she is awarded the trip, the interests of justice may not require reimbursement for the champagne because she would have incurred this expense anyway.

3. New luggage and costly new golfing clothes

Under contract theory, Polly did not bargain for luggage and clothing, so these would not be considered part of her expectation damages. As consequential damages, the issue would be whether the new luggage and costly new golfing clothes were reasonably foreseeable. Although new luggage may be reasonably foreseeable, costly golfing clothes may not. It does not seem objectively reasonable or foreseeable to buy costly clothing to be used for a one-week trip.

Under a reliance theory, the analysis would be similar. Polly is not likely to be compensated for costly new golf clothes but may receive the cost of the luggage as an out-of-pocket expense, unless she is awarded the trip.

If she owns the trip — No consequentials because she would have incurred those expenses anyway.

4. Quitting her job

Quitting a job for a one-week vacation is not reasonable and not foreseeable. Polly will not be compensated for this regardless of the theory used.

5. The value of the trip to Scotland

As indicated, the value of the trip would represent Polly's expectation damages and would be awarded under a contract theory. Because money damages would be adequate to compensate Polly, she would not be entitled to specific performance.

Under a reliance theory, Polly would be entitled to her reasonably foreseeable out-of-pocket expenses as discussed above, but may not get the value of the trip. She would certainly not get both. Contract allows recovery of expectation plus consequential damages and incidentals. Reliance damages are more limited and are designed to put the person in the position they would have been in had there been no contract. Compensating Polly for the expenses she incurred would accomplish the goal of reliance damages. However, in the court's discretion, she could be awarded the value of the trip and not the out-of-pocket expenses that she would have incurred anyway had she been awarded the trip.

Consequentials must be reasonably Foreseeable.

— Contract allows recovery of Expectation plus consequentials + incidentals.

— Reliance damages are more limited and are designed to put the person in the position they would have been in had there been no contract.

FEBRUARY 2000 CALIFORNIA BAR EXAM -- QUESTION 5

1-Hour Exam

In January, in response to an inquiry, Seller sent Buyer a letter offering to sell 10,000 tires, assorted sizes to be selected by Seller and delivered at the rate of 1,000 each month for ten months. This letter stated the price for each size and specified that payment was due on delivery of each shipment. Buyer sent a letter agreeing to purchase 10,000 tires, assortment to be specified by Buyer. Buyer's letter contained its standard provision that any disputes arising under the agreement were to be resolved by commercial arbitration. *Arbitration clause* The letter also contained Buyer's specification of the size assortment for the first month's shipment of tires.

On February 1, Seller's driver arrived with the first installment, which consisted of the assortment specified in Buyer's letter. The driver left the tires without asking for payment. Four days later Buyer sent Seller a check for the first installment and a letter specifying the assortment for the second installment. On March 1, Seller's driver arrived with the second installment, again containing the assortment specified in Buyer's letter. Again the driver left the tires without getting payment.

Three days later Buyer sent a check for the second installment and specifications for the third installment. On April 1, Seller's driver arrived, but the assortment was not exactly what Buyer had specified. Buyer accepted the tires anyway and seven days later sent a check for the third installment, along with specifications for the fourth installment.

On May 1, Seller's driver arrived, again with an assortment that was not exactly what Buyer had specified. Buyer agreed to take delivery, but Seller's driver insisted on payment. When Buyer was unable to pay, Seller's driver refused to leave the tires and took them back to Seller's warehouse.

Buyer called Seller to complain about the driver's refusal to leave the tires and insisted upon immediate redelivery. Buyer said he would pay "as usual, a few days after delivery." Seller refused and told Buyer, "If you don't like it, why don't you take me to arbitration?" Buyer replied, "Look, I have no intention of arbitrating this dispute. But I'm not accepting that last shipment unless it meets my specifications precisely and unless you allow me the same leeway for payment as with past shipments."

Seller sued Buyer for breach of contract. Buyer simultaneously filed a counterclaim against Seller and moved the court for an order staying the suit and compelling arbitration. Seller opposed the motion.

1. How should the court rule on the motion for an order staying the suit and compelling arbitration? Discuss.

2. What are the rights and obligations of Seller and Buyer, and who should prevail on the merits of the litigation? Discuss.

February 2000 California Bar – Question 5
Model Answer Written by Professor Dennis P. Saccuzzo

CALL 1 – Motion Compelling Arbitration

UCC

The UCC applies to contracts for the sale of goods, which means things moveable at the time of identification to the contract. Because tires are moveable things, the UCC will apply.

Merchant

The UCC has special rules for merchants. A merchant is a person who deals in goods of the kind involved in the transaction. Seller and Buyer negotiated and then dealt with a contract involving a large quantity of tires (10,000). They will be held as merchants and the special UCC rules for merchants will apply to them.

Is there a contract?

[handwritten margin note: Always analyze whether there's a valid contract.]

In order to determine if the arbitration clause applies it is necessary to ascertain whether the clause was part of a valid contract. A valid contract requires offer, acceptance, and consideration.

Offer

An offer is a manifestation of present intent to enter a bargain communicated to an offeree in definite and certain terms. An offer confers the power in an offeree to create a contract. Under the UCC, the only essential term of an offer is the quantity term. The court can use gap fillers to fill in missing terms based on course of performance, course of dealing, trade usage, and principles of good faith and fair dealing.

The facts indicate that Buyer sent Seller a letter offering to sell 10,000 tires, assorted sizes to be selected by Seller, and delivered in 10 equal monthly installments. The offer letter contained the quantity term and was communicated to the offeree. Thus, there was a valid offer, the terms of which will be discussed below.

Acceptance and Effect of Different and Additional Terms

[handwritten margin note: UCC – keep Acceptance can be given in any reasonable manner.]

Acceptance is an unconditional assent to be bound by the offer. Under the UCC an offer is construed as inviting acceptance in any reasonable manner.

Buyer sent a letter agreeing to purchase 10,000 tires, assortment to be specified by the buyer, along with an arbitration clause. Under the UCC, an expression of acceptance is valid even though it states terms additional to or different from the offer, unless acceptance is made conditional upon them. Thus, although Buyer's term that Buyer specifies assortment is different from Seller's (Seller specifies) and the arbitration clause is an additional term, Buyer's acceptance is valid since Buyer did not make his acceptance conditioned upon the additional and different terms.

Consideration

Consideration is promises or acts in exchange for promises or acts in which there is legal detriment. Buyer and Seller bargained a promise of money for a promise of tires. Buyer has the legal detriment of paying for the tires, Seller the legal detriment of delivering the tires. Thus there is consideration.

Conclusion: A valid contract exists. The issue is, did the arbitration clause become a term of the contract.

Additional Terms: Arbitration Clause

Between merchants, additional or different terms will become part of the contract unless (1) the offer expressly limits acceptance to the terms of the offer; (2) the terms materially alter it; or (3) the seller objects in a reasonable time.

No facts indicate that Seller's offer expressly limited acceptance to its terms or that Seller objected. In fact, Seller appears to have endorsed arbitration and may have waived his rights to object when he goaded Buyer to take him to arbitration. The issue is whether the addition of an arbitration clause materially alters the contract. Under the UCC a material alteration occurs where it results in surprise or hardship if incorporated without the express awareness of the other party, such as a clause negating warranties. Here, the clause refers to a remedy that is widely accepted and used in commercial and noncommercial settings. Further, the clause does not affect the basis of the bargain. Therefore it does not materially alter the contract and should become part of it.

Conclusion: The court will rule for Buyer and compel arbitration.

CALL 2. Rights and Obligations of Buyer and Seller

Different Terms   under UCC

As indicated, the existence of different terms does not negate the contract. Even if it did, under the UCC conduct by the parties that recognizes the existence of a contract is sufficient to establish a contract. Where the terms differ, the terms will be those on which the parties agree supplemented by other UCC provisions, including course of performance, course of dealing, and trade usage.

The parties agreed to the sale and purchase of 10,000 tires of assorted sizes to be delivered in installments of 1,000 for each of 10 months. These terms are thus part of the contract because both parties agreed on them.

The terms to which both parties did not expressly agree are: (1) assorted sizes to be selected by Seller versus assortment to be specified by Buyer; and (2) payment on delivery (Seller's term; Buyer silent on this issue).

(1) Assortment selected by . . .

The court will strike the terms upon which the parties disagree and attempt to fashion a contract based on course of performance, course of dealing, and trade usage.

On Feb. 1 and March 1, first and second installments were as specified by Buyer. However, on April 1 and May 1, assortment was not as specified by Buyer but Buyer accepted anyway. Because of these conflicts, course of performance does not present a clear picture. No facts indicate a prior course of dealings. The arbitrator could use trade usage. However, neither party is in a clear breach under the facts.

(2) Payment on delivery – Waiver

Waiver

Seller's terms called for payment on delivery. Even if this term was part of the contract, Buyer will successfully argue that Seller waived his rights to the provision under the contract. A waiver is a voluntary relinquishment of a right. No consideration is required. On Feb. 1, Mar. 1, and Apr. 1 the driver left without asking for payment. Buyer subsequently sent a check that Seller accepted without complaint. Seller waived his rights.

Estoppel

A waiver may be retracted at any time. Seller will argue that he retracted the waiver on May 1. The arbitrator will hold in favor of Buyer if Buyer can show that he detrimentally relied on the earlier waiver. Facts show that Buyer needed leeway and Seller gave him leeway on Feb. 1, Mar. 1, and Apr. 1. Thus, he had a right to expect some leeway and Seller will be estopped from retracting his waiver. The condition will be excused, and Seller will be in breach. Facts indicate he needed leeway. He was given the leeway on Feb. 1, Mar. 1 and Apr. 1. Thus he had a right to expect some leeway, and Seller will be estopped from retracting his waiver.

Breach

A breach is an unjustified failure to perform an absolute duty.

Material breach goes to basis of the bargain.

Seller had an absolute duty to deliver 1000 tires. Buyer agreed to accept an installment of 1000 tires that had been selected by Seller and that did not meet Buyer's specifications. Seller delivered the tires but then took them back. He breached his agreement. The breach is material because it goes to the basis of the bargain.

Remedy in Installment Contract

In an installment contract divisible units of the contract are delivered and accepted in separate lots. Buyer will have a right to sue under the breached May 1 installment and receive his expectation of 1000 tires or the cost of cover plus incidentals. Buyer may then continue under the contract if he chooses.

In order to cancel an installment contract entirely, Buyer must show that Seller's breach substantially impaired the whole value of the contract. This is unlikely because a problem with one lot of 1000 probably does not affect another.

Conclusion: Seller waived his right to payment on delivery and breached on the May 1 installment. Buyer is entitled to his expectation, as discussed, and can continue the contract with assortment selected according to trade usage or as can be determined by the arbitrator on the basis of principles under the UCC, including commercial reasonableness, fair dealing, and good faith.

1-Hour Exam

Susan is the Chief Operating Officer of WestTel, a telecommunications company. Felix is the Chief Executive Officer of CodeCo, a software company. About a year ago, Susan and Felix negotiated and signed a valid written contract under which WestTel purchased from CodeCo a license to use and sell software that prevents interception of telephone communications during transmission. Susan was assisted in the negotiations by Larry, an in-house attorney then employed by WestTel.

Throughout the negotiations, WestTel insisted that the license from CodeCo be an exclusive license for WestTel to use and sell the software in the national cellular telephone market. The only language bearing on the subject in the contract stated that, "WestTel shall have the use" of the software. The contract contained a clause stating that the written contract represents the entire agreement of the parties.

Susan was given oral assurances by Felix that the language quoted above would be interpreted by CodeCo to mean that WestTel was granted the exclusive license and that CodeCo would not license the software to others in the national cellular telephone market. Larry advised Susan that he was satisfied with Felix's oral assurances.

Last week, Susan saw an ad in a trade journal announcing that NewCom, a competitor of WestTel, was marketing a new national cellular phone service using the same anti-interception software produced by CodeCo. She immediately called Felix to inquire about the NewCom ad and remind him of WestTel's exclusive license. Felix confirmed that CodeCo had licensed the same software to NewCom and denied that WestTel had an exclusive license.

Susan then called NewCom and informed its chief executive officer that WestTel had the exclusive license for the use of the software and that, if NewCom went forward with its plan to use the software in the national market, WestTel would sue NewCom. She was told that if she wanted to discuss it further she should talk to Larry, NewCom's in-house attorney who had negotiated the NewCom/CodeCo contract.

It turns out that at the time Larry was assisting Susan with the WestTel/CodeCo negotiations, NewCom had contacted Larry and offered him a job. NewCom knew when it offered him the job that Larry was participating in the WestTel/CodeCo negotiations. Larry quit WestTel about six months ago and joined NewCom's legal staff.

When Susan confronted Larry and reminded him of his advice about the exclusivity of the WestTel/CodeCo deal, Larry responded only with, "Well, you signed it."

1. What theories, if any, might WestTel reasonably assert against CodeCo to establish and enforce a right to an exclusive license and what is the likely outcome on each theory? Discuss.

2. Should WestTel prevail in actions for tortious interference with the WestTel/CodeCo contract against: (a) CodeCo? Discuss. (b) NewCom? Discuss. (c) Larry? Discuss.

3. What, if any, ethical duties has Larry breached? Discuss.

Model Answer Written by Professor Dennis P. Saccuzzo

CALL 1 – Theories to enforce an Exclusive License

To enforce an exclusive license WestTel must have an equitable remedy. Their first major problem will be to find a way of introducing extrinsic evidence in the face of an integration clause and the Parol Evidence Rule.

Valid Contract

The facts stipulate the existence of a negotiated and signed valid written contract.

Parol Evidence Rule

According to this rule, evidence of any prior agreement or contemporaneous oral agreement is inadmissible to vary the terms of the contract if the written contract is intended as a complete and final expression of the parties.

The contract contained an integration clause, which means on its face the parties agreed that the written contract was the final integrated agreement. Absent an exception to the Parol Evidence Rule, WestTel will be unable to introduce extrinsic evidence that throughout negotiations WestTel insisted on an exclusive license, that Felix gave Susan oral assurances that the language of the contract would be interpreted by CodeCo to mean WestTel had an exclusive license, and that WestTel's attorney advised Susan that the oral assurance would suffice even though the attorney had a conflict of interest (as discussed below).

Exceptions to the Parol Evidence Rule

(1) Fraud in the Inducement (False Misrepresentation)

The court will allow parol evidence to show fraud. There must be a false material assertion and justifiable reliance.

Extrinsic evidence will show that CodeCo knew of WestTel's belief that they would have an exclusive license. Such a license was discussed throughout negotiations, and there is little doubt that the exclusive license is material because it goes to the basis of WestTel's bargain not to have competition in the national market. When Felix asserted that CodeCo would interpret the language of the contract to mean WestTel had an exclusive license, he made a false material assertion. Further, WestTel's reliance was justified given that their attorney, Larry, was "satisfied" and they had no reason to doubt his legal advice. Thus, the court will hear the evidence based on fraud.

Reformation

Where fraud is shown, the court may reform the contract to conform to the original agreement. As such, the court could rewrite the contract to unequivocally grant WestTel an exclusive license. WestTel could also sue in tort for damages, but their goal is to have an exclusive license. (Westel can also sue in tort for damages, but their goal is to have an exclusive license.)

(2) Ambiguity

The courts will always allow extrinsic evidence to interpret ambiguous language. Here, the clause "WestTel shall have use" of the software is ambiguous because it is subject to more than one interpretation. Again, the court will allow the extrinsic evidence and if it believes WestTel, CodeCo will be in breach by voluntary disablement, which is anticipatory repudiation by conduct, as well as by anticipatory repudiation by language.

Voluntary disablement is shown by the ad in the trade journal announcing NewCom was using the same software because by granting NewCom a license CodeCo repudiated its duties under the contract. Anticipatory repudiation is further shown by CodeCo's actual denial that WestTel had an exclusive license and confirmation that CodeCo had licensed the same software to NewCom..

WestTel can suspend its duties, treat the repudiation as a present breach, and sue for specific performance to enforce the agreement.

Specific Performance

To get specific performance WestTel will have to show the following:

(1) Inadequacy of Legal Remedy

WestTel bargained for an exclusive agreement to avoid competition. This would allow them to get a foothold in the market and develop a name and goodwill. Money damages cannot compensate for such benefits and would be uncertain in any case. Thus, the legal remedy is inadequate.

(2) Definite and Certain Terms

If the ambiguity is interpreted by the court to mean exclusive license, terms are definite and certain.

(3) Feasibility of Enforcement

The court can use the power of contempt through a mandatory injunction to force CodeCo to abide by the agreement.

(4) Mutuality

Specific performance would be available to both, so this element is met.

(5) Absence of Defenses

CodeCo would have no valid defenses.

Conclusion: WestTel has two valid theories to enforce the exclusive license in a court of equity.

CALL 2 – Tortious Interference

To establish a claim for tortious interference with contract a plaintiff must show (1) a valid relationship or business expectation, (2) that defendant had knowledge of the relationship or expectation, (3) intentional interference by defendant inducing breach or termination of expectancy and (4) damages.

Two of these elements (Numbers 1 and 4) apply to all three parties. WestTel had a valid contract with CodeCo for an exclusive license and WestTel suffered damages in that their exclusive rights advantage was impaired arguably by the announcement in trade journal and by the actual granting of a license to NewCom.

CodeCo

Although CodeCo certainly had knowledge of WestTel's expectation, no facts indicated that they intentionally interfered. To show this, WestTel would have to produce facts that CodeCo sought out NewCom to intentionally interfere with WestTel's agreement with them. This is unlikely in that CodeCo will argue they did not believe there was an exclusive agreement.

NewCom

No facts specifically indicate that NewCom had knowledge that WestTel had an expectancy in an exclusive license because the contract term in the original contract was admittedly ambiguous. However, facts do state that NewCom knew when it offered him the job that Larry was participating in the WestTel/CodeCo negotiations. These facts should be more than sufficient to avoid summary judgment and allow sufficient discovery to determine if NewCom had knowledge and intentionally interfered.

Larry

Larry knew of the expectancy. He participated in the original negotiations and assured Susan the oral assurances gave her an exclusive contract. In addition, he intentionally interfered. The facts indicate it was Larry who negotiated the agreement with NewCom. Larry will be held liable for tortious interference with contract.

CALL 3 – Larry's Ethical Duties

Competence

An attorney has a duty to be reasonably competent; he must prepare or affiliate.

Larry advised Susan to accept Felix's fraudulent misrepresentation despite the ambiguous language and integration clause. A reasonably competent attorney would have known that WestTel's rights would be in jeopardy. Larry failed to protect

What would a reasonably competent attorney do?

WestTel's rights and a generous interpretation was that he simply didn't know what he was doing. If he did, then he was guilty of fraud.

Communication

A lawyer has a duty to keep clients informed. By advising Susan he was satisfied with Felix's oral assurances, Larry failed to inform her that WestTel was contracting for a lawsuit as discussed.

Confidentiality

A lawyer shall not reveal a matter relating to representation except after obtaining the client's consent after consultation or to prevent imminent death or bodily harm. Nor shall confidential communication be used to disadvantage a client or former client.

Larry assisted in the original WestTel/CodeCo negotiations. Facts also indicate NewCom knew that Larry was participating in such negotiations. Larry subsequently quit and negotiated a deal for NewCom. The clear inference is that it was Larry who informed NewCom about the negotiations and later used that information against his former client, WestTel. Larry will be held for a violation of his duty of confidentially to WestTel.

Duty of Loyalty

A lawyer shall not represent a client if that representation involves a concurrent conflict of interest unless (1) she has a reasonable belief that she can be diligent and competent with both, (2) the case does not involve a claim by one client against another in the same litigation, (3) each gives informed consent confirmed in writing, and (4) it is not prohibited by law. A concurrent conflict of interest exists when either representation is directly adverse to another client or the representation involves a significant risk of material limitation on representation because of Lawyer's responsibilities to another client, 3rd person, or Lawyer's own personal interests.

As indicated, Larry was apparently negotiating with NewCom for a job on its legal staff while he was employed by WestTel as general counsel. If so, he violated his duty of loyalty because his representation of WesTel in negotiating the NewCom contract was limited by his own personal interests in obtaining employment with NewCom.

Former Client

A lawyer shall not represent a client on a matter that is substantially related and materially adverse to a former client unless the client gives written informed consent.

Larry clearly is in violation here. The matter of NewCom's exclusive license is substantially related and materially adverse to WestTel's interests, yet it was Larry who negotiated the deal for NewCom. The facts negate the possibility that WestTel was consulted by Larry and consented to his professional betrayal.

Mandatory Withdrawal

The lawyer shall withdraw if representation will violate a professional rule or law. As indicated, by representing NewCom, Larry violated several professional rules. He should have excused himself from any negotiations for NewCom concerning the exclusive license.

Misconduct

A lawyer shall not engage in conduct involving dishonesty, fraud, deceit, or misrepresentation. Larry was at best deceitful because he apparently was having discussions with NewCom while he was assisting in negotiations for WestTel. At worst, he committed fraud by inducing Susan to accept Felix's oral assurances, knowing that he could later negotiate a deal for the license for NewCom.

Conclusion: Larry should be disciplined.

FEBRUARY 1999 CALIFORNIA BAR EXAM -- QUESTION 5

1-Hour Exam

Maker manufactures printing presses. News, a publisher of a local newspaper, had decided to purchase new presses. Rep, a representative of Maker, met with Boss, the president of News, to describe the advantages of Maker's new press. Rep also drew rough plans of the alterations that would be required in the News pressroom to accommodate the new presses, including additional floor space and new electrical installations, and left the plans with Boss.

On December 1, Boss received a letter signed by Seller, a member of Maker's sales staff, offering to sell the required number of presses at a cost of $2.4 million. The offer contained provisions relating to the delivery schedule, warranties, and payment terms, but did not specify a particular mode of acceptance of the offer. Boss immediately decided to accept the offer, and telephoned Seller's office. Seller was out of town, and Boss left the following message: "Looks good. I'm sold. Call me when you get back so we can discuss details."

Boss next telephoned Pressco and rejected an outstanding offer by Pressco to sell presses to News similar to those offered by Maker. Using the rough plans drawn by Rep, Boss also directed that work begin on the necessary pressroom renovations. By December 4, a wall had been demolished in the pressroom and a contract had been signed for the new electrical installations.

On December 5, the President of the United States announced a ban on imports of foreign computerized heavy equipment. This removed from the American market a foreign manufacturer which had been the only competitor of Maker and Pressco. That afternoon, Boss received a telegram from Maker stating, "All outstanding offers are withdrawn." In a subsequent telephone conversation, Seller told Boss that Maker would not deliver the presses for less than $2.9 million. A telephone call by Boss to Pressco revealed that Pressco's entire output had been sold to another buyer.

1. Was Maker obligated to sell the presses to News for $2.4 million? Discuss.

2. Assume Maker was so obligated. What are News' rights and remedies against Maker? Discuss.

Model Answer Written by Professor Dennis P. Saccuzzo

CALL 1 – Was Maker Obligated to Sell to News for 2.4 Million?

UCC

The UCC applies to contracts for the sale of goods, which means things moveable at the time of identification to the contract. Because printing presses are moveable things, the UCC will apply.

Merchant

The UCC has special rules for merchants. A merchant is a person who deals in or has special knowledge of the kinds of goods involved in the transaction. Maker manufactures and sells printing presses; printing presses are integral to News' business. Both are merchants and the special UCC rules will apply to them. *(Note: Give full credit for concluding that News is not a merchant. However, the answer must be consistent and use a theory other than the rules involving merchants under 2-207 of the UCC—e.g., detrimental reliance/firm offer rule).*

Is there a Contract?

Whether Maker is obligated to sell the presses to News for 2.4 million depends on whether they formed a contract for which there are no valid defenses. A valid contract requires offer, acceptance, and consideration.

Offer

An offer is a manifestation of present intent to enter a bargain communicated to an offeree in definite and certain terms.

On Dec. 1, following preliminary negotiations between a representative of Maker (Rep) and the President of News (Boss), in which Rep drew rough plans of alterations News would have to make to accommodate new presses, Maker sent Boss a signed letter. The letter offered to sell the required number of presses at a cost of $2.4 million. Thus, terms were communicated and definite with regard to subject matter (presses), quantity (required number), and price (2.4 million). The offer also contained provisions relating to delivery schedule, warranties and payment terms that demonstrated Maker's present intent to be bound. Because a reasonable person would believe that Maker had conferred on News the power to create a contract by accepting, the offer is valid. *(Note: Give credit if an argument is made for a "firm offer" under the UCC.)*

Acceptance

The offer did not specify a particular mode of acceptance. Under the UCC absent such a specification, acceptances may be made in any manner and by any medium reasonable under the circumstances.

Boss decided to accept the offer by telephone and did so immediately. Seller was out of town, so Boss left a message stating "Looks good. I'm sold. Call me when you get back so we can discuss details."

Boss responded in a reasonable time (immediately), and did so by telephone, which is a reasonable medium. Thus, his acceptance was valid. The issue is, what effect did the statement concerning "details" have on the acceptance.

Acceptance and Effect of Different or Additional Terms

Buyer's mention of details can be construed as an attempt to add different or additional terms. Under the Common Law, attempts to accept with different or additional terms were deemed rejections of the offer and counter offers under the mirror image rule. Under the UCC, however, an expression of acceptance is valid even though it states terms additional to or different from the offer, unless acceptance is made conditional upon them. Thus, even if Buyer's statement is construed as an attempt to insert different or additional terms, the acceptance is valid since Boss did not make his acceptance conditional upon Maker's acceptance of any "details."

Consideration

Consideration is promises or acts in exchange for promises or acts in which there is legal detriment for both parties. Buyer and Seller bargained a promise of money for a promise of printing presses. Buyer has the legal detriment of paying for the printing presses; Seller the legal detriment of delivering the presses. Thus there is consideration.

Conclusion: A valid contract was formed.

Defenses to Formation – Statute of Frauds

Contracts for the sale of goods for $500 or more are covered by the Statute of Frauds and are therefore unenforceable absent a writing or a valid exception.

The contract was for goods at a cost of $2.4 million. The contract will be unenforceable unless Buyer can satisfy the Statute of Frauds.

Exception to Statute of Frauds – Sufficient Memo

A sufficient memo signed by the parties to be charged will satisfy the Statute of Frauds. Seller sent a letter to Buyer. As indicated, the letter confirmed all the essential terms of the agreement. It was signed by Seller, a member of Maker's staff. Thus, Buyer will be able to satisfy the Statute of Frauds against Maker with a memo signed by Maker.

Exception to Statute of Frauds – Estoppel

Even if the memo is not found sufficient, Buyer can show the existence of a contract and satisfy the Statute of Frauds by the doctrine of estoppel. Under this doctrine the Statute will be satisfied if Buyer can show detrimental reliance and enforcement is necessary in the interest of justice.

Here, after accepting the contract, Boss rejected an outstanding offer to sell presses to News similar to those offered by Maker, and thus changed his position in reliance on Maker's offer. In addition, by Dec. 4 Buyer had demolished a wall in the press room and contracted for new electrical installations in accord with the rough plans of alterations drawn up by the Maker representative. Buyer's reliance was justified given Maker's clear offer, and it is foreseeable that Buyer would make the necessary changes in advance due to the duration it would take to complete them.

Conclusion: Buyer has two valid exceptions to the Statute of Frauds. Seller has no defenses to formation of the contract.

Breach by Anticipatory Repudiation

Anticipatory repudiation is definite and unequivocal language that a party intends not to perform. The aggrieved party can either await performance or treat the repudiation as a breach and resort to breach remedies.

On Dec. 5, Maker sent Boss a telegram stating all outstanding offers are withdrawn. In a subsequent telephone conversation Seller told Boss that Maker would not deliver the presses for less than $2.9 million. The telegram and telephone conversation unequivocally show Maker's intent not to perform. Given that firm stand, News should be advised to treat the repudiation as a present breach. In that case, News may suspend its performance, can sue for full performance, and any of News' conditions will be excused. Maker then has a present duty to deliver the presses in a commercially reasonable manner, given that delivery details were not specified.

Maker's Defenses: Impossibility and Impracticability

To argue impossibility, performance must be objectively impossible, which means no on could do it. Maker can perform; it just wants more money, so this defense won't work.

objectively impossible means no one could do it.

Commercial impracticability will discharge a contractual duty if due to an unforeseen event performance is commercially impracticable. The courts usually require a cost increase of 5 to 10 times to make this defense valid. Here, costs have not gone up; Maker is just trying to take advantage of a situation to make more profit.

Conclusion: Maker is obligated to sell the presses to News for $2.4 million. Maker has no defenses and is in breach.

CALL 2. News' Rights and Remedies against Maker

Damages – Expectation

News can sue for expectation damages, which would be measured by the cost of cover plus incidentals, or the difference between the contract and market price. Cover is not available since there are no available presses. The contract /market price difference is $2.9 million versus $2.4 million, or $500,000.

Consequential Damages

These are damages foreseeable at the time of contract formation. As discussed, given the plans drawn by Maker's representative on needed changes and the time needed to make these changes, it was foreseeable at the time of contract that News would demolish a wall and sign a contract for electrical installations. Therefore, News can also recover for these expenses.

Specific Performance

News can also specifically enforce the contract if it can meet the following elements:

(1) Legal remedy inadequate
The facts indicate the new presses would have certain "advantages" for News. Presently, due to the ban on imports and the depletion of Pressco's entire output, no other presses are currently available. If News can argue that money damages cannot compensate them for the advantages of the new presses, their legal remedy would be deemed inadequate.

(2) Definite and Certain Terms
As indicated, most of the relevant terms were specified in Seller's offer. Those that were not specified can be supplemented under the various gap fillers and other principles of the UCC.

(3) Feasibility of Enforcement
The courts can easily enforce specific performance under its power of contempt through a mandatory injunction requiring seller to deliver the presses.

(4) Mutuality
News' performance of payment can likewise be enforced through the court's contempt power, thus meeting the security of performance test.

(5) Defenses
Maker has no defenses. To argue hardship would be ludicrous since Maker will be getting its original contract price and is only being barred from taking unfair advantage of the import ban.

Conclusion: News can specifically enforce Maker's performance.

[handwritten: * Both parties could get an injunction]

FEBRUARY 1996 CALIFORNIA BAR EXAM -- QUESTION 1

1-Hour Exam

On June 1, 1994, Owner signed a contract with Ace Painting to paint the exterior of Owner's house by September 1, 1994 for a contract price of $4,700. On July 1, Owner called Ace by telephone and told Ace that it was particularly important that the house be painted by September 1 because his employer had transferred him and he was putting the house up for sale.

The weather was unusually rainy, and Ace fell behind on all of its painting jobs. Ace could have hired additional painters or subcontracted out some of its jobs to stay on schedule, but Ace would have lost money on several jobs. Ace did not finish painting Owner's house until September 20. As a consequence, Owner did not list the house for sale until September 21.

The house stood empty, and Owner made no effort to rent or otherwise make use of it, until it was finally sold in May 1995. Most realtors in the area agree, and would testify, that the "selling season" in the area runs from May 1 to October 1 and that Owner's house would have been more likely to be sold in 1994 if it had been painted and ready to show by September 1.

Owner has refused to pay Ace for the work. Ace has sued Owner for $4,700. Owner denies liability and counterclaims against Ace for $6,000, asserting that the delay in Ace's completion was the cause of his missing the "selling season." The interest payments on the mortgage on Owner's house from October 1994 to May 1995 totaled $6,000.

What claims and defenses may Owner and Ace reasonably assert against each other, and what is the likelihood of success on each? Discuss.

Model Answer Written by Professor Dennis P. Saccuzzo

What Claims and Defenses May Owner and Ace Reasonably Assert Against Each Other?

(1) Owner v. Ace

Applicable Law

Owner and Ace have entered into an agreement in which Ace will paint the exterior of O's home. This is a service contract. Therefore the common law will apply.

Valid Contract

A valid contract requires offer, acceptance, and consideration.

Offer and Acceptance

An offer is manifestation of a present intent to enter a bargain communicated to an offeree in definite and certain terms. Acceptance is unconditional assent to be bound by the offer.

Although no facts indicate who was the offeror and offeree, the facts stipulate that O signed a contract with Ace. Terms are definite. Ace will paint the exterior of O's house by Sept. 1, 1994 for a contract price of $4700. We can thus assume that there was a valid offer and acceptance, and the two parties achieved mutual assent to reach an agreement.

Consideration

To be enforceable by law, agreement must be based on consideration. Consideration is promises or acts in exchange for promises or acts in which there is legal detriment. O and A appear to have bargained for a promise that A will paint O's house for a promise that O will pay $4700. O has the legal detriment of paying money and Ace the legal detriment of painting O's house. Thus there is valid consideration.

Conclusion: Ace and O entered into a valid services contract on Sept. 1.

Terms

The terms indicate that A will paint the house by Sept. 1 and O will pay $4,700. There is no time is of the essence clause or other express conditions that indicate order of performance, so these will be implied.

Conditions

A condition is an event that must be excused or satisfied before a duty to perform becomes absolute. Due to the absence of any express order of performance of duties, such an order will be implied. When one party's performance takes longer, the law will imply that that party's performance is a constructive condition to the other party's performance.

It takes longer to paint a house than to pay money, so it will be implied that Ace should perform first, and that Ace's performance is a constructive condition of Owner's duty to pay.

Attempted Modification – Time is of the Essence

On July 1, one month after formation of the contract on June 1, O called Ace and told him that it was particularly important that the house be painted by September 1 because his employer had transferred him and he was putting the house up for sale. In this conversation, O was attempting to modify the contract by inserting a time is of the essence clause, an express condition that would require Ace to complete the job by Sept. 1 or be in major breach of the contract.

Requirement of Consideration

Under the common law, contract modifications require new consideration. No facts indicate that O offered Ace, or that Ace accepted any consideration for this attempted modification. Therefore it will fail, and the conditions will remain implied as stated.

Substantial Performance

Where conditions are implied, the law will allow performance duties to be discharged by substantial performance. Ace must show that (1) O got substantially what he bargained for, (2) O can be reimbursed for what he did not receive, (3) great hardship for Ace if the duty is not discharged, and (4) any deviation from perfect performance was not willful.

Here, the weather was unusually rainy, and Ace fell behind on all of its painting jobs. Ace did not complete the work until Sept. 20 – 19 days late. Now O has refused to pay. Ace will successfully argue substantial performance.
   (1) O got substantially what he bargained for; the exterior of his house was painted as specified.
   (2) O can be reimbursed for what he did not receive. In fact, O's house was painted as specified, so he need not be reimbursed.
   (3) There would be great hardship to Ace if he is not paid. He expended time and materials to paint O's house.
   (4) The deviation was not willful. Ace got behind because the weather was unusually rainy. Although Ace could have hired additional painters or subcontracted other jobs to finish, Ace would have lost money on several jobs.

Conclusion: Ace's duties were satisfied by substantial performance.

Discharge of Duties

Ace may further claim his duties were discharged under the doctrine of impossibility and impracticability, however these arguments will fail.

Impossibility

To succeed on an impossibility claim, performance must be objectively impossible, meaning no one could perform the duties. This was not the case; facts stipulate that Ace could have completed the job by hiring extra painters.

Commercial Impracticability:
This UCC term has been accepted by the common law in a majority of jurisdictions. It requires a severe financial hardship, and no facts indicate that this was the case.

O's Claim for Damages

Even if Ace did breach a duty, O has no basis to claim damages.

Expectation Damages

As indicated, O got his house painted as specified, albeit 19 days late.

Consequential Damages

O claims $6,000 against Ace, asserting that he missed the selling season and now O wants to recoup interest from Oct. 1994 to May 1995. This claim will fail.

Consequential damages are damages other than expectation and incidental damages that are foreseeable at the time of contract. That the house would remain empty was not foreseeable at the time of contract because O did not know he was going to be transferred by his employer until one month after formation of the contract. Therefore O is not entitled to interest on the home because it sat vacant.

Duty to Mitigate

Even if O did have a claim for consequential damages, such damage must be certain and unavoidable.

O failed in his duty to mitigate. The facts stipulate that O made "no effort" to rent or otherwise make use of the house until it sold in May. O could have rented the property to mitigate damages and made no effort to do so. Further, although it might have been "more likely" the house would have been sold had the house been ready 19 days earlier on Sept. 1, this is highly speculative. The court will not award speculative damages.

Conclusion: Ace will prevail in the Owner v Ace action.

(2) Ace v Owner

Major Breach

In a major breach, the nonbreaching party does not receive the substantial benefit of his bargain.

Ace contracted for $4,700 for painting O's house. Ace painted the house and substantially performed under the contract. O has refused to pay. O is in major breach. When A substantially performed, he satisfied his implied condition, which triggered an absolute duty in O to pay. Because Ace's bargain was for money, O's failure to pay deprives Ace of the substantial benefit of his bargain. O is in breach and Ace will be entitled to remedies.

Damages

Ace will be entitled to his expectation damages plus incidentals. The court will order O to pay $4700 plus collection and other minor expenses incurred by Ace. Ace is not entitled to consequential damages under the facts.

[Handwritten margin note: Consequential Damages must be certain & unavoidable]

[Handwritten margin note: ☆ the court will not award speculative damages.]

TORTS

Crossover Questions:

    Torts + Constitutional Law

    Torts + Professional Responsibility:

JULY 2004 CALIFORNIA BAR EXAM -- QUESTION 6

1-HOUR ESSAY

Jack owned the world's largest uncut diamond, the "Star," worth $1 million uncut, but $3 million if cut into finished gems. Of the 20 master diamond cutters in the world, 19 declined to undertake the task because of the degree of difficulty. One mistake would shatter the Star into worthless fragments.

One master diamond cutter, Chip, studied the Star and agreed with Jack in writing to cut the Star for $100,000, payable upon successful completion. As Chip was crossing the street to enter Jack's premises to cut the Star, Chip was knocked down by a slow moving *[negligence]* car driven by Wilbur. Wilbur had driven through a red light and did not see Chip, who was crossing with the light. Chip suffered a gash on his leg, which bled profusely. Though an ordinary person would have recovered easily, Chip was a hemophiliac *[eggshell skull]* (uncontrollable bleeder) and died as a result of the injury. Chip left a widow, Melinda.

Jack, who still has the uncut Star, engaged Lawyer to sue Wilbur in negligence for the $2 million difference between the value of the diamond as cut and as uncut. Lawyer allowed the applicable statute of limitations to expire without filing suit. *[P.R. Competence]*

1. What claims, if any, may Melinda assert against Wilbur, and what damages, if any, may she recover? Discuss.

2. What claims, if any, may Jack assert against Lawyer, and what damages, if any, may he recover? Discuss.

[Handwritten notes: Melinda v. Wilbur; Jack v. Lawyer; 1. Claims 2. Damages]

Model Answer

Dennis P. Saccuzzo and Nancy E. Johnson

Call 1. Melinda v. Wilbur

Under common law, most claims extinguish upon one's death. Moreover, third party negligence claims are extremely limited. In the case of spouses, most states have survival statutes to permit surviving spouses to recover under a wrongful death theory. In any case, the first step in any analysis would be to determine whether the decedent spouse had a valid claim.

[handwritten left margin: Wrongful Death]

Negligence

Negligence is the breach of a duty of care that is the actual and proximate cause of plaintiff's damages.

[handwritten left margin: 1. Duty 2. Breach 3. Causation 4. Damages]

Duty *[handwritten: act as reasonably prudent person under the circumstances]*

As a driver of an automobile, Wilbur had a duty to act as a reasonably prudent driver would under the circumstances. A reasonably prudent driver would obey traffic laws, stop at red lights, and be on the lookout for pedestrians so as not to injure them.

Breach

Wilbur breached his duty of a reasonably prudent driver when he drove through a red light and failed to see Chip, knocking Chip down and causing Chip injury.

Special Duty – Violation of a Statute

[handwritten left margin: Special Duty]

Wilbur was also under a special duty to obey traffic laws. If a statute establishes civil liability, it conclusively establishes a duty of care. If a statute establishes criminal liability, it is necessary to show that the injured party was within the class of persons intended to be protected and that the intent of the statute was to protect the plaintiff from the type of harm suffered.

Traffic lights are designed to protect pedestrians and other drivers. As a pedestrian crossing the street, Wilbur was within the class of persons intended to be protected.   The type of risk protected by traffic lights is injury to pedestrians. Wilbur was knocked down and injured; thus he was within the class of risk.

Conclusion: Wilbur would also be liable under the special duty not to violate a statute. The result would be negligence per se, in which both duty and breach are established.

Actual Cause *[handwritten: "But for"]*

But for Wilbur running the red light and knocking down Chip, Chip would not have suffered the gash on his leg that bled profusely and ultimately led to Chip's death. Therefore, Wilbur is the actual cause of Chip's injury and death.

Proximate Cause

Proximate cause is a legal doctrine used to limit a defendant's liability for unforeseeable results. The general rule is that a defendant is liable for all foreseeable harmful results of his conduct.

It is foreseeable that if a driver runs a red light and fails to see a pedestrian then the driver may cause injury to a pedestrian. In this case, Chip suffered a gash on his leg that bled profusely.

However, a normal person would have recovered easily. Wilbur will argue that Chip's death was unforeseeable and that he should be liable only for the gash Chip suffered. This argument will fail.

Eggshell Plaintiff

Under this doctrine, a defendant must take the plaintiff as he/she is. Chip was a hemophiliac, and he died as a result of his injury. Therefore proximate cause will not limit Wilbur's liability to the gash. Wilbur would be liable for all damages that flow *from the tort* from Chip's death.

Damages

Chip was knocked down and suffered a gash on his leg. The gash no doubt caused him pain and suffering, including severe anxiety because he was a hemophiliac and bled profusely until he eventually died as a result of the injury. Chip's damages include any medical bill, pain and suffering, emotional damage, and lost earnings due to his death.

Lost Earnings

Damages must be certain. If Melinda is able to collect damages based on Chip's earnings, she would have to show with certainty what Chip's lifetime earnings might have been. In Chip's case, because he was a hemophiliac his life expectancy may be reduced. As a diamond cutter, his earnings probably varied, so Melinda might have to use an average over a reasonable period of time.

Value of the $100,000 Contract to Cut the Star

Damages must be certain. The court will not award speculative damages.

Chip had a contract with Jack to cut the Star diamond for $100,000. Of 20 master diamond cutters in the world, 19 declined to undertake the task because of the degree of difficulty. Chip's payment of $100,000 was payable only upon successful completion. As such, the $10,000 payment was speculative in view of the degree of difficulty, the fact that of all the master diamond cutters all but Chip declined, and because one mistake would shatter the Star into worthless fragments. Therefore, even if Melinda is able to recover for Chip's damages, she would <u>not</u> collect under the $100,000 contract because these damages are speculative and uncertain.

The Court will not award speculative damages.!

If a client does not suffer losses as a result of the attorney's conduct, the client cannot recover from the attorney.

Call 2. Jack v. Lawyer

When an attorney is being sued for malpractice, it is necessary for a plaintiff to prosecute a case within a case. First, attorney liability must be established by a showing that the attorney fell below the standard of care, causing plaintiff damages. Next, damages must be assessed examining the underlying case. If a client does not suffer losses as a result of the attorney's conduct, the client cannot recover from the attorney. When the underlying case is a civil lawsuit, the client must show that but for the attorney's conduct, the client would have been awarded damages (or more damages than those actually received). In this case, Jack received nothing.

Malpractice

Malpractice is a professional negligence claim, as defined above.

Duty

Lawyer has the duty to act as a reasonably prudent general practitioner. A reasonably prudent practitioner would not allow the applicable statute of limitations to expire without filing suit.

Breach

Lawyer breached his duty when he allowed the applicable statute of limitations to expire without filing suit.

Actual Cause *"But For"*

But for Lawyer's failure to file, Jack would not have lost his opportunity to bring his case to a court of law and sue for his losses.

Proximate Cause *"it is foreseeable"*

It is foreseeable that if an attorney fails to file on time, his client will lose his opportunity to bring suit for his losses.

Damages

Jack lost his right to sue for his losses. To determine if Jack will be awarded damages against Lawyer, it is necessary to look at Jack's underlying claim.

Jack's Underlying Claim: Jack v. Wilbur – Negligence

Duty

Assuming Jack could convince a jury that he was foreseeable, the next issue is whether Wilbur owed a duty to Jack. As indicated, Wilbur owed a duty to drive carefully, follow traffic laws, stop at red lights, and not injure pedestrians or other motorists. If Jack was in his premises, it is doubtful that Wilbur owed a duty to Jack.

Breach

Although Wilbur breached his duty to Chip when he failed to drive carefully, this breach affected Jack only insofar as Jack had a contract with Chip.

It is doubtful whether Jack can show Wilbur breached a duty of care owed to Jack. Even if he can, Jack must show causation and damages.

Actual Cause   "Butfor"

But for Wilbur injuring and killing Chip, Chip would have been able to attempt to cut Jack's diamond. Therefore, Wilbur is the actual cause of Jack losing the opportunity to have someone successfully cut his diamond.

Proximate Cause   "Was it foreseeable"

Jack will have a difficult time proving it is foreseeable that when a motorist fails to drive carefully and observe traffic laws, the only diamond cutter in the world willing to take on a task would be killed and cause injury to a diamond dealer. Moreover, it is questionable whether Jack was a foreseeable plaintiff.

Foreseeable Plaintiff

When a defendant breaches a duty to one plaintiff and causes injury to a second, the second plaintiff must be foreseeable. The standard for foreseeability is that the second plaintiff must be within the zone of danger.

Wilbur caused the death of Chip. In so doing, he indirectly caused injury to Jack because Chip was the only diamond cutter in the world willing to cut Jack's diamond. Uncut, the diamond was worth one million dollars. Cut properly, it would be worth three million.

When Chip was injured by Wilbur, he was crossing the street to enter Jack's premises. No facts indicate Jack was outside or anywhere near the accident scene. Therefore, it is unlikely that Jack would be a foreseeable plaintiff because he was not in the geographic zone of danger.   _geographic zone of danger_

Damages

Damages must be certain and not speculative. In addition, the court will not award damages in tort for purely economic injury.

As discussed above, it was uncertain and highly speculative whether Chip could successfully cut the diamond. Only one of 20 master cutters would even attempt the task and one mistake would shatter it into worthless fragments. Therefore, Jack's claim of a two million dollar loss is highly speculative and uncertain.

Moreover, Jack suffered no personal or property injury as a result of Wilbur's negligence. Therefore, Jack's injuries are purely economic, and the court will not ward damages in tort for them.

Conclusion: Jack will recover nothing because his negligence claim is dubious, and even if he could show he was a foreseeable plaintiff and establish duty, breach and causation, Jack will not be able to establish damages. Because Jack did not suffer a loss as a result of Lawyer's conduct, Jack will not succeed in his claim against Lawyer and Jack will not be awarded damages from Lawyer.

The court will not award damages in tort for purely economic injury!

— Must have personal injury or injury to property.

1-Hour Essay

Paula is the president and Stan is the secretary of a labor union that was involved in a bitter and highly-publicized labor dispute with City and Mayor. An unknown person surreptitiously recorded a conversation between Paula and Stan, which took place in the corner booth of a coffee shop during a break in the contract negotiations with City. During the conversation, Paula whispered to Stan, "Mayor is a crook who voted against allowing us to build our new union headquarters because we wouldn't pay him off."

The unknown person anonymously sent the recorded conversation to KXYZ radio station in City. Knowing that the conversation had been surreptitiously recorded, KXYZ broadcast the conversation immediately after it received the tape.

After the broadcast, Paula sued KXYZ for invasion of privacy in publishing her conversation with Stan. Mayor sued Paula and KXYZ for defamation.

1. Is Paula likely to succeed in her suit against KXYZ? Discuss.

2. Is Mayor likely to succeed in his suit against Paula and KXYZ? Discuss.

Written by Dennis P. Saccuzzo & Nancy E. Johnson

Commentary

Defamation appears frequently on Bar exams across the country. The California Bar, for example, tests defamation repeatedly. Prior to this July 2003 exam, defamation was tested in California in July 2002, February 2000, July 1995, and July 1992. Past California Bar defamation hypotheticals have combined it with privacy torts, as in the present hypothetical, malicious prosecution, (February 2002 and July 1995), and professional responsibility (July 2002).

The present fact pattern emphasized the privacy torts more than did any previous California Bar essay. The facts presented afforded an opportunity to discuss all 4 of the major privacy torts covered in the Bar Secrets^{TM} substantive law books.

Few Bar candidates saw all 4 privacy issues, so careful study of the model is recommended. Also note that there are 3 conflict pairings (P v KXYZ, M v P, and M v KXYZ) and that the language "is . . . likely to succeed" raises both the prima facie case and defenses. Within each of 3 conflict pairings, it was necessary to discuss the relevant prima facie cases raised by the facts, as well as the defenses to each prima facie case.

Central to the defenses was that the matter at issue was of public concern and that 2 of the parties (Paula and Mayor) were public figures. Also note the important nuance that there were no facts to indicate that the radio station (KXYZ) recorded the message. KXYZ is not subject to liability for the illegal recording under the Constitution.

KXYZ also had a good defense to intrusion upon seclusion because it did not directly or personally intrude. However, this defense triggered 2 subtle issues, respondeat superior and joint venture.

An important feature of the current model is its illustration of sub-headnoting. When dealing with torts and other issues that are fact-rich, it is a good idea to enumerate each element, sub-headnote that element, and then discuss the relevant facts that go to that issue. Such an approach not only intends to increase one's score, but also help the candidate come to the correct conclusion.

Of particular note is the discussion of damages in defamation. It is usually necessary to discuss both libel and slander per se when discussing damages in defamation in order to provide the proper background law, as the following model illustrates.

Paula v. KXYZ – Invasion of Privacy

Paula is suing KXYZ for invasion of privacy after KXYZ broadcasted a conversation of hers that had been surreptitiously recorded. Paula may reasonably allege each of the following four privacy torts. The issue is whether she is likely to succeed on any of them.

1. Appropriation of Name and Likeness

To succeed in this privacy tort, Paula must show that KXYZ used Paula's name and likeness without her authorization for commercial advantage, and that KXYZ had no defenses.

Unauthorized Use

Facts indicate Paula whispered the broadcasted information, indicating her interest and intent to keep the information private. Moreover, the conversation was surreptitiously recorded, without Paula's knowledge, and no facts indicate that Paula agreed to the broadcast. Therefore, Paula will succeed in showing unauthorized use.

[handwritten margin note: acts that show]

Commercial Advantage

Paula will argue that the broadcast was made in an effort by KXYZ to gain the attention of listeners and hence boost its ratings and KXYZ's value to potential advertisers. However, as discussed below, KXYZ will argue that the information broadcasted was a matter of public concern and that the main intent of the broadcast was to inform the public rather than to commercially exploit. As indicated below, KXYZ is likely to succeed in defending itself based on this argument, even if Paula can show commercial exploitation.

KXYZ Defenses – Matter of Public Interest/Free Speech

[handwritten margin note: Defense – Free Speech]

Facts indicate that Paula is the president of a labor union and Stan, the individual to whom she whispered the information, is the union's secretary. The union was involved in a bitter and widely publicized labor dispute with City and Mayor. Consequently, Paula qualifies as a public figure because she has voluntarily assumed a central role in a particular controversy. Moreover, the statement concerned alleged corruption by City's Mayor. Therefore, the broadcast is a matter of public interest and concern.

[handwritten margin note: Public Figure]

Where a news publication is a matter of public interest or concern, the plaintiff must show actual malice, which means knowledge of the falsity of what was published or a reckless disregard for the truth.

A problem for KXYZ is that they broadcast the information immediately after they had received the taped conversation, indicating that they failed to conduct any investigation or corroborate the information. The fact that the tape was surreptitiously recorded and that KXYZ was aware of this, however, does not subject KXYZ to liability for illegal recording because under the Constitution a broadcaster cannot be held liable for broadcasting illegally obtained information as long as the broadcaster was not the perpetrator.

From the standpoint of Paula's privacy interests, even though KXYZ probably failed to investigate, Paula cannot claim either knowledge of the falsity or reckless disregard for the truth because the statement was made by Paula and no doubt reflected her beliefs.

Qualified Privilege

KXYZ may defend under a qualified privilege, which requires that the published information be socially useful, relevant, and in good faith.

Given the highly publicized and bitter dispute, and the public's right to know whether their mayor is a crook, KXYZ can successfully show that the broadcast was socially useful, and it was certainly relevant to the highly publicized dispute. Good faith is KXYZ's weakest link, because they immediately broadcast what they knew to be a surreptitiously recorded conversation.

Conclusion: Paula will succeed in this claim only if she can show that the broadcast was more for commercial exploitation than a matter of free speech regarding a matter of public concern, and that KXYZ did not act in good faith. However, KXYZ has the better argument.

2. Intrusion Upon Seclusion

To succeed on this tort, Paula must show that KXYZ intruded upon her reasonable expectation of privacy, that the prying is objectionable to a reasonable person, and that KXYZ has no defenses.

Reasonable Expectation of Privacy. The statement was recorded in the corner booth of a coffee shop, a public place. Generally, one does not have an expectation of privacy in a public place. Moreover, the conversation took place during a break in the contract negotiations, increasing the chance that it might be overheard. Paula's argument that she whispered the statement and therefore intended to keep it private rings hollow, given that she spoke loudly enough to be recorded and was in a public place. Thus, Paula had no reasonable expectation of privacy and will fail on this claim.

Prying Objectionable. Arguably, any surreptitious recording is objectionable. However, as indicated, the statement was regarding a matter of public concern and was made by a public figure. The recording gave Paula's true views about Mayor, and revealed either a bias on Paula's part or the fact that Mayor is corrupt. In either case, Paula has a weak argument.

KXYZ did not directly or personally intrude: Vicarious Liability

It was an unknown person, not KXYZ who intruded, assuming there was an intrusion. To hold KXYZ liable, Paula would have to show that KXYZ was vicariously liable for the recorder's acts.

She could try a number of theories, but all are likely to fail. If she could show that the person who did the recording was an employee or agent of KXYZ, she could try a respondeat superior theory, in which the master (here KXYZ) may be held vicariously liable for the torts of employees or agents that occur within the scope of employment or agency. The stipulated facts show no such relationship.

Joint venture. Paula may have a better chance of showing vicarious liability under a joint venture theory, in which each member of a partnership or joint venture is vicariously liable for the torts of another committed within the scope of the partnership or venture.

She would have to show an agreement, a common (business) purpose, and equal rights of voice and control. Even if we assume an implied agreement and can infer a common business purpose, Paula would have to produce the person who recorded to have any hope of proving equal rights of voice and control.

Conclusion: Paula will not succeed on an intrusion claim because she can't meet all elements of the claim and she can't show that KXYZ was responsible for the intrusion.

3. Public Disclosure of Private Facts
The law provides a civil claim against defendants who disclose private facts that are highly offensive and widely publicized. Truth is no defense.

Highly Offensive. Although perhaps not highly offensive from the standpoint of Paula's views, the broadcast has subjected Paula to tort liability, and from this standpoint may be viewed as highly offensive.

Publicity Widespread. The broadcast was heard by all listeners to a radio station, so it was widespread.

Private Facts. The standard is that the facts revealed are not a matter of public knowledge. Paula will have to show two things: first, that it was not a matter of public knowledge that the mayor acted as he did because the union wouldn't pay him off, and second that her belief that mayor is a crook was not a matter of public knowledge. These will be difficult burdens, and no facts are given that would suggest that Paula might succeed. Indeed, given her role as union president and the adversarial nature of her widely publicized dispute, Paula's views about Mayor are likely to be known by many.

Conclusion: Paula might prevail on this tort, but she will have a heavy burden and must produce additional evidence not presented in the fact pattern.

4. False Light
This tort is used where a defendant attributes to plaintiff views she does not have or actions she did not take. The information must be highly offensive, and the publicity widespread. If it is a matter of public interest, the plaintiff must show actual malice, and truth is a defense.

Highly Offensive. As indicated, it is arguable whether the statement is highly offensive from the standpoint of reflecting Paula's views. Given the bitter dispute and Paula's role, it should come as no surprise that she thinks the mayor is a crook. Thus, the statement fails to put Paula in a false light.

2. Widespread. The broadcast was on a radio station, so no doubt it was widespread.

3. Malice. As indicated, it is arguable whether Paula can show malice, given that what she whispered to Stan no doubt reflected what she believed to be the truth about Mayor and so her views were not misrepresented.

4. Truth is a defense. The statement reflected what Paula believed to be the truth. The issue would not be the truth of the statement per se, but whether Paula's views were misrepresented. Here they were not, so KXYZ can succeed in raising truth as a defense.

Conclusion: Paula will fail in her claim for false light.

2. Mayor v. Paula -- Defamation

To succeed, Mayor must show that Paula made a defamatory statement of or concerning Mayor that was published to a third party and resulted in damages. If the plaintiff is a public figure or the matter is one of public concern, Mayor must also show falsity and fault as part of his prima facie case.

1. Defamatory Statement. The statement must adversely affect plaintiff's reputation. Accusing Mayor of being a crook would certainly affect Mayor's reputation, as it would lower his esteem in the community.

2. Of or Concerning. Paula whispered, "Mayor is a crook who voted against us . . . because we would not pay him off." That leaves little doubt that the statement pertained to the mayor of City, with whom Union was embroiled in bitter labor negotiations.

3. Publication. To meet this element the publication merely must be to one person other than the plaintiff. Here the statement was whispered to Stan. Paula could argue that because she whispered only to another officer of the same union and in confidence, there was no publication to a third party. She would lose that argument, however, because her comment was overheard by the person taping her, and indeed was loud enough to register on the tape. Her comment was published.

4. Damages. Damages are presumed for libel (written defamation) and slander per se. Slander per se statements accuse the plaintiff of a crime, loathsome disease, lack of chastity or impotence, or business incompetence. Paula's statement was spoken, and it accused Mayor of the crime of corruption. A competent mayor would vote according to the merits and not on whether he was being paid off, therefore Paula's comment arguably accuses the mayor of professional incompetence. Thus, the statement was slander per se, and damages will be presumed.

As indicated, because the mayor is a public figure and the matter is of public concern, Mayor must show falsity and fault.

1. Falsity. Mayor will have to prove that he is not a crook and that his vote was not influenced by a refusal to pay him off. No facts are given, but Mayor's character will be at issue in this suit and Paula will have an opportunity to impugn Mayor's reputation.

2. <u>Fault.</u> <u>Where plaintiff is a public figure, as here, plaintiff must show actual malice,</u> <u>which is knowledge of the falsity or reckless disregard for the truth.</u> Again, no facts are given, but Mayor will have to bring forth convincing evidence that Paula either knew Mayor was not a crook or that she recklessly disregarded the truth by not conducting a sufficient investigation. <u>His burden will be high.</u>

Conclusion: Insufficient facts are given to determine whether Mayor can make a prima facie case against Paula.

<u>Defense:</u> Even if he did, Paula can raise the defense of <u>qualified privilege,</u> defined *Socially useful, relevant + in good faith* above. Mayor's character is certainly relevant, and if <u>Paula indeed made her statement in</u> <u>good faith, then Paula will prevail.</u>

Mayor v. KXYZ – Defamation

<u>Each repetition of a statement is a separate publication.</u> KXYZ broadcasted the statement and so may be liable for defamation.

The analysis for Mayor's prima facie case for defamation will be similar to that in Mayor v. Paula. As indicated, <u>Mayor can show that KXYZ made a defamatory statement</u> <u>concerning him that was published and that resulted in damages as slander per se.</u> As <u>further indicated, Mayor will have the burden of showing falsity,</u> for which no facts are given, and actual malice.

<u>Because KXYZ aired the tape immediately, they showed reckless disregard for</u> <u>the truth of the material in the tape.</u> Therefore, <u>Mayor can establish actual malice on the</u> <u>part of KXYZ.</u>

<u>Like Paula, KXYZ can raise the defense of qualified privilege.</u> Given that the <u>public needs to know about the integrity of its public officials, the broadcast was socially</u> <u>useful as long as it was not false.</u> The activities of Mayor in this highly publicized dispute are certainly relevant. <u>KXYZ will have to show good faith, and their immediate</u> <u>publication is evidence against them.</u>

<u>First Amendment Free Speech Privilege</u>
In addition, <u>KXYZ can argue it was exercising its First Amendment right of free</u> <u>speech.</u> Although <u>the press has no special privilege other than those afforded to any</u> <u>citizen, as indicated, it is not unconstitutional to broadcast illegally obtained information.</u>

This <u>entire case will center on the truth of the statement</u> and Mayor's integrity. If <u>the statement was false, or not made in good faith, or made with reckless disregard for the</u> <u>truth, then Mayor will prevail.</u>

1-HOUR ESSAY

Prodcts Liability

Manufacturer (MFR.) advertised prescription allergy pills produced by it as "the modern, safe means of controlling allergy symptoms." Although Mfr. knew there was a remote risk of permanent loss of eyesight associated with use of the pills, Mfr. did not issue any warnings. Sally saw the advertisement and asked her Doc (Doc) to prescribe the pills for her, which he did.

As a result of taking the pills, Sally suffered a substantial loss of eyesight, and a potential for a complete loss of eyesight. Sally had not been warned of these risks, and would not have taken the pills if she had been so warned. Doc says he knew of the risk of eyesight loss from taking the pills but prescribed them anyway because "this pill is the best-known method of controlling allergy symptoms."

harm

Bud, Sally's brother, informed Sally that he would donate the cornea of one of his eyes to her. Bud had excellent eyesight and was a compatible donor for Sally. This donation probably would have restored excellent eyesight to one of Sally's eyes with minimal risk to her. The expenses associated with the donation and transplantation would have been paid by Sally's medical insurance company. Sally, however, was fearful of undergoing surgery and refused to have it done. Thereafter, Sally completely lost eyesight in both of her eyes.

Duty to mitigate?

Sally filed a products liability suit against Mfr. seeking to recover damages for loss of her eyesight. She also filed a suit for damages against Doc for negligence in prescribing the pills.

What must Sally prove to make a prima facie case in each suit, what defenses might Mfr. and Doc each raise, and what is the likely outcome of each suit? Discuss.

Sally v. M   = Prodcts Ciability

Sally v. D   Negligence

JULY 2002, QUESTION 5
TORTS

-- Written by Dennis P. Saccuzzo & Nancy E. Johnson

Commentary:

This is a products liability question, which is obvious not only from the call of the question but also from the presence of a manufacturer. The Bar tests products liability periodically. Prior to the July 2002 Bar exam, the last time products liability was an issue was February 1997 (Question 1). The Bar also tested products liability in Feb. '86 and again in Feb. '87. In Feb. '87 the defective product was also an ultrahazardous material (an insecticide), which meant that you had to discuss ultrahazardous material as well as products liability.

In order to be well prepared for the Bar exam, you must know how to handle questions such as these, and it is essential to practice at least one because it is difficult to finish when confronting them for the first time. Our analysis of selected answers released by the California Bar Examiners indicates that the Bar expects candidates to discuss a minimum of 3 or 4 theories in any products liability question, including: strict liability in tort, negligence, misrepresentation, and warranties. Notice that each selected answer for the July 2002 Bar exam, provided by the Bar on its website, contains at least 5 theories. From our observations of answers from candidates who failed this Bar exam, answers that contained only 1 or 2 theories scored in the 50-60 range on this question.

An effective approach for handling a products liability question is covered in the Bar Secrets: The Multistate Subjects (section 6 of the torts chapter). It is best to begin with a strict liability in tort theory, and discuss the various elements. Critical to the analysis is to identify the defect, which may be a manufacturing defect, design defect, or failure to warn. In Feb. 1997 the fact pattern indicated one or two clear design defects as well as a failure to warn. In July 2002 there was arguably a design defect and a clear failure to warn, complicated by the general rule that a manufacturer of prescription drugs is generally required to warn only the prescribing physician.

Sally v. Mfr.

Sally has several legal theories against Mfr., including strict liability in tort, negligence, breach of implied and express warranties, and intentional misrepresentation.

Strict Liability in Tort

A commercial seller who places a defective product in the stream of commerce is strictly liable in tort for injury to persons or property caused by a foreseeable use of the product. Sally must show that Mfr is a commercial seller who put a defective product in the stream of commerce. Sally must have been a foreseeable plaintiff who made a foreseeable use of the product. The product must have been defective at the time that it left the manufacturer's control, and that defect must have been the actual and proximate cause of Sally's injuries.

Commercial Seller:

A commercial seller is one engaged in the business of selling or distributing products. Facts stipulate that Mfr offered prescription allergy pills it produced for sale, therefore Mfr is a commercial seller. The pills were sold to individuals who had doctors' prescriptions and therefore the product was released into the stream of commerce. As a commercial seller, Mfr has a duty not to release a defective product.

Foreseeable Plaintiff/Foreseeable Use

The product was advertised as a modern and safe method of controlling allergy symptoms. Sally, as an allergy sufferer, is therefore a foreseeable user. Sally took the pills, and no facts indicate that she failed to take the pills as prescribed by her doctor. Therefore, her use was also foreseeable.

Defective Product

There are three types of defects: (1) a manufacturing defect in which a product is not made as intended; (2) a design defect in which the product is made as intended but the foreseeable risks are avoidable by using a reasonable alternative design; and (3) a failure to warn.

No facts indicate that the pills were not made as intended. However, Sally can argue that the risk of loss of one's eyesight, although "remote," is avoidable through an alternative that does not cause blindness. In fact, there are many effective allergy medications that do not carry a risk of blindness. Therefore, Sally has an arguable claim for a design defect. Even if this claim fails, facts stipulate that Mfr knew of the risk and did not issue any warnings. Sally has a very strong argument that such warnings should have been issued and that Mfr's failure to include this known risk of permanent loss of eyesight in its ad increased the foreseeable risk of harm to her. Sally will prevail on her claim of a defect due to a failure to warn because she would not have taken the pills had she known of the risk.

Failure to warn.

Actual Cause ~~But for~~ "But for"
 But for Mfr's failure to warn, Sally would not have taken the pills. Therefore, failure to warn was the actual cause of Sally's loss of her eyesight.

Proximate Cause
 The issue is foreseeability. It is foreseeable that if a manufacturer fails to post an adequate warning, then individuals such as Sally would take the medication and suffer loss of eyesight that could have been avoided.

Intervening Factor: Mfr has two counter-arguments against proximate cause, but both will fail. First, Mfr can argue that the Doctor's failure to warn was an intervening factor that should break the chain of causation and defeat Sally's claim. However, as discussed below, Doctor's failure to warn was ordinary negligence. Generally, ordinary negligence by a doctor is considered foreseeable and therefore will not limit Mfr's liability.

Learned Intermediary: Mfr may also argue under the so-called learned intermediary doctrine in which courts have held that manufacturers of prescription drugs do not have a duty to warn if the Doctor is informed of the risks. Although facts stipulate Doc knew of the risks, Sally learned directly about the pills from Mfr's ad. Therefore, it is doubtful that this exception to the duty to warn will apply.

Damages
 Sally suffered complete loss of eyesight. She was seriously injured.

Defenses
 Learned Intermediary Exception:
 As noted above, this exception will not apply because Sally learned of the pills directly from Mfr's own ad.

 Assumption of the Risk
 This defense requires that the plaintiff voluntarily encountered a known risk. This defense will fail because Sally did not know of the risk and if she had, she would not have voluntarily taken the pills.

 Failure to Mitigate
 Plaintiffs have a duty to mitigate damages. Sally might have avoided permanent loss of her eyesight because her brother Bud, a compatible donor, volunteered to donate the cornea of one of his eyes. The procedure "probably" would have restored excellent eyesight (to one eye) with "minimal" risk, and would have been paid for by insurance. Nevertheless, it is unlikely that a court would punish Sally for refusing to undergo major surgery on her eye when she was fearful and there was risk, even though minimal.

In conclusion, Sally will prevail on her strict liability in tort claim and Mfr has no defenses.

Negligence

Sally can also assert a negligence claim. The analysis would be similar except that unlike her strict liability claim, in negligence claim Sally must find fault on Mfr's part. Specifically, she must show a breach of duty to a foreseeable plaintiff that is the actual and proximate cause of her damages.

[handwritten margin note: Breach Duty Causation Damages]

Duty to Foreseeable Plaintiff

As indicated above, Sally is a foreseeable user of allergy medications. Mfr has a duty to act as a reasonably prudent manufacturer. This would include the duty to post adequate warnings of side effects in its ads to alert consumers to potential risks and dangers.

Breach

Mfr breached its duty when it failed to warn Sally and advertised its product as modern and safe, knowing there was a remote risk of permanent loss of eyesight.

Actual Cause, Proximate Cause, and Damages

The analysis is similar to that above for strict liability in tort. But for the failure to warn in its ads, Sally would not have taken the medication. Thus, Mfr is the actual cause of Sally's blindness.

Moreover, it is foreseeable that when a manufacturer pushes its products as modern and safe without adequate warnings, an unsuspecting consumer will take the product and suffer the risks.

[handwritten margin note: Damages =] Finally, as indicated, Sally lost her eyesight. *[handwritten note: harm resulted]*

Defenses – Comparative Negligence

In addition to the defenses discussed above, Mfr can try to raise comparative negligence, where Sally's damages may be reduced to the extent that she contributed to her own damages. Here, this defense will fail, as Sally was not aware of the risks, she would not have taken the drug had she known, and no facts indicate any abuse or misuse of the drug.

As indicated, Doc's negligence will not relieve Mfr of its liability, nor will the fact that Doc knew of the danger. Mfr advertised the product as modern and safe and had direct contact with Sally. As also indicated, it is doubtful the court will reduce Sally's damages because she did not have an operation, given Sally's aversion to even remote risk.

Breach of Implied Warranties

Merchantability: Under this warranty, a product must be of fair and average quality; fit for ordinary purpose. Sally will successfully argue that the absence of a warning caused a breach of this warranty because without the warning, Sally was unaware of the known risks. The analysis for causation and damages would be the same as for strict liability in tort. There are no defenses, as discussed in the negligence analysis.

Intended Use: Under this warranty, the product must be fit for its intended use and the buyer must rely on seller's recommendation. Here, Sally relied on Mfr's recommendation that the product was modern and safe. It was not safe, so Sally will prevail on this theory as well, with causation, damages, and defenses as discussed above.

Breach of Express Warranty

A statement of fact or promise by a commercial seller creates an express warranty that becomes part of the basis of the bargain. Mfr stated that their product was safe, with no warning of the risks. Facts stipulate that Sally would not have purchased the product had she known the risks. Thus, Mfr's promise of safety went to the basis of Sally's bargain and this warranty was breached as well. Causation, damages, and defenses are the same as discussed above.

Misrepresentation

A commercial seller is liable for misrepresentation of fact. The representation must be material with intent to induce reliance, justifiable reliance, causation, and damages.

Mfr's claim that the product was safe even when it knew of a risk of permanent loss of eyesight induced Sally to purchase its product. As indicated above, the promise of safety was material. The statement was a misrepresentation because Mfr knew of the risks but in the ad described the product as "safe," without reference to known adverse consequences. Sally's reliance on the ad was justifiable because she had no reason to believe there was a risk of serious injury. Causation, damages, and defenses are the same as discussed above.

In sum, Sally can meet the elements of a prima facie case for strict liability in tort, negligence, breach of implied warranties, breach of express warranties, and misrepresentation.

Sally v. Doc

Negligence (defined above)

Duty: Doc has a duty to act as a reasonably prudent doctor in his community. A reasonably prudent doctor would warn his/her patients of serious risks such as permanent blindness and obtain the proper informed consent.

Breach: Doc breached his duty when he failed to warn Sally of the danger of permanent loss of eyesight.

Actual Cause: But for Doc's failure to warn Sally, she would not have taken the drug and suffered permanent loss of her eyesight.

Proximate Cause: It is foreseeable that when a doctor fails to warn and adequately inform his/her patients of a known risk, the patient will take the medication believing it is safe. Mfr's failure to warn in the ad will not cut off Doc's liability, as he had an independent duty to warn Sally.

<u>Foreseeable Plaintiff</u>: Sally is a foreseeable plaintiff because she is a patient of Doc's and therefore in the zone of danger for any of his negligent acts that may cause her injury.

<u>Damages</u>: Sally suffered permanent loss of her eyesight. She is now blind.

<u>Defenses</u>: As indicated, Sally did not voluntarily assume the risk, nor did she contribute in any way to her own condition. Doc can argue failure to mitigate, but as indicated above, undergoing eye surgery to mitigate is risky and the court is unlikely to punish Sally for failure to take that risk.

Under Proximate Cause — Discuss foreseeable Plaintiff.
        └→ Zone of Danger

JULY 2001 CALIFORNIA BAR EXAM -- QUESTION 5
(Torts + P.R.)

1-HOUR ESSAY

Ann, an attorney, represented Harry in his dissolution of marriage proceedings, which involved an acrimonious dispute over custody of Harry and Wilma's minor children.

Ann advised Harry that a favorable custody ruling would be more likely if he could show that Wilma had engaged in improper behavior. Two days after receiving this advice Harry came to Ann's office with his wrist heavily bandaged. Harry told Ann that, when he went by the family home the prior evening to get some of his things, Wilma had tried to run over him with her car, actually hitting him. This was the first suggestion of any violence between Harry and Wilma. After listening to Harry's story, Ann urged Harry to sue Wilma for assault and battery. Ann said:
"Filing this suit will improve our bargaining position on custody." Ann did nothing to investigate the truth of Harry's story.

Just before the hearing on custody, Ann filed a tort action on Harry's behalf alleging ~~Frivolous~~ Wilma had committed an assault and battery on Harry. Ann referred to the tort action at the custody hearing, and Wilma denied that the incident ever occurred. The judge, however, believed
Harry's version and awarded sole custody to Harry.

Three months later, Ann learned that Harry had fabricated the story about how he injured his wrist. Ann did not report Harry's lie to anyone and merely failed to prosecute the tort action, which, as a result, was dismissed with prejudice. Wilma then sued Ann for malicious prosecution, abuse of process, and defamation. Wilma also filed a complaint against Ann with the State's office of lawyer discipline. _P.R._

A: What is the likelihood that Wilma can succeed on each of the claims she has asserted in her civil suit against Ann? Discuss.

B: Did Ann's conduct violate any rules of professional ethics? Discuss.

JULY 2001, QUESTION 5
TORTS/P.R.

-- Written by Dennis P. Saccuzzo

Commentary:

This question tests one of the California Bar's favorite torts, defamation. Since 1995, defamation has been tested in July 2003, July 2001, February 2000, and July 1995. The July 1995 fact pattern is the most similar to the present (July 2001, Q5) in that both called for a discussion of defamation, malicious prosecution, and abuse of process. The present fact pattern (unlike July 1995) also contained a professional responsibility crossover.

Ann, an attorney, represented Harry in a marriage dissolution involving a custody dispute. Ann advised Harry he could improve his legal position if he could show that Wilma had engaged in improper conduct. Harry subsequently fabricated a story that his estranged wife, Wilma, had tried to run him over. Ann failed to conduct an investigation, even though this was the first suggestion of any violence between Wilma and Harry. Ann subsequently filed a complaint on Harry's behalf alleging assault and battery. Ann also referred to the alleged assault and battery at the judicial custody hearing, and Wilma lost custody of her children. The primary issue is whether Ann can be held liable for defamation.

Note that the first call of the question asks whether Wilma can succeed on each of the claims she has asserted in her civil suit against Ann. In the preceding sentence, we are told that Ann has sued for (1) malicious prosecution, (2) abuse of process, and (3) defamation. This was the proper order to discuss these torts, and that is what most candidates did. Answers that began with defamation tended to be downgraded, no doubt because such answers stood out as different and because they failed to follow the directions implied by the question. As such, these answers were no doubt subjected to greater scrutiny.

A second common problem was rejecting the tort of malicious prosecution solely on the grounds that this was a civil, not a criminal proceeding. Even though one element could not be perfectly met, all other in this tort could. The only difference between malicious prosecution and wrongful civil proceedings is that the former involves criminal complaints, the latter civil. All other elements are the same. Candidates who simply went to the bad element failed to show their knowledge and understanding of the law by discussing the elements that could be met and for which there were numerous facts that needed to be analyzed.

Defamation has been tested so often on the California Bar exam that the expected approach is well established. This approach is presented in the outline/flowcharts in the substantive Bar Secrets™ law books (see Bar Secrets: The Multistate Subjects or Bar Secrets: The 1L Book). The approach is also illustrated in the following model. Note that the issue of matter of public concern/public figure was addressed even though neither of these sub-issues applied to Wilma. This is because there were facts that raised the elements that go to these sub-issues, as illustrated herein. Please also study the discussion of damages. Far too many Bar candidates lost points because unlike the model, their answers discussed damages only in terms of Wilma's loss of her child and out-of-pocket expenses. Remember, in defamation an important aspect of recovery is for reputational damages, and these are presumed for libel and slander per se.

The professional responsibility call was straightforward. Notice that Attorney Ann *failed to conduct an investigation.* Such a failure occurs commonly, not only in PR questions but also in corporations and trusts questions, where a director or trustee fails to conduct an investigation. This failure is a serious omission, and you are expected to articulate it and discuss it thoroughly whenever it occurs. Your role in answering questions in the areas of PR, corporations, trusts, and crimes is that of a protector of the public, therefore you are expected to hold the professional/wrongdoer accountable whenever possible.

Call A. Wilma v. Ann

Malicious Prosecution/Wrongful Civil Proceedings

Malicious prosecution involves the institution of criminal proceedings against a plaintiff. Ann did not file criminal proceedings against W, but instead filed a tort action, which is a civil proceeding. The proper tort action for W is wrongful civil proceedings, where the elements are the same as in malicious prosecution except for the filing of criminal proceedings.

A wrongful civil proceeding is the initiation of civil proceedings against a plaintiff that terminates in plaintiff's (P's) favor and for which there is no probable cause and an improper purpose resulting in damages to P. W must show the following elements:

(1) *Institution of Civil Proceedings Against P*

> Ann urged Harry to sue W for assault and battery (A&B). Further, she filed a tort action on H's behalf alleging A&B. Thus she initiated civil proceedings against W.

(2) *Termination in P's favor*

> Facts stipulate that the case was dismissed with prejudice because Ann did not prosecute. Thus, the case was terminated in W's favor, and the 'with prejudice' judgment carries full *res judicata* effects so that H will be barred from ever bringing this action again.

(3) *Absence of Probable Cause*

> Ann relied on H's story as her only basis to bring this case. The fact that two days earlier Ann had advised H that he would be more likely to get a favorable custody ruling if he could show wrongful conduct on W's part, coupled with the fact that this was the first suggestion of any violence between H and W, would have caused any reasonable person to doubt H's story. In fact, H had fabricated the whole thing, and Ann failed to investigate. The court will find an absence of P.C.

(4) *Improper Purpose*

> It is improper to file a suit to improve one's bargaining position in another action. Ann in fact used the suit in the custody action, and her improper purpose succeeded in gaining H an award of sole custody.

(5) *Damages*

> The judge believed H and awarded sole custody to him, depriving W of her rights as a parent and no doubt causing considerable emotional damage to her (not to mention the child). W also had to prepare to defend against the tort action and answer the complaint, which caused her out-of-pocket expenses.

Conclusion: W will prevail on wrongful civil proceedings.

Abuse of Process

This tort involves use of civil process for purposes for which it was not intended, involving an ulterior purpose and definite acts or threats to accomplish the purpose.

(1) *Wrongful Use of Process.*   Ann's advice to H prompted H to fabricate a story that Ann failed to question despite, as discussed above, contrary evidence. Ann should have conducted a reasonable investigation. Her stated goal of filing the suit was to "improve H's bargaining position" in the custody action. Because it is wrong for an attorney to file or threaten to file a suit to improve a position in another action, the court will rule in favor of W on this element.

(2) *Ulterior Purpose.*   As indicated, Ann's purpose was not to recover damages for a tort, but to improve her client's chances and bargaining position in the custody action.

(3) *Threats or Acts to Accomplish the Purpose.*   To accomplish her purpose, Ann filed the suit, and then referred to the tort action in the custody hearing.

(4) *Damages.*   As discussed, W suffered emotional and monetary damages.

Conclusion: W will prevail on her abuse of process claim.

Defamation

Defamation is a defamatory statement of or concerning a plaintiff published to a third party that results in damages.

(1) *Defamatory Statement.*   Ann alleged that W had committed domestic violence (DV) against H. Because being a perpetrator of DV would tend to adversely affect W's reputation and lower her esteem in the community, this allegation is defamatory. Indeed, the effect of the allegation was such that the judge awarded full custody to H.

(2) *Of or Concerning.*   The claim was filed in a court of law and therefore would have clearly identified W, leaving no doubt that the statement was of or concerning W.

(3) *Publication.*   The allegation was filed with the court in a written complaint, making it a matter of public record. It was also referred to by Ann in the court room for the judge and all others present to hear.

(4) *Damages.*   Damages are presumed for libel (written statements) and for slander per se, when the defamatory statement goes to a crime, loathsome disease, chastity (in a woman, and in California, impotence in a man), or business (incompetence).

Here, the defamatory statements were written in a complaint, and so were libelous. Further, the spoken statements make in court accused A of domestic violence, which is a crime. Therefore, damages will be presumed.

(5) *Matter of Public Concern*. If W were a public figure, she would also have the burden of proving falsity and fault (actual malice). A public figure is one who has achieved pervasive fame or voluntarily assumed a central role in a particular controversy. No facts indicate W was a public figure.

Even if she were, W would still make a prima facie case because the statement was fabricated and therefore false, and Ann showed a reckless disregard for the truth when she failed to question H despite the fact that this was the first suggestion of violence in the relationship. Ann's malice is also evident in her failure to conduct a reasonable investigation.

Conclusion: Absent a defense, W will prevail.

Defense: Privilege. Statements made in judicial proceedings carry an absolute privilege. Because a complaint filed with the court is a statement to the court, and Ann's spoken statements were in court, Ann's written and spoken statements will be privileged. She will have a complete defense to defamation.

Call B. Violation of Rules of Professional Responsibility

Then state what a

Competence. An attorney has a duty to be reasonably competent. A competent attorney would question suspicious facts such as H's fabricated story when there was no previous history of violence. Because Ann failed to conduct a reasonable investigation, she violated her duty of competence.

Scope. An attorney should not assist in criminal or fraudulent conduct. In California a member should not advise the violation of any law. Ann assisted H in conduct that was both criminal and fraudulent. She implicitly encouraged him to fabricate a story in her advice that H would be more likely to prevail if he could show improper behavior by W. Then, as discussed, she showed a reckless disregard for the truth when she failed to question suspicious facts or conduct a reasonable investigation. She allowed H to perpetrate his fraud, even to the point of referring to the tort claim to win H sole custody.

Ann's conduct is tantamount to suborning perjury. Under the ABA rules, an attorney is required to inform the court if a client perjures himself. In California, the attorney may not blow the whistle, but is specifically prohibited from referring to perjured statements. In this case, Ann specifically referred to the tort action.

Ann violated several duties under both the ABA and California rules.

Diligence. Ann did not act with reasonable diligence when she failed to conduct a reasonable investigation and ignored suspicious facts.

Confidentiality.   Generally a lawyer may not reveal a matter relating to representation. ABA rules allow an attorney to inform a defrauded party if the attorney's services were used as part of the scheme to defraud, but as discussed, in California violations of confidentiality are not permitted even when a client perjures himself. However, the California Evidence Code exempts from the attorney-client privilege any client information where the attorney's services are used to perpetrate a fraud.

When Ann learned that H had fabricated his story, she was in a conflict. She then knew that H had used her services to perpetrate a fraud on W and the court, and inappropriately win sole custody. She should have confronted H, and under ABA rules she could have informed the court if H failed to rectify. Under California rules there would be no privilege and Ann is in a major conflict due to her duty of candor to the court. However, California rules do not permit a "noisy" withdrawal.

Withdrawal.   Withdrawal is mandatory if representation will lead the attorney to violate a professional rule or law, or if the client engages in illegal acts.

Continued representation of H would have caused Ann to continue to assist H in his fraud. Ann may have persuaded H to withdraw his claim. Instead, she did nothing. While the dismissal with prejudice may have been the right result, Ann's inaction subjected her to tort liability from W, as discussed above. She remained a party to H's wrongful conduct and made no attempt to mitigate the damages. By not withdrawing, Ann violated still another duty.

competent attorney
would have done.

JULY 2000 CALIFORNIA BAR EXAM -- QUESTION 6

1-HOUR ESSAY

Dan operates a plant where he makes pottery. To provide a special high-capacity power source to his pottery kilns, Dan recently installed on the electric company's power pole outside of his building an electrical transformer that would increase the electrical current entering his plant from the main power line. He did this without the knowledge or consent of the electric company. Dan did not know that the power line on which he installed the transformer also feeds power to the adjacent office buildings.

Peter occupies one of those adjacent office buildings. In the building, he has an extensive computer network that he uses in his business of providing advanced computer services to local commercial enterprises. Peter has been in this business for ten years. He employs several highly paid computer operators and technicians.

Dan's installation of the transformer caused power surges each time his kilns were turned on and off. Soon after Dan had installed the transformer, Peter's computers began to malfunction and eventually were severely damaged by the repeated power surges. As a result, Peter lost a large amount of data stored in his computers. He laid off some employees without pay and shut down his business for two weeks while the computers were repaired and while the remaining employees restored the lost data.

During the shutdown, Peter lost considerable income because he was unable to furnish computer services to his customers.

Peter and the laid-off employees have filed suit against Dan.

1. In an action against Dan, what theories, if any, might Peter assert and what defenses might Dan raise if Peter seeks to recover:

   a) The cost of repairing his computers? Discuss.

   b) The cost of restoring the lost data? Discuss.

   c) His lost income? Discuss.

   d) Loss of goodwill and other incidental effects of the disruption of his business? Discuss.

2. May Peter recover punitive damages? Discuss.

3. May the laid-off employees recover lost wages and benefits from Dan under any theory? Discuss.

CALL 1. Peter v. Dan – Theories and Defenses

Negligence

Negligence is a breach of a duty of care which is the actual and proximate cause of a plaintiff's damages.

To establish a claim for negligence against Dan, Peter must show that Dan owed him a duty as a foreseeable plaintiff, that Dan breached that duty, and that Dan's breach was the actual and proximate cause of Peter's damages. Finally, Dan must not have a valid defense.

Duty to Foreseeable Plaintiff

Peter occupies a building adjacent to Dan's. Peter is within the zone of danger because it is foreseeable that businesses adjacent to Dan's would use electrical power and might suffer damages from improper handling of the electrical transformers that power the building.

Dan owes Peter a duty to act with the care that a reasonably prudent person would exercise under the circumstances. A reasonably prudent person in Dan's circumstances would have obtained the knowledge and consent of the power company, hired skilled help, and conducted an investigation so that he would have knowledge of the effect of his actions.

Breach of Duty

Dan breached his duty when he installed a dangerous electrical transformer without the knowledge and consent of the power company, without skilled help, and without knowledge of the effect his actions may have on Peter.

Actual Cause

Facts stipulate that it was Dan's installation of the transformer that caused the power surges. But for the repeated power surges, Peter's computers would not have malfunctioned and become severely damaged. Dan is the actual cause of Peter's damages.

Proximate Cause

The issue is foreseeability. It is foreseeable that when one attempts to modify an electrical power source without permission or proper knowledge, harm may result to other users of electrical power. Dan's ignorance that the transformer he installed also feeds power to adjacent buildings will not excuse him because a reasonable person would have investigated sufficiently. Dan should have known the possible effects of his actions on adjacent buildings. Further, the link between the installation, power surges and Peter's damages is direct, with no intervening factors. Therefore Dan is the proximate cause of Peter's damage.

Damages

Peter's computers were damaged and he lost data. He shut his business down and lost income and good will. He had to repair his computers. He suffered damages, and his possible recovery will be discussed below.

Defenses: Comparative Negligence

Dan will argue that a reasonably prudent owner of expensive computers with valuable and sensitive data would protect them by using special power surge devices. In failing to use such devices Peter contributed to his own injury and therefore Dan should not be liable.

This argument will fail. No facts indicate that Peter did anything to contribute to his own injury. Further, the courts will not reduce Peter's award because he failed to predict that Dan would install damaging equipment without the consent or knowledge of the electrical company.

Peter's Recovery

Dan will be liable for general damages (those that flowed from Dan's negligence) as well as additional special damages that Peter can prove are causal, foreseeable, certain, and unavoidable.

(a) The cost of repairing the computers

These damages are general damages that flow directly from Dan's negligence. To make Peter whole it will be necessary to repair his computers and return them to their original condition. Damages for repairs can be proved with certainty by producing all the repair bills for labor, parts, and tax if any. No facts indicate Peter could have taken steps to mitigate his losses. Peter will recover all of his repair bills.

(b) Cost of restoring lost data

There is a direct link between the computer malfunctions and lost data, so these are general damages that flowed from Dan's negligence. As such, they are, as discussed above, both causal and foreseeable. Further, the cost of replacing the lost data can be determined with certainty as long as Peter kept reasonably good records to document his losses. Dan is not obligated to pay for an improved data system; however, he must replace what his negligence destroyed. Peter will document these damages by the bills from data specialists and other necessary consultant and labor costs.

(c) Lost Income

During the shutdown Peter lost considerable income because he was unable to furnish computer services to his customers. Peter will have more difficulty recovering lost income for a number of reasons. First, the causal link between the computer failure and the lost income is more attenuated. Did Peter actually need the lost data in order to serve his customers? If so, shouldn't he have routinely created some sort of back-up files for exactly this kind of emergency? Could he have mitigated his damages through some temporary or back-up service? Was it really necessary to shut down? Peter will have the burden of proof for all of these questions because they will be raised by the defense. However, if he can succeed, then as an established, 10-year business, Peter can probably produce sufficient records and documentation to show certainty of damages.

Mitigation

(d) Loss of goodwill and other incidentals

The loss of goodwill is even more attenuated than lost income, and is highly speculative. Unless Peter can prove these damages with certainty, the court is unlikely to provide relief. Peter's best attempt might be to call experts in this line of work to testify as to the

The court will not award speculative damages.

specific economic impact of this loss. However, the court will not award speculative damages.

Other Possible Actions

Although his property was destroyed, Peter cannot argue trespass to chattel or conversion because these are intentional torts, and Dan did not intentionally interfere with or take control of Peter's property. Similarly, a trespass theory will not work because Dan did not actually enter or intentionally cause electricity to enter Peter's business. However, Peter can sue under a nuisance theory.

Nuisance

Nuisance is substantial, unreasonable interference with another's use and enjoyment of property where the interference is non-trespassory and the utility does not outweigh the harm.

As discussed, Peter's computers were severely damaged and he was forced to shut down for repairs. The interference was substantial. Further, it was unreasonable for Dan to alter the power lines without consent or knowledge. As discussed, the electricity was non-trespassory. There is little utility to improperly altering a dangerous electrical power source and all adjacent buildings had risks similar to Peter's or worse – a power surge might have caused someone to suffer an electrical burn or even death.

Conclusion: Peter will prevail with both his negligence and nuisance claims.

CALL 2 – Punitive Damages

Punitive damages are awarded only where conduct was willful and malicious. Under such circumstances, punitive damages are recoverable, although the Supreme Court has ruled that due process protects defendants from excessive punitive damages and punitive damage awards will be reviewed under a *de novo* standard of review. The court will weigh the wrongfulness or reprehensibility of the conduct, proportionality to actual damages, and the wealth of the defendant in assessing amounts.

Here, Dan was careless and negligent. The issue is whether his failure to get consent and his reckless disregard for the consequences of his actions rises to the level of willful or malicious. This is unlikely. Dan did not even know the power lines on which he installed the transformer also feed power to adjacent office buildings. Peter will not recover punitive damages.

CALL 3 – Laid-Off Employees

To recover, the employees must have an appropriate theory. Nuisance will not work because the employees did not have possession and control of the land.

Negligence

Defined and discussed *supra*, the employees' best hope is a negligence claim. Dan will argue that the employees were not foreseeable plaintiffs. Even if they were, their damages were purely economic and as a general rule courts will not award purely economic damages. Further, the causal link between the power surge and the lay-offs, though logical, is attenuated. Given the absence of any direct impact, their purely economic claim, and their likely unforeseeability as plaintiffs, the employees' claim will likely be dismissed on a summary judgment.

JULY 1998 CALIFORNIA BAR EXAM -- QUESTION 4

1-HOUR ESSAY

Transco, a common carrier, hauls toxic chemicals by train through an area where Paul operates a commercial greenhouse. Concerned about the risks if there were spillage from one of the boxcars containing the chemicals, Transco hired Diana, a consultant, to assess that risk. Diana concluded there was little or no risk to nearby property owners if any such spillage occurred, and she so advised Transco.

intervening? Thereafter, one of Transco's trains containing a known toxic chemical derailed because the train engineer suffered a heart attack while operating the engine. The engineer was obese and, five years earlier, had taken a leave of absence because of a mild heart attack he had suffered. The derailment caused chemical spillage near Paul's property, and Paul closed his greenhouse business out of fear that the spillage would damage his greenhouse plants and cause him to get cancer. In fact, no lasting damage resulted from the spill. *No harm*

Six months after the accident, Paul moved back into his previously vacated premises and began operating the greenhouse again. Paul's fear for his health from possible exposure to the chemical continued, however, and subsequently he suffered severe anxiety and depression because of this fear.

On what theory or theories, if any, can Paul recover damages from, and what defenses may reasonably be raised by:

1. Transco? Discuss. *S.L. Negligence*

2. Diana? Discuss.

Paul v. Transco

Paul v. Diana

Paul v. Transco

Vicarious Liability: Respondeat Superior

In vicarious liability, liability may be imputed to a third party. Respondeat superior is a type of vicarious liability in which an employer (master) is held liable for the torts of an employee (servant) that occur within the course and scope of employment.

The train derailed because the engineer suffered a heart attack while operating the engine. Assuming the engineer was an employee of Transco, this accident occurred during the engineer's employment and was within the scope of it. Therefore, Paul can hold Transco liable for its own torts as well as those caused by the engineer's negligence.

Negligence

Negligence is a breach of the duty of care to a foreseeable plaintiff which is the actual and proximate cause of plaintiff's damages.

Duty

Because Paul was not a patron of Transco, Transco will not be held to the higher standard of duty of common carriers, but instead will be held to the duty of a reasonably prudent hauler of toxic chemicals.

Breach of Duty

Paul will argue that Transco breached its duty by allowing toxic chemicals to be driven by an obese engineer who Transco knew had taken a leave of absence because of a mild heart attack five years earlier. Paul can also argue that Transco is liable under a respondeat superior theory because the engineer breached a duty when he remained or became obese following a heart attack, yet continued to operate the engine, subjecting it to increased risk of derailment. Transco will counter that the past heart attack was mild and remote (it occurred five years ago).

Breach is arguable. However, Paul can also use the doctrine of *res ipsa loquitur*.

Res Ipsa Loquitur

A plaintiff can show a breach under this doctrine by showing that (1) an accident or injury does not normally occur absent negligence; (2) defendant's negligence was more likely responsible than not; and (3) the plaintiff did not contribute to his own injury. Paul can meet each of these elements. First, trains do not normally derail absent negligence. Second, the train was under Transco's and/or their engineer's exclusive control, and Paul had nothing to do with the forces that led the train to crash. Therefore it is most likely that Transco was responsible. Finally, Paul didn't do anything to contribute to this injury; the chemicals spilled due to the derailment.

Effect:

The effect is negligence per se and Paul will avoid a directed verdict; he can get his case to the jury even if a direct breach cannot be established.

Actual Cause   *But for*

But for the train derailment, there would not have been a spillage and Paul would not have closed his greenhouse or developed a fear for his health and subsequent severe anxiety and depression.

Proximate Cause

Foreseeable Plaintiff

It is foreseeable that a train hauling toxic chemicals might have a spillage in areas along its route. The spillage occurred along its route through an area where Paul operates a greenhouse. Therefore Paul is a foreseeable plaintiff.   *Zone of Danger*

A defendant is liable for all foreseeable harmful results of his conduct.

It is foreseeable that a chemical spill would cause Paul to shut down because of the potential damage toxic chemicals might cause to plants. Therefore Transco is the proximate cause of this damage.

However, it is of doubtful foreseeability that Paul would develop severe anxiety and depression because of his fears, especially six months later and given that there was no lasting damage. Therefore, the court is not likely to hold Transco liable for Paul's subsequent severe emotional damages.

Damages

Paul suffered damages. He closed his greenhouse and suffered severe distress.

Defenses

Contributory Negligence – As discussed, Paul did not contribute to his own injury, so this defense will fail.

Assumption of the Risk – A defendant assumes the risk of liability where he has knowledge of the danger and voluntarily encounters it. Paul did not voluntarily encounter the risk of a toxic chemical spill. At best, Transco could argue that he returned even though his fear was great and so assumed the risk of emotional disorder. As previously discussed, Paul is unlikely to prevail on his claim for emotional distress in any case.

Conclusion: Paul will succeed in his claim for negligence, but Transco will only be liable for Paul's losses that he can prove with certainty and which flowed from the six months that he shut down his business.

Ultrahazardous Activity

One who maintains an abnormally dangerous activity may be liable despite the exercise of reasonable care. To succeed on this claim, Paul must show the following:

(1) The activity involves a serious risk of harm.
> Here, Transco hauls toxic chemicals. Such chemicals generally involve a serious risk of harm to persons and certain property such as greenhouses, despite the claims of Diana, Transco's hired consultant, that there was little or no risk to property owners.

(2) *Defendant unable to eliminate risk even with reasonable care.*

A risk of derailment exists regardless of how careful Transco might be, so Paul can meet this element.

(3) *Balance of danger versus value favors the plaintiff.*

This element is arguable, and there are no facts to indicate the value of toxic chemicals. Transco will argue the danger was small based on Diana's report and the fact that no actual lasting damages occurred.

(4) *Causation & Damages.*

Discussed *supra*, Transco caused Paul's damages and has no defenses.

Conclusion: Paul can probably prevail under this tort if he wins the balancing argument.

Negligent Infliction of Emotional Distress

Paul can assert this claim and the analysis would be similar to his general negligence claim. The duty is not to cause distress to another by creating a foreseeable risk of physical injury through impact or threat of impact. Here, Paul suffered no impact or threat of impact, so he is unlikely to prevail on this tort.

Intentional or Negligent Trespass

Paul will not prevail on either of these torts because the spillage occurred near his property; it did not enter his property.

Nuisance – Unreasonable Interference with Plaintiff's Use & Enjoyment of Property

Paul is unlikely to prevail since this was a single, one-time impact injury for which negligence and strict liability are the two appropriate torts.

Negligent Hiring and/or Supervision

Paul can argue that Transco was negligent in hiring Diana and/or the engineer and negligent in supervision of the engineer. The analysis would be similar to the general negligence discussed above and below and arguable for the reasons discussed.

Paul v. Diana

Negligence

Defined *supra*, Paul can assert a negligence claim against Diana. It is foreseeable that a recommendation by Diana might influence Transco's decision to haul the chemicals that eventually spilled near Paul's property and damaged him, as discussed above. Therefore Paul is a foreseeable plaintiff.

Duty

Diana has a duty to act as a reasonably prudent consultant. However, she owes this duty to Transco and not to Paul. Even if Paul could establish a duty, Diana would not be liable because she did not proximately cause his damages (as discussed below).

Breach

It does not appear that Diana breached a duty. She assessed the risk; advised Transco. As she advised, no lasting damage resulted from the spill.

Causation & Damages

Even if Diana is the actual cause of the damages, the relationship between Paul's damages and her report is highly attenuated, at best. Between Diana's report and Paul's damage were too many superseding factors, including the engineer's obesity and heart attack and Paul's abnormal fears.

Conclusion: Paul will not succeed in his claim against Diana.

Indemnity and contribution

Even if Paul did succeed, Diana can try to claim indemnity from Transco, since they were the ones who hired her to do the report.

Employee vs. Independent Contractor

To counter her indemnity claim, Transco will argue that Diana was an independent contractor. Generally, a principal is not liable for the torts of an agent if the agent is an independent contractor. The issue will be the extent to which Transco maintained control over Diana's activity. If Transco can prove that Diana was an independent contractor and that her negligence was a proximate cause of Paul's damages, then they may claim indemnity and contribution from her. However, as discussed, this is unlikely.

JULY 1995 CALIFORNIA BAR EXAM -- QUESTION 3

1-HOUR ESSAY

Booker is the owner of The Bookstore. Walker, a clerical worker in a nearby office, came into The Bookstore every day at lunchtime to browse. Booker became annoyed because Walker read books and magazines but never bought anything. Finally, Booker told Walker that he would call the police if Walker came into the store again.

Walker returned the next day, and Booker called the police. Booker made a citizen's arrest of Walker for violation of the local vagrancy ordinance that made it a misdemeanor to "loiter in an annoying fashion in any place open to the public." Walker objected loudly to the arrest, yelling, "You can't arrest me, I didn't take anything." *[handwritten: False Imprisonment]*

Reporter overheard Walker's remarks. Reporter worked for The News, the local newspaper, and recognized Walker because one year earlier Walker had led a movement to remove certain books from the local high school library. Reporter thought that the police were arresting Walker for shoplifting and rushed back to the paper to file a story on the arrest. *[handwritten: Defamation]*

The next day, The News reported that Walker had been arrested for shoplifting, in a story headlined: "Book Burner Arrested for Book Theft." *[handwritten: Libel + slander per se]*

Walker was charged with vagrancy. The charge was dismissed on the ground that the vagrancy ordinance had long been construed to require actual disturbance of the peace, and in this case there was no actual disturbance.

1. What claims, if any, does Walker have against Booker? Discuss.

2. What claims, if any, does Walker have against The News? Discuss.

Question 3, July 1995 California Bar Exam
Written by Dennis P. Saccuzzo

Call 1. Walker v. Booker

False Imprisonment

False imprisonment is intentional confinement of another within fixed boundaries.

By arresting Walker and calling the police, Booker voluntarily acted to intentionally confine Walker. Walker was confined within the fixed boundaries of the store because a reasonable person in Walker's shoes would not feel free to leave. Thus, Booker is liable for false imprisonment.

Booker's Defenses – Shopkeeper's Privilege

A shopkeeper has a privilege to detain a suspected shoplifter for a reasonable time if he has reasonable grounds, uses reasonable force, and conducts a reasonable investigation.

Walker came into Bookstore every day at lunch to browse. Booker became "annoyed" because Walker read books and magazines, but never bought anything. There are no facts to suggest that Booker ever suspected Walker of shoplifting. In fact, he relied on a vagrancy ordinance, therefore Booker had no reasonable grounds to suspect Walker of shoplifting.

Thus, the shopkeeper's privilege does not apply.

Lawful Arrest

Booker may claim the privilege of lawful arrest. A private citizen is not liable for an arrest made without a warrant as to a breach of the peace committed in his presence. Such an arrest is lawful even if the defendant is reasonably mistaken in his belief that a breach of the peace was being committed.

Here, the ordinance refers to loitering in an "annoying fashion;" it does not relate to breach of the peace. Indeed, the court found that there had been no actual breach of the peace. Further, as discussed, Booker had no belief that Walker had shoplifted. If Booker claims mistake, it will be found unreasonable.

Conclusion: Booker is liable for false imprisonment and has no defenses.

Malicious Prosecution

To establish malicious prosecution, Walker must show the following five elements:

1. Institution of Criminal Proceedings

Here, Booker called the police and made a citizen's arrest. Thus, he instituted criminal proceedings against Walker.

2. Termination in Plaintiff's Favor

The charge was dismissed on the grounds that the vagrancy ordinance had long been construed to require actual disturbance of the peace, and in this case there had been no actual disturbance.

3. Absence of Probable Cause

As previously discussed, Booker had no grounds to suspect Walker of shoplifting, and no cause to believe Walker was breaching the peace. Walker was in a bookstore. He merely read books and magazines, which is the type of conduct one expects from bookstore customers. He came in every day. Therefore, a reasonable person would have no basis to believe that Walker was "loitering in an annoying fashion."

4. Improper Purpose

Booker called the police and arrested Walker because he was "annoyed" that Walker never bought anything. His purpose was improper.

5. Damages

Booker suffered the indignity of arrest. It was his lunch hour, so he probably missed work. He also appears to have suffered shock; he yelled "you can't arrest me, I didn't take anything."

Conclusion: Booker is liable for malicious prosecution.

Abuse of Process

To establish abuse of process, Walker must show the following three elements:

1. Wrongful Use of Process

Booker's actions were motivated by his own annoyance because Walker never bought anything. His purpose appears to be to punish or retaliate against Walker. Thus, he misused the legal process for his own vindictive ends.

2. Definite Acts or Threats

Booker "threatened to call the police;" actually did call the police; and made a citizen's arrest of Walker which led to Walker being intentionally confined by Booker, as discussed above. Thus, Booker made definite acts and threats.

3. For Ulterior Purpose

Booker's ulterior purpose was that he wanted to keep Walker out of the store.

Conclusion: Booker is liable for abuse of process.

Intentional Infliction of Emotional Distress

Conduct of an extreme and outrageous nature calculated to cause and does cause severe emotional damage.

While Walker may have suffered severe emotional damage, he will not prevail on this tort because Booker's actions were neither extreme nor outrageous as they were not beyond the bounds of ordinary human decency and no facts indicate Walker had special sensitivities or a special relationship with Booker.

Battery

Intentional harmful or offensive touching.

No facts indicate Booker actually touched Walker to arrest him. If he did, then Walker would be liable for battery.

Call 2. Walker v. News

Respondeat Superior

A master is vicariously liable for the torts of servants that occur within the course and scope of employment.

Here, Reporter worked for the News. Therefore News is his master. Because Reporter was acting within his capacity as a reporter for News, his actions were within the course and scope of employment.

Therefore, News is vicariously liable for Reporter's acts.

Defamation

Defamation is a defamatory statement of or concerning plaintiff, published to a third party, that results in damages.

1. Defamatory Statement

News reported that Walker had been arrested for shoplifting books. Being accused of shoplifting books would definitely tend to lower anyone's reputation in the community. Because Walker had led a movement to remove certain books from the library, the damage to his reputation would be even greater. Therefore, the statement was defamatory.

2. Of or Concerning Plaintiff

The article referred specifically to Walker, and further identified him as a book burner, leaving no doubt that the statement referred to Walker. Because a reasonable person would understand that the defamatory statement applied to Walker, this element is established.

3. Publication

The defamatory statement was printed in a newspaper that is available to the public. Thus, the statement was published.

4. Damages to Plaintiff's Reputation

Damages are presumed for libel, which is a written statement. Damages are also presumed for slander per se, where the spoken defamatory statement goes to a crime, loathsome disease, the plaintiff's business, or chastity (of a woman).

Because the statement was written in the newspaper, it is libel, and damage to Walker's reputation is presumed.

Matter of Public Concern

If the defamatory statement is a matter of public concern, the plaintiff must also prove falsity and fault. News will successfully argue that Walker's arrest on criminal charges is a matter of public concern, especially since Walker had previously taken a public stand by leading a movement to remove books from the public library. Thus, Walker will have the additional burden of showing falsity and fault.

Falsity

News reported that Walker had been arrested for shoplifting. In fact, he was arrested for violation of the local vagrancy ordinance and charged with vagrancy. Therefore, the defamatory statement was false.

Fault

The test for fault depends on whether the plaintiff is a public figure. The standard for public figures is actual malice, which requires the defendant to have knowledge of the falsity, or a reckless disregard for the truth. The standard for a private figure is negligence.

Public Figure

A public figure is one who has achieved pervasive fame or voluntarily injected themselves into the public eye.

News will argue that Walker voluntarily injected himself into the public eye when he led a movement to remove certain books from the library, and that therefore he is a public figure.

However, Walker had been involved in the movement one year earlier. Thus, it is unlikely that Walker was still in the public eye.

[handwritten margin note: One year too long]

Even if Walker is found to be a public figure, News showed a reckless disregard for the truth when it erroneously published its defamatory statement, because a reasonable investigation would easily have revealed that Walker was not being charged with shoplifting.

Therefore, whether or not Walker is deemed to be a public figure, News is liable for defamation.

Intentional Infliction of Emotional Distress

Discussed and defined supra. Here, the defamatory statement, though false, was neither extreme nor outrageous. Therefore, News is not liable for this tort.

Invasion of Privacy – False Light

To establish a prima facie case for False Light, the plaintiff must show publication of highly offensive information on a widespread basis. If the matter is of public interest, malice must also be shown. However, truth is a defense.

1. Highly Offensive

Here, the statement "Book burner arrested for book theft" is highly offensive because presenting Walker in such a manner would be objectionable to a reasonable person.

2. Widespread

The statement was printed in a public newspaper.

3. Malice

As discussed above, News showed malice in their reckless disregard for the truth.

Defense – Truth

The statement was not true (discussed above). Therefore News has no defense.

Thus, News is liable for invasion of privacy under a False Light theory.

1-HOUR ESSAY

Dina, aged sixteen, lives at home with her mother, Mary, in a state where the age of majority is eighteen. Mary is aware that Dina has recently exhibited a sometimes violent and delusionary nature diagnosed as schizophrenia, and has attacked persons in the neighborhood. Medication that can control Dina's behavior has been prescribed, but without Mary's knowledge Dina has stopped taking it.

A week after Dina stopped taking her medication, she approached a neighbor, Paul, as he walked along the sidewalk fronting Mary's home. When she was face to face with Paul, Dina, without provocation, gestured threateningly and screamed, "I know you're out to get me and I'm going to get you first," and then strode away. *Threat*

Paul, who had no knowledge of Dina's mental illness, phoned Mary about the incident. Mary told Paul that "Dina has sometimes made threats to others, but I do not think that she will try to hurt you and I assure you that this will not happen again." Paul believed Mary's assurances and, for that reason, did not seek to avoid Dina.

Mary questioned Dina about the incident, scolded her, and asked if Dina was taking her medication. When Dina said she was, Mary did not pursue the matter. *Negligence*

Two days later, after Dina confronted Paul, Dina saw him raking leaves which had fallen into the street fronting their adjoining homes. Dina got on her bike and rode it as rapidly as she could directly at Paul. Although Dina swerved away from Paul at the last moment, Paul reacted by diving to one side. He struck his head on the curb and suffered a severe concussion and facial injuries.

Paul had sued Dina and Mary, alleging tortious causes of action.

1. Is Paul entitled to recover against Dina for:

   a. Assault? Discuss. *Threat*
   b. Battery? Discuss.

2. Is Paul entitled to recover against Mary:

   a. On the ground that Mary was negligent as to Paul? Discuss.
   b. On the ground that Mary is vicariously liable for Dina's conduct? Discuss.

TORTS
July 1993 California Bar Exam – Question 1
Analysis by Professor Dennis P. Saccuzzo

CALL #1 – Paul v. Dina *Act with intent to cause reasonable apprehension of imminent harmful or offensive touching*

(a)(1) Assault – Verbal Threat (for definition, see schema)

Act: Dina approached Paul voluntarily, then without provocation gestured threateningly & screamed ". . . I'm going to get you first."

Intent: Shown by express threat "I know you're out to get me and I'm going to get you first."

Reasonable Apprehension: A reasonable person would experience apprehension when face-to-face with someone gesturing threateningly.

Of Imminent: This is the main issue. Dina's threat was a future threat. Conditional or future threats and words alone are not enough. This can be argued both ways because Dina used threatening gestures and future threats.

Harmful and Offensive Touching: The gestures and future threats alone probably would not cause a reasonable person (objective standard) to experience imminent apprehension of harmful touching.

Conclusion: Dina is probably not liable for assault for the verbal threat.

(a)(2) Assault – Riding the Bike

Act: Dina got on her bike and rode it as rapidly as she could directly at Paul.

Intent: Dina had made expressed threats; rode the bike directly at Paul.

Reasonable Apprehension: A reasonable person in Paul's shoes would have a reasonable apprehension.

Of Imminent: She was riding directly at him as fast as she could.

Harmful or Offensive Touching: The issue is whether the Dina's swerving at the last moment saves Dina. It does not. Paul's reaction was normal.

Conclusion: Dina is liable for assault.

(a)(3) Competency/Infancy

These are hidden issues. The facts state Dina is 16 in a state where majority age is 18. Thus she is a minor.

Facts also indicate Dina is schizophrenic; sometimes violent and delusional. The law is that infancy and insanity are no defense to intentional torts.

(a)(4) Self-Defense

(See schema for definitions)

Facts indicate Dina, in her delusional state, believed Paul was out to get her. Arguably she was acting in self-defense. This argument will fail when the facts are applied to the elements. There are no facts indicating Dina was in imminent threat of harm. She was not privileged to use self-defense. Further, Dina was the aggressor. She had promised to get Paul first.

(b) Battery – Riding the Bicycle (See the schema for definitions)

Intentional harmful or offensive touching of another w/o consent

Intent: Dina rode her bike directly at Paul as fast as possible.

Transferred Intent: A hidden issue; Dina's intended assault could be transferred to the battery if the jury believes her argument that she didn't actually intend to cause harmful touching because she did in fact swerve away.

Harmful or Offensive: The issue is whether Dina actually caused the touching. She did, though indirectly. Paul's reaction of diving away was a natural and direct result of Dina's actions.

Self-Defense: See discussion above.

Conclusion: Dina is liable for battery.

CALL 2: Paul v. Mary

Breach of Duty of care which is the actual + proximate cause of P's damages.

(a) Negligence (See schema for definition)

Duty: Duty is the major issue. First, Mary may have a special duty because Dina is a child of known dangerous propensities. Even if she did not, she had a duty as a reasonable parent of a violent and delusional daughter to provide adequate supervision and control. She also had a duty to check whether Dina was actively taking her medications. Further, she had notice from Paul. Finally, she assured Paul he would not be harmed, and thereby arguably assumed a duty.

Breach: Mary breached all of the above duties. She did not supervise Dina, even after Paul put her on notice. She did not check to determine whether Dina was taking her medication even after Paul put her on notice and after she assured Paul.

Actual Cause: But for Mary's failure to supervise and make sure Dina was taking her medication, Dina would not have attacked Paul.

Proximate Cause:

Foreseeable Plaintiff: Paul lived in the neighborhood; he was in the zone of danger. Moreover, Mary had notice.

It is foreseeable the when one fails to properly supervise and check on a delusional schizophrenic adolescent that she might attack someone. It is also foreseeable that when one provides assurances to another, that person would rely on those assurances and would not take precautions to protect himself. Mary's argument that Dina was an intervening factor will fail because as Dina's parent Mary had the authority and means to control Dina.

Damages: Paul suffered a severe concussion and facial injuries. He will be entitled to all damages that flow from the tort.

Defenses: Mary's argument that Paul contributed to his own injury by not taking precautions will fail because it was reasonable for Paul to rely on Mary's assurances.

(b) Vicarious Liability

The general rule is parents are not liable for the acts of their children.

The exception is a child of known dangerous propensities. Dina had such propensities. Modernly, many states also have parental responsibility laws.

Conclusion: Mary would be vicariously liable either based on Dina's known propensities or under a modern statute if one existed in her state.

1-HOUR EXAM

Owner hired Plummer, a plumbing contractor, to repair the plumbing in a store that Owner planned to lease. In performing the repair, Plummer used a connector on a hot water pipe made of a different metal than the pipe itself. As a result of the incompatibility of the two metals, the connector corroded and weakened. This condition was not obvious because the weakened connection was located within a wall. After the repair was completed, the store was leased to Amy's a swimwear retailer.

Two years after Plummer finished the repairs, the connector burst. Hot water broke through the wall and sprayed into the store, scalding Carrie, a customer who was in the store at the time. The water also ruined swimsuits on display in the store. While repairs were being made, Amy's had to close for two months during the summer, causing significant financial loss. Emma, an employee of Amy's lost her job because of the closure.

1. What rights, if any, does Carrie have against Owner and against Plummer? Discuss.

2. What rights, if any, does Amy's have against Plummer? Discuss.

3. What rights, if any, does Emma have against Owner and against Plummer? Discuss.

Model Answer Written by Professor Dennis P. Saccuzzo

Note: *This question is similar to the July 2000 and July 1998 California Bar Tort questions with the addition of landowner liability.*

CALL #1 – Carrie's Rights

(a) Carrie v. Owner (O)

Negligence of Landowner/Special Duty

A landowner owes invitees a duty to warn of all known dangers or those discoverable by inspection. He must make a reasonable inspection of the premises.

As a business customer, Carrie is an <u>invitee</u> of Amy and Amy leased the property after Owner hired Plummer. As the landowner, O had a duty to make a reasonable inspection and warn of known or discoverable dangers. However, because the condition was located within a wall and therefore not obvious, it is unlikely that it would be discovered by an ordinary inspection. Therefore, O probably did not violate his duty as a landowner.

Negligence/Negligent Hiring of Plummer

Negligence is a breach of a duty of care which is the actual and proximate cause of a plaintiff's damages. To establish a claim for negligence Carrie must show that O owes her a duty of care as a foreseeable plaintiff, that O breached that duty, and that O's breach was the actual and proximate cause of C's damages. Finally, O must not have a valid defense.

O's property was commercial. He leased it to Amy and it is foreseeable that Amy would have customers such as Carrie. As a customer Carrie was in the zone of danger and therefore was a foreseeable plaintiff.

As discussed above, O probably did not breach his duty as a landowner. However, he also has a duty to act with the degree of care that an ordinary landowner would exercise under the circumstances. A reasonable Owner would do sufficient checking and research to hire a competent Plummer. No facts indicate that O exercised any care at all in hiring Plummer. If a reasonable checking would have revealed that Plummer was incompetent and had caused similar accidents, Carrie may be able to show that O breached his duty by hiring Plummer.

Causation and damages that may have resulted from Plummer's work will be discussed below because O's liability for negligent hiring will depend upon whether Plummer was in fact negligent in his work.

Respondeat Superior vs. Independent Contractor

C may attempt to hold O vicariously liable for Plummer's work under a respondeat superior theory. According to this theory the master is vicariously liable for torts of employees within the course and scope of employment.

The issue is whether Plummer's work was within the course and scope of employment under O. Facts indicate Plummer was a contractor. The general rule is that a principal is not liable for the torts of an agent if the agent was an independent contractor. Because P was a contractor, absent an exception O will not be held vicariously liable for Plummer's actions.

Exception: Non-delegable Duty

These are duties that are so important to the community that the employer will not be permitted to transfer his duties to another. Although there is no general rule for what is non-delegable, generally courts will hold matters of safety to be non-delegable.

Here, because safety is an issue, the courts will probably hold that the duty was non-delegable and therefore hold O liable.

Carrie's Damages

Carrie was scalded. If she prevails on any of the above theories, O will be liable for all her medical costs as well as pain and suffering. He will also be liable for any special damages that were causal, foreseeable, and certain.

Carrie v. Plummer

Negligence

Defined above, Carrie is a foreseeable plaintiff because any customer would be in the zone of danger of Plummer's work on a commercial building.

Plummer has a duty to act as a reasonably competent Plummer in the community. Carrie may also successfully argue that as a professional, Plummer owed a higher duty.

Duty and Breach

To determine the standard of care for plumbers, Carrie may bring in experienced experts who can testify as to the standard in the community. The court may also use custom as evidence of standard, or it may balance utility versus risk of the conduct.

Here, Plummer was working on a hot water pipe and used a connector made of a different metal. Because hot water pipes can be dangerous, it is likely that the reasonably prudent or professional plumber would take care not to use incompatible metals that might corrode. Moreover, the utility of using what is perhaps a cheaper metal is small compared to the risks of scalding someone. Therefore it is likely that Plummer breached a duty and fell below the standard of care when he conducted the work as he did.

Actual Cause

But for Plummer's use of incompatible metals, the connector would not have weakened and eventually burst, causing hot water to scald Carrie. Plummer is the actual cause of Carrie's injury.

Proximate Cause

It is foreseeable that a negligently installed system could burst and cause injury. Therefore, Plummer is the proximate cause of Carrie's injuries. Plummer will argue that the passage of time (2 years) was an intervening factor that should cut off his liability. This argument will fail because the link between Plummer's conduct and the burst pipe is direct, and no outside factors disrupted the causal chain.

Damages

Discussed above, Carrie suffered injury and is entitled to recovery.

Conclusion: Carrie has a stronger case against Plummer but could probably recover from either Plummer or Owner.

Contribution

If Carrie sues only O, O may implead Plummer for contribution.

CALL 2: Amy v. Plummer

Negligence

Discussed above, the issue is whether Amy is a foreseeable plaintiff. Plummer was working on a commercial building. It is foreseeable that the building would be leased to Amy. Therefore Amy is a foreseeable plaintiff because she is in the zone of danger.

As discussed above, Plummer breached a duty of care. Further, but for Plummer's breach, Amy's store and goods would not have been damaged, and it is foreseeable that such damage could result from faulty repair of a hot water pipe. As discussed, there were no factors other than time to break the causal link. Plummer is the actual and proximate cause of Amy's damages.

The Swimsuits

As a direct result of Plummer's breach, hot water ruined Amy's swimsuits on display in the store. The goal in tort law is to make the plaintiff whole. Amy will be entitled to all damages that flowed directly from Plummer's negligence. She will be entitled to replacement cost for the swimsuits. She will also be entitled to cost of repairs to the store.

Lost Profits

Amy suffered significant financial loss because she had to close for two months during the summer. Such losses do not flow directly from the tort. They are special damages which must be causal, foreseeable, certain, and unavoidable. The courts will not award speculative damages and the burden of proof will be on Amy.

The store was ruined by the hot water and needed to be repaired. Further, as discussed, such damage is foreseeable. The issue is whether Amy's lost profits can be proved with certainty. Amy has owned the store for only two years. It is unlikely that she can demonstrate a clear track record of profits that would convince the court that her losses are certain and not speculative. Even if she could succeed, she would still have to show that she could not have avoided the substantial loss and that the closure was necessary.

Duty to Mitigate

CALL 3: Emma's Rights versus Owner and Plummer

Emma's right to damages must be based on the negligence claims discussed above. She will have two problems.

First, Emma was an employee. As such, it is arguable that she is not a foreseeable plaintiff to whom Plummer or Owner owed a duty. Emma will probably win on this point because it is foreseeable that employees will be hired to work in commercial property.

More difficult for Emma will be her claim for financial loss. The courts generally do not award purely economic damages where there was no impact. Because Emma was not directly affected by the bursting pipe and her claim is purely economic, she is unlikely to prevail in her claim for lost wages. Moreover, her claim could be speculative because it is unclear how long she would have remained employed, even if the pipes didn't burst.

FEBRUARY 1989 CALIFORNIA BAR EXAM -- QUESTION 3

1-HOUR ESSAY

In May 1985, Dick, who was driving a truck owned by Ace Co., his employer, failed to stop at a red light at a busy intersection. Phil was lawfully bicycling through the intersection at the time. Dick collided with Phil. The force of the collision knocked Phil to the ground. Phil's legs were broken and his bicycle destroyed. Although the cycling helmet he wore shattered when he fell, Phil escaped head injuries.

A month after the accident, Phil retained an attorney, Len. Len assured Phil that he would pursue an action against Ace Co. and Helmet Co., the manufacturer of the shattered helmet. Three years later, in June 1988, Len revealed to Phil that he had been too busy to pursue settlement or file a lawsuit in his case. Phil was furious and told Len so.

In July 1988, Len filed a complaint in state court on behalf of Phil alleging negligence against Ace Co. and Helmet Co. Len believed Phil's case was barred by his state's two-year statute of limitations for negligence actions. However, he filed the complaint to placate Phil and served the summons and complaint on Ace Co. and Helmet Co.

Ace Co. and Helmet Co. hired attorneys to defend them and filed appropriate motions to dismiss. The state court dismissed Phil's damage action against Ace Co. and Helmet Co. on the ground that it is barred by the applicable statute of limitations.

What, if any, liability does Len have to:

1. Phil? Discuss.

2. Ace Co.? Discuss.   Wrongful Civil ~~prosecution~~ Proceedings

3. Helmet Co.? Discuss.   Abuse of Process

Analysis by Professor Dennis P. Saccuzzo

CALL #1 – Phil v. Len

This will require a suit within a suit. Phil must not only prove malpractice against Len, he must show that he would have prevailed in his original claim in order to establish damages.

Phil's Original Claim: Negligence Against Ace

Respondeat Superior (See schema for definitions)
Phil's claim against Ace will be based on a vicarious liability theory. Because Dick was acting within the course and scope of employment when he drove Ace's truck, Ace will be held liable for Dick's negligence under this theory.

Negligence (see schema and past models for definitions)

Duty: Dick had a duty to drive as the reasonably prudent truck driver.

Breach: Dick breached this duty when he failed to stop at a red light at a busy intersection.

Actual Cause: But for Dick's failure to stop, Dick would not have collided with Phil, causing him to be knocked to the ground.

Proximate Cause:

Foreseeable Plaintiff: Phil was lawfully bicycling through the intersection.

It is foreseeable that when a driver fails to stop at a red light somebody may be impacted. There were no intervening factors to break the causal chain.

Damages: Phil's legs were broken and his bicycle destroyed. Phil will be entitled to be made whole. He will receive all damages that flowed from the tort including medical bills, pain and suffering and property loss (bicycle and helmet). He will also be entitled to any special damages that are causal, foreseeable, certain, and unavoidable. No facts indicate special damages.

No contributory negligence or voluntary assumption of the risk here

Defenses: Phil did not contribute to his own injury; nor did he voluntarily encounter it. Ace has no defenses.

Conclusion: Ace would have been liable to Phil for damages. If Phil can prove Len was negligent, he can recover these damages from Len.

Phil's Original Claim: Product Liability Action Against Helmet Company

Phil may assert three theories in a products liability action against Helmet Co: strict liability in tort; negligence; and breach of warranty.

Strict Liability in Tort/Negligence/Warranty (See definitions in schema)

There are two main issues: Phil must show that the helmet was defective for his strict liability claim and that he suffered damages for all three claims.

No facts indicate a defect. Although the helmet shattered, Phil escaped head injuries. The helmet performed as expected. Again, Phil suffered no damages. He has no claim against Helmet Company.

Phil v. Len:

Malpractice (Negligence)

Duty: Len has a duty to conduct himself as a reasonably prudent attorney in the community. Expert evidence can easily show that a competent attorney would not allow the statute of limitations to lapse. Rules of professional conduct such as competence, diligence, and communication can also be used to show Len's duties.

Breach: Len breached his duties when he failed to file Phil's claim within the statute of limitations.

Actual Cause/Proximate Cause: But for Len's failure to file, Phil would have prevailed. It is foreseeable that a failure to file will cause Phil damage.

Foreseeable Plaintiff: As a client, Phil is a foreseeable plaintiff.

Damages: Phil lost his case. Len will be liable for all the damages he could have recovered against Ace.

Misrepresentation (Negligent)

(See definitions/elements in schema). Len is also liable under this theory. His representations as an attorney induced Phil's reliance in not seeking further legal advice and resulted in damages.

CALL 2: Ace v. Len

Wrongful Civil Proceedings

(see schema for rules)

Len did not have probable cause to file a suit because the statute had run. The court dismissed the action. Len's purpose was improper. He knew the case was barred but he filed to "placate" Phil. Len will be liable for this tort.

Abuse of Process

(See schema for rules).

This tort will fail because no facts show definite threats to accomplish the ulterior purpose.

CALL 3: Helmet Co. v. Len

Helmet Co. has the same claims as Ace. However, they have the additional argument that Len knew not only that the claim was barred but also that he never had a claim in the first place. Len will be liable to Helmet Co. for wrongful civil proceedings.

Professional Responsibility Issue

In California, Len is required to report this malpractice action to the state Bar. He is subject to discipline.

PROPERTY

Pure Property:

Property with Remedies:

Crossover Questions:

Property + Wills/Trusts:

FEB 2004 CALIFORNIA BAR EXAM -- QUESTION 4

1-HOUR ESSAY

Lori owns a small shopping center. In April 1999, Lori leased a store to Tony. Under the lease Tony agreed to pay Lori a monthly fixed rent of $500, plus a percentage of the gross revenue from the store. The lease term was five years. In part the lease provides:

Landlord and Tenant agree for themselves and their successors and assigns:
* * *

Do these covenants run to assignees?

4. Tenant has the right to renew this lease for an additional term of five years, on the same terms, by giving Landlord written notice during the last year of the lease.
5. Tenant will operate a gift and greeting-card store only. Landlord will not allow any other gift or greeting-card store in the center.
* * *

Assignee

In July 2000, Tony transferred his interest in the lease in writing to Ann. Ann continued to operate the store and pay rent.

In February 2003, a drugstore in the shopping center put in a small rack of greeting cards. Ann promptly complained, but Lori did nothing.

Beginning in March 2003, Ann stopped paying the percentage rent, but continued to pay the fixed rent alone. Lori took no action except to send a letter in April 2003 requesting payment of the percentage rent that was due.

In January 2004, Ann sent a letter to Lori requesting that Lori renew the lease according to its terms. Lori denied that she had any obligation to renew.

1. Is Ann entitled to a renewal of the lease? Discuss.

2. Is Lori entitled to the past-due percentage rent from:

    a. Ann? Discuss.
    b. Tony? Discuss.

Model Answer
Dennis Saccuzzo & Nancy E. Johnson

Call 1. Ann's Right to Renew

Tenancy for Years

A tenancy for years has the beginning and end of the estate fixed at the outset. It expires automatically without notice.

The Lori-to-Tony lease began in April 1999 and runs for 5 years, until March 31, 2004. It is a tenancy for years because its beginning (April 1999) and end (March 31, 2004) were set at the outset.

Lori-to-Tony lease – Statute of Frauds (S of F).

Leases for greater than 1 year are covered by the S of F. The S of F requires that the agreement be reduced to a writing signed by the parties.

The lease runs for 5 years so S of F applies and a writing is required. The existence of written clauses 4 & 5 indicates a writing. Assuming both Lori and Tony signed the lease agreement, the S of F would be satisfied.

July 2000 transfer from Tony to Ann: Assignment.

An assignment is a complete transfer of all interest.

Facts stipulate that Tony transferred his interest to Ann, indicating an assignment. The effect of an assignment is that the assignor (Tony) remains in privity of contract with the landlord (Lori). This means that Tony will be liable to Lori for all of his duties under the lease, including the duty to pay rent for the entire duration of the lease. The assignee (Ann) is in privity of estate with Lori, the landlord, and is subject to all covenants that run with the land.

Because the Tony-to-Ann assignment involved a lease greater than one year (July 2000 to March 31, 2004), a writing would have been required to satisfy the S of F. No facts indicate a writing, but such can be assumed. Thus, the assignment is valid.

Covenant to Renew

A covenant is a promise in a deed or lease that binds the promisor and promisee to act or refrain from certain conduct.

Paragraph 4 of the lease contained a provision allowing Tenant (Tony) the right to renew the lease for an additional 5 years. This provision is a promise to allow the Tenant to renew and is written in the lease. Thus it is a covenant. The issue is whether the benefit of the covenant to renew runs to Ann.

Does the benefit run to Ann?

For a benefit to run to successors in interest, there must be intent, the covenant must touch and concern the land, and there must be vertical privity.

Intent: The lease stipulates Lori & Tony agree for themselves and their **successors and assigns**, indicating intent for the covenant to run with the land to successors in interest such as Ann.

Touch and Concern (T & C): The covenant must make the land more valuable or useful. The right to renew lends some stability to the operation of the gift and greeting card store and operates as a valuable option contract, so it makes the land more valuable to the tenant. Therefore it touches and concerns the land.

Vertical Privity: The entire interest must be transferred. Facts indicate Tony transferred his interest to Ann, meeting this requirement.

Conclusion: The covenant to renew the lease runs with the land and Ann can enforce it against Lori, absent any valid defenses.

Defense: Breach of Covenant by Ann

The lease agreement contained a covenant that the Tony would pay a fixed rent of $500 plus a percentage of gross revenue. Ann failed to pay a percentage of the gross revenue. The issue is whether this burden to pay a fixed percentage is a covenant that runs with the land and can be enforced by Lori against Ann as a successor in interest.

Burden of a Covenant to run?

For the burden of a covenant to run, there must be intent, notice, T & C, and privity.

Intent. Discussed above. The language of the lease indicates the parties intended the covenant to run to successors and assigns.

Notice. Ann complied with the terms from July 02 to Feb 03, so she knew about the promise. *Knowledge of promise, constructive notice,*

T & C. The covenant to pay rent is central to any lease and the ability of real property to generate rents is a major factor in its value. Therefore Ann's duty to pay rent made the land more valuable to Lori.

Privity. Must be both horizontal and vertical.
Horizontal privity exists when the original parties have an interest in land at the same time. Lori and Tony were the original parties and were in a L/T relationship. Thus, they had a common interest, meeting this element.

Vertical privity is discussed above; the entire interest was transferred.

Conclusion: When Ann stopped paying the percentage, she breached the covenant.

Effect of Ann's Failure to Pay the Required Rent

When a tenant fails to pay rent the landlord can terminate the lease, sue for damages and evict the tenant.

As discussed above, Ann has failed to pay rent as required. Ann's failure to pay the requisite rent places her in breach, and absent a defense by Ann, Lori can exercise her right to evict Ann and sue for damages. If Ann cures by paying past due rent plus interest, then Ann may be able to enforce the covenant that would allow her to renew the lease. Otherwise, Ann has no right to renew.

1. Ann's Defense: Waiver

A waiver is a voluntary relinquishment of a right. Generally, a waiver can be retracted at any time unless there has been detrimental reliance. When Lori took no action and accepted the reduced rent payments, she arguably waived her rights. No facts indicate detrimental reliance. Therefore, Lori has the right to retract her waiver and exercise her rights to terminate the lease, as discussed above.

2. Ann's Defense: Breach of Covenant by Lori to exclude any other card store

Paragraph 5 of the lease states that Landlord will not allow any other gift or greeting card store in the Center. It is a covenant because it is a promise by Lori to protect the Tony from competition. Presumably, this promise is linked to Tony's agreement to pay a percentage of gross revenues from the gift and greeting card store Tony promised to operate. To determine if the covenant has been breached, it is necessary to determine whether the benefit it confers runs to Ann, Tony's successor in interest.

Does the benefit run to Ann?

Intent: As discussed, the Lease stipulates Lori & Tony agree for themselves and their **successors and assigns**, indicating intent that the covenant runs with the land to successors in interest such as Ann.

Touch and Concern (T & C): Here, the covenant would prevent competition, making it more valuable to Ann.

Vertical Privity: Discussed above; the entire interest was transferred.

Conclusion: The covenant runs with the land and Ann can enforce it against Lori.

Breach of Covenant by L: Small rack of greeting cards – Lori did nothing.

Ann promptly complained after a drugstore put in a small rack of greeting cards. If this rack is construed as "a store," Lori breached the covenant when she did nothing.

Effect of Breach: Suit for damages or equitable servitude.

Assuming a breach, Ann's remedies would be to sue for damages (*e.g.,* loss of income due to competing entity) under a real covenant theory, or pursue a remedy in equity under an equitable servitude. However, she cannot take self-help measures and unilaterally refuse to pay rent.

An equitable servitude requires intent, notice, and T & C. As indicated above, there was intent and T & C. Notice to Lori was actual, as she was a party to the original lease agreement.

Conclusion: Assuming a breach by Lori if the rack of cards is construed as a store, A is entitled to damages or a court order that would cause Lori to take steps to eliminate the competition caused by the drugstore. However, Ann took unilateral action and refused to pay rent as specified in the lease. Therefore the argument of a breach of covenant by Lori will not serve as a defense against Lori's argument to terminate the lease, precluding Ann's right to renew.

Therefore breach of covenant by L is no defense.

Call 1 conclusion: Ann's request to renew:

Ann will not be entitled to renew the lease because she breached her duty to pay rent under the covenant and therefore has subjected herself to eviction and termination of the lease by Lori.

Call 2.

a) Lori v. Ann

Covenant: Duty to Pay Rent

In order for Lori to recover from Ann, she will have to show that the covenant providing for a payment of a percentage of the gross revenues is a covenant, the burden of which would run to Ann. As indicated, as a result of the valid assignment, Ann was in privity of estate with Lori. Moreover, the above analyses demonstrate that the burden to pay the percentage does in fact run to Ann, who has breached that covenant.

Assuming Lori did not waive her rights by accepting only the $500 fixed rent, Lori can sue Ann for damages to recover the rents from Ann.

Ann's Defenses: Constructive Eviction

Ann can claim constructive eviction as a defense. She will have to show that (1) Lori is at fault (2) for a substantial interference that made the premises uninhabitable.

Here, A remained on the premises and there is no indication that the drugstore small rack of greeting cards made the premises uninhabitable.

Even if Ann were constructively evicted, under this theory Ann would be required to vacate within a reasonable time in order to have her rental obligation excused. Ann did not leave. She continued to stay on the premises and requested a renewal of the lease.

The warranty of habitability will not work because it applies only to residential property. Ann was using the premises for commercial purposes (to sell cards).

Conclusion: Lori is entitled to rent from Ann and Ann has no defenses.

Ann's Counterclaim: Breach of Covenant

As indicated above (see Call 1), Ann has a claim for damages under a real covenant theory. Ann can counterclaim against L in the event of a lawsuit.

Ann can reasonably sue for lost profits due to the drugstore card rack. Her losses may therefore offset any lost rent L may claim.

b) Lori v. Tony

As indicated, following the assignment, Lori and Tony remained in privity of contract. Therefore, Lori may sue Tony under the lease in which Tony agreed to pay a percentage of gross profits from the store.

No facts indicate a novation, in which Lori agreed to accept Ann and thereby relieve Tony of his obligation under the lease. Therefore, Tony will also be liable to Lori. Tony, in turn, may sue Ann for any breach of his assignment contract, assuming he had one. If Tony did not have a written agreement, then Ann can successfully assert the S of F as a defense, because the Tony-Ann agreement involved a lease greater than one year.

FEBRUARY 2003 CALIFORNIA BAR EXAM -- QUESTION 2

1-HOUR EXAM

Olga, a widow, owned Blackacre, a lakeside lot and cottage. On her seventieth birthday she had a pleasant reunion with her niece, Nan, and decided to give Blackacre to Nan. Olga had a valid will leaving "to my three children in equal shares all the property I own at my death." She did not want her children to know of the gift to Nan while she was alive, nor did she want to change her will. Olga asked Bruce, a friend, for help in the matter.

Bruce furnished Olga with a deed form that by its terms would effect a present conveyance. Olga completed the form, naming herself as grantor and Nan as grantee, designating Blackacre as the property conveyed, and including an accurate description of Blackacre. Olga signed the deed and Bruce, a notary, acknowledged her signature. Olga then handed the deed to Bruce, and told him, "Hold this deed and record it if Nan survives me." Nan knew nothing of this transaction.

As time passed Olga saw little of Nan and lost interest in her. One day she called Bruce on the telephone and told him to destroy the deed. However, Bruce did not destroy the deed. A week later Olga died.

Nan learned of the transaction when Bruce sent her the deed, which he had by then recorded. Nan was delighted with the gift and is planning to move to Blackacre.

Olga never changed her will and it was in effect on the day of her death.

Who owns Blackacre? Discuss.

FEBRUARY 2003, QUESTION 2
PROPERTY

-- Written by Dennis P. Saccuzzo & Nancy E. Johnson

Commentary:

This is a very difficult and unusual fact pattern, and there is no easy approach. Every Bar exam includes at least one or two "freak-out" questions like this one. To handle such questions, it is best to concentrate on identifying the major and subsidiary issues raised by the facts and discuss them.

Here, there is a big obvious issue of delivery of the deed, and the validity of a conditional delivery. Secondary to these larger issues are issues pertaining to the contents of the deed, the Statute of Frauds, and acceptance of the deed. In property questions it is particularly important to carefully define all terms of art and explain the subsidiary issues. Therefore, our model defines deeds and thoroughly covers the Statute of Frauds before getting into the central issue of delivery.

The problem in this fact pattern is that delivery is to a 3rd party with a condition (record only if Nan survives me). Thus the issues of delivery to a third party and conditional delivery had to be covered. Underlying both of these issues is whether Bruce, the 3rd party, was an independent or personal agent of Olga, owner of Blackacre. The following model illustrates the relevant on-point rules of law and provides an example of how one might have applied the facts to these rules.

The Bar considered this question to be a property/wills crossover. Indeed, minor property issues often appear in the context of a wills/trust problem. But here the property issues outweighed the wills issues, which is unusual.

Because the fact pattern made explicit reference to a will and gave relevant facts, wills law had to be discussed. The most difficult part of this question was seeing the hidden possibility that the form deed could be construed as a holographic will or codicil. Seeing this issue, you could then apply wills law to whether the holograph was validly revoked.

Careful study of this fact pattern is particularly important for California Bar candidates, as it shows new approaches to the essays for which candidates should prepare themselves.

Summary of Issue:

Olga had a valid will leaving Blackacre (BA) to her 3 children. She subsequently wanted to give BA to Nan as a gift at her death and completed a deed form naming Nan as grantee. The main issue is who owns BA.

Conveyance

In giving BA to Nan, Olga attempted a conveyance. Conveyance requires a valid deed that complies with the Statute of Frauds, an effective present delivery, and acceptance. Olga gave the completed form deed to her friend Bruce with instructions to record the deed if Nan survived her.

Deed and Statute of Frauds

A deed is the normal and ordinary way of transferring property. As an interest in property, the deed must be in writing to satisfy the Statute of Frauds. The contents of the deed must include the identity of the parties, a description of the land, consideration (if any), and the signatures of the parties to be charged.

Olga, owner of BA, was furnished with the form deed by her friend, Bruce. The first issue is whether the deed contained the proper contents. When Olga named herself as grantor and Nan as grantee, she clearly identified the parties. Facts stipulate that Olga included an accurate description of BA on the form deed, meeting the second element. Because this was a gift from Olga to Nan, there was no consideration; nor is consideration a necessary element of a conveyance. Olga signed the deed and Bruce, who was a notary, acknowledged her signature. Therefore the deed is valid and satisfies the Statute of Frauds.

Delivery

Proper delivery requires the intent of the grantor to make a present transfer. Once delivery (*i.e.* intent to transfer) is found, it cannot be retracted. Physical delivery is not necessary. In fact, the grantor may deliver the deed to an independent third party for future delivery according to the grantor's specific instructions or effectuate delivery through his or her own agent. However, should the grantor try to effectuate delivery through her own agent with conditional instructions, there is no delivery and there is no effective conveyance until the condition has been fulfilled and the deed has been delivered to the grantee. This is because, in this situation, the grantor has not relinquished control: by definition, the grantor's own agent is subject to her continuing control until the deed is delivered to the grantee.

Several key facts indicate a present intent to deliver. After a pleasant reunion with her niece, Nan, Olga "decided" to give BA to Nan. She asked her friend Bruce for help in transferring BA to Nan without the knowledge of her children who were equal beneficiaries under her valid will. By its terms, the deed would effectuate a present conveyance. Olga did not physically deliver the deed but instead entrusted it to her friend Bruce to record on behalf of Nan. However, Olga then told Bruce to record the deed only on the condition that Nan survives her.

Although delivery to an independent third party with instructions constitutes a valid delivery, as indicated, present delivery with conditions cannot be effectuated by one's own agent until the condition has been fulfilled. The next issue then is whether Bruce was an independent agent or a personal agent of Olga.

Independent versus personal agent

A common practice is deposit of the deed with an independent third party, or escrow agent, who releases the deed on fulfillment of conditions such as payment. The deed must be irrevocably delivered to the escrow agent and the agreement must be in writing. Bruce was a notary but no facts indicate he was an escrow agent or that he was independent. In fact, Bruce was Olga's friend and was assisting her in the conveyance. No facts indicate the deed was irrevocably delivered. Moreover, the instructions to record if "Nan survives me" were given orally, and not in writing. Thus, the delivery to Bruce does not meet the requirements of escrow. There is a strong argument that Bruce was not independent and would best be construed as an agent of Olga's.

Bruce as Olga's Personal Agent

Assuming Bruce was Olga's personal agent and the verbally given conditions were effective, there was no effective delivery when Olga handed the deed to Bruce with instructions to hold it and record it if Nan survived her, because under these conditions Olga maintained control. Therefore, in order to find an effective delivery Nan will have to look to another theory.

Fulfillment of Conditions

One theory is that even if Bruce is Olga's personal agent, present delivery with conditions by one's own agent can be effectuated when the conditions have been fulfilled. In this case, Nan survived Olga, therefore the condition was fulfilled. Arguably, when Bruce recorded the deed after Olga's death, present delivery was fulfilled and Nan is the owner of BA.

Bruce as Independent Agent

A second theory is that Bruce was independent, as demonstrated by his conduct in ignoring Olga's telephoned instruction that he destroy the deed. As an independent agent, when Bruce accepted the deed Olga relinquished control and therefore there was present intent and valid delivery. Under this theory, upon Olga's death, when Bruce properly recorded, Nan became the owner of BA.

Present Intent to Transfer a Future Interest

Nan can also argue that Olga had the present intent to convey a future interest when she handed the deed to Bruce with instructions. Under this theory, Olga's transfer to Bruce, the third party, demonstrated her present intent to create a life estate for herself and a contingent remainder for Nan. A life estate is a present possessory interest that terminates at the death of someone (in this case, Olga). A remainder is a future interest capable of becoming possessory immediately upon the termination of the preceding estate (in this case, Olga's life estate). A remainder is contingent if there is an unascertainable beneficiary or a condition precedent. Here, the condition precedent is that Nan survive Olga. Should Nan fail to survive, Olga would have a reversion and again have a fee simple in BA.

If Bruce is Olga's personal agent, this theory will not work to demonstrate present intent to transfer for the reasons stated above: Olga maintained dominion and control over the deed, thereby refuting any argument of a present transfer. To give effect to the present transfer under these conditions would essentially allow Olga to effectuate a testamentary transfer while evading the formalities of the Statute of Wills: it would mean that Olga had irrevocably transferred all but her life estate, putting the deed beyond her dominion and recall. In that case, Bruce could not be her agent because an agent is always subject to the control of his principal.

Although this theory has flaws, Nan has a good case based on (1) personal agency with fulfillment of conditions and (2) independent agency.

Acceptance

Assuming valid delivery, Nan has a good argument for acceptance. Generally acceptance by the grantee is presumed whether or not she has knowledge. Although Nan knew nothing of the transaction between Olga and Bruce, when Bruce sent her the deed she was delighted with the gift and planned to move in. These facts would suggest an acceptance.

Olga's Attempted Revocation

Olga lost interest in Nan and one day called Bruce and instructed him to destroy the deed. If Bruce was Olga's agent and Olga, as indicated, maintained control, Bruce was legally obligated to follow her instructions. He did not, and has at least two valid theories to support his conduct. First, as an independent agent who accepted delivery, he now has dominion and control. Second, the instructions to destroy were not in writing and because they involved an interest in real property, they would not be effective under the Statute of Frauds absent a writing.

Conclusion: Nan has some strong, valid arguments to support her claim for BA. However, these arguments hinge on complex legal issues of agency. Nan can also attempt to make arguments under wills law.

Alternative Theory – Testamentary Disposition

Wills Formalities

A valid will requires testamentary intent, capacity, and wills formalities. These formalities require that the testator sign in the presence of two attesting witnesses who are present at the same time and who knew it was a will. Nan can argue that the form deed completed by Olga was a formal will or codicil (amendment to a will, which requires the same formalities). This argument will fail for a number of reasons. There was only one signature (Bruce's) and Bruce did not believe this was a will -- he knew it was a deed.

Valid Holograph

Nan can also argue that the form deed represented a valid holographic codicil, assuming Olga completed the form deed in her own handwriting. A holographic will or codicil is valid if it contains the signature of the testator, the material provisions are in T's handwriting, and testamentary intent is found. In this case, it was signed and the material provisions named Olga as grantor and Nan as grantee, described BA, and designated BA as the property to be conveyed. Unfortunately for Nan, even if the material provisions were in Olga's handwriting, there is no testamentary intent. In fact, the deed form by its terms effected a present conveyance. Olga's verbal instructions to record if Nan survives would not provide the requisite testamentary intent because those instructions were not written and not part of the document.

Revocation

If the document had been valid as a holographic will or codicil, Olga's attempt to revoke it would not have been successful. Olga called Bruce and told him to destroy the deed. Treating the deed as a holograph, this would have been an attempted revocation by physical act by a third party. Such revocation requires intent to revoke and a physical act in the presence of T, at the direction of T. Although Olga demonstrated the intent to revoke when she directed Bruce to destroy the deed, there was no physical act in her presence. Therefore, there was no valid revocation by physical act.

Conclusion

Nan has a strong case for ownership of BA under property law, but not under wills law. By contrast, the children have a valid will devising BA to them. The outcome will be a close call.

1-HOUR ESSAY

Able owned Whiteacre in fee simple absolute. Baker owned Blackacre, an adjacent property. In 1999, Able gave Baker a valid deed granting him an easement that gave him the right to cross Whiteacre on an established dirt road in order to reach a public highway. Baker did not record the deed. The dirt road crosses over Whiteacre and extends across Blackacre to Baker's house. Both Baker's house and the dirt road are plainly visible from Whitacre.

In 2000, Able conveyed Whiteacre to Mary in fee simple absolute by a valid general warranty deed that contained all the typical covenants but did not mention Baker's easement. Mary paid Able $15,000 for Whiteacre and recorded her deed.

Thereafter, Mary borrowed $10,000 from Bank and gave Bank a note secured by a deed of trust on Whiteacre naming Bank as beneficiary under the deed of trust. Bank conducted a title search but did not physically inspect Whiteacre. Bank recorded its deed of trust. Mary defaulted on the loan. In 2001, Bank lawfully foreclosed on Whiteacre and had it appraised. The appraiser determined that Whiteacre had a fair market value of $15,000 without Baker's easement and a fair market value of $8,000 with Baker's easement. Bank intends to sell Whiteacre and to sue Mary for the difference between the sale price and the loan balance.

The following statute is in force in this jurisdiction:

> Every conveyance or grant that is not recorded is void as against any subsequent good faith purchaser or beneficiary under a deed of trust who provides valuable consideration and whose interest is first duly recorded.

1. What interests, if any, does Baker have in Whiteacre? Discuss.

2. What interests, if any, does Bank have in Whiteacre? Discuss.

3. What claims, if any, may Mary assert against Able? Discuss.

JULY 2002, QUESTION 2
PROPERTY

-- Written by Dennis P. Saccuzzo & Nancy E. Johnson

Commentary:

The key to a good answer for a property fact pattern is to carefully and thoroughly address each issue needed to respond to a call of the question. Where there is only one general call (e.g., "What are Mary's rights? Discuss."), a simple but effective response is to address each issue as it arises.

It is very important to define any term of art and explain the effect of each and every transaction. For example, as the following model shows, to explain Baker's interests it was necessary to explain and define easement, express easement, easement by grant, easement appurtenant, dominant estate, servient estate, and the effect of B's failure to record. Then, to explain the effect of failure to record, it was necessary to define and explain recording statutes, types of recording statutes, BFP, and the three types of notice.

In the property chapter in the Bar Secrets™ book (Bar Secrets: The Multistate Subjects), the cluster of issues that arise for any given issue (e.g., easement) are presented together as a group to help candidates structure answers and cover all the relevant (related) issues that must be addressed. The book also provides definitions for the various terms of art.

A major but common mistake is the failure to define terms of art. Bar candidates seem to reason that the Bar Examiners know what an easement is, so why should I define it? The point is, the Bar Examiners want to know that you know the definition and can apply the facts in the fact pattern to it.

Interestingly, this question on the July 2002 Bar exam was almost identical to Question 3 on the February 1994 Bar exam. In that question, Al (rather than Able) executed a valid quitclaim deed to Betty (rather than Baker), granting Betty an easement. Eventually the servient estate was sold for value to a purchaser who recorded but who did not qualify as a BFP because he was on inquiry notice of B's easement. This purchaser then had to sue the seller of the encumbered property under the general warranty deed.

Call 1: Baker's Interest in Whiteacre (WA)

Express Easement by Grant

An easement is and interest in land and, as such, is covered by the Statute of Frauds. An affirmative easement is the right to make limited use of the land. A negative easement is the right to restrict the use of the land.

In 1999 Able, an adjacent property owner, gave Baker a valid deed granting him an easement. A deed is a written instrument that is the normal and ordinary way of transferring property. Therefore the Statute of Frauds is satisfied and the easement is valid. Because the easement was created by a writing, it is known as an express easement. Able, the grantor, specifically conveyed the easement to B, so the express easement was by grant.

Easement Appurtenant

There are two basic types of easements. Easements appurtenant are tied to the land. To form such easements by law requires two pieces of land and an intent to benefit the land. Easement in gross requires only one piece of land with an intent to benefit a particular person.

Baker's easement involved Whiteacre (WA), owned by Able, and Blackacre (BA), owned by Baker. Thus, it involved two pieces of land. Evidence of the intent of the easement to benefit BA can be found in that the two pieces of land are adjacent, and the easement was a dirt road that extended over WA across BA to Baker's house. The easement benefited BA by providing an access route from BA to the public highway. Thus, the easement was appurtenant.

In an easement appurtenant the dominant estate is the one that benefits; the burdened estate is the one whose use is restricted. Here, BA is the dominant estate because BA benefits by having an access road to the public highway; WA is the burdened estate because the owner of this parcel cannot prevent the owner of BA from crossing over WA along the easement.

Effect of B's Failure to Record

Recording acts are designed to give notice to subsequent purchasers. The basic policy is to protect subsequent bona fide purchasers (BFPs) from unrecorded transfers and interests. In general, all prior interests in land are void if not duly recorded as to a subsequent BFP for value.

Recording Act Statutes

There are 3 types of recording acts. In a race jurisdiction, the first to record prevails, irrespective of notice. In a notice jurisdiction, a subsequent BFP without notice prevails against any grantee who fails to record. In a race notice jurisdiction, to prevail one must be the first BFP without notice to record.

Race-Notice Statute

The statute in force in B's jurisdiction is a race notice statute, because a conveyance not recorded is void as to a BFP who "first duly records." In 2000 Able, owner of WA in fee simple, conveyed WA to Mary by a valid deed. Mary paid $15,000, meeting the requirement of valid consideration. She then recorded her deed. Because B never recorded, Mary was the first to record.

BFP

The issue is whether Mary is a BFP without notice. A BFP acts in good faith without notice of an earlier transaction. Notice may be actual, constructive, or inquiry.

No facts indicate Mary had actual notice. In fact, A did not mention B's easement. Further, because B failed to record, Mary did not have constructive notice.

Inquiry notice exists where a reasonable person would ask about an earlier transaction and discover such with a reasonable inspection. Here, both B's house and the dirt road are plainly visible from WA. As such, a reasonable person in Mary's shoes had a duty to inquire about the road, and a reasonable inspection would have revealed B's easement.

Hence, Mary was on inquiry notice and does not qualify as a BFP. Her recording of the deed would therefore not extinguish B's easement.

Conclusion: B has a valid easement over WA.

Call 2: Bank's Interest

Mortgage

A mortgage is a conveyance to a creditor. It is a device to secure a loan on real property. The debtor is called the mortgagor because it is she who made the conveyance. The lender is the mortgagee.

Here, Mary named Bank as beneficiary of WA under the deed of trust, thereby creating a mortgage. Mary is the mortgagor because she borrowed $10,000. Bank is the mortgagee to whom Mary owes $10,000.

Deed of Trust and Mary's Default | Foreclosure

In a deed of trust, the deed is given by the mortgagee to a third party. Such deeds allow the lender to cause a private sale of the real property that secures the debt on default by the borrower. Mary defaulted on the loan, and Bank exercised its right to foreclose and sell WA.

Bank's Interest in B's Easement

The fair market value of WA without the easement is $15,000, but with the easement it is only $8,000, or $2000 less than Bank's interest. Bank conducted a title search, which means it evaluated all transactions on WA within the chain of title. Because B never recorded, B's easement would not be found within the chain of title.

Unfortunately, Bank failed to conduct a reasonable inspection. Like Mary, Bank was on inquiry notice, and therefore does not qualify as a BFP, even assuming Bank properly recorded the mortgage. Therefore, Bank's interest in WA is limited to its value with B's easement, or $8000. It can sell WA for $8,000 and bring a deficiency suit against Mary for the remaining $2,000.

Deficiency Suit.

Call 3: Mary's Claims Against Able

General Warranty Deed

When A sold WA to Mary, he did so under a general warranty deed. Such a deed has 6 covenants; three present that do not run with the land and are personal to the grantee (seisin, convey, encumbrances), and three that do run with the land (quiet enjoyment, warranty, and further assurances). Mary may make claims against A under these covenants.

Seisin: This covenant says that the seller had a claim of ownership to the property. Although A had a claim of ownership in WA, her claim was limited by B's valid easement appurtenant. A failed to mention the easement and therefore did not have the interest in WA implied when he sold WA in fee simple absolute with a general warranty deed. Therefore, Mary can bring a claim under this covenant and sue A fro damages, which is easily measured by the difference in the value of WA with and without B's easement ($7,000).

Convey: This covenant says seller had a right to convey. A owned WA and did have a right to convey it, subject to B's easement.

Encumbrances: This covenant says the property is free of encumbrances. An easement is an encumbrance. Hence, A breached this covenant because he sold WA when it was encumbered by B's easement. M can sue A for damages under this covenant.

Quiet Enjoyment: This covenant says buyer will not be disturbed by lawful claims of title. B has a lawful claim of title, which B will no doubt assert in any action by Bank or Mary pertaining to B's easement. Mary will then have a claim against A and can sue for damages.

B has lawful claim of title regarding the easement

Warranty: This warranty says seller will defend buyer against lawful claims. A will be required to defend Mary against any future action B might bring.

Further Assurances: Under this covenant, seller must do what is needed to perfect title. A can do this by purchasing B's easement. If he cannot, A will be liable for the difference between the value of WA with B's easement and without.

Conclusion: Mary has a claim for damages against A under the covenants of the general warranty deed.

JULY 2001 CALIFORNIA BAR EXAM -- QUESTION 2

1-HOUR ESSAY

Artist owns a workshop in a condominium building consisting of the workshops and sales counters of sculptors, painters, potters, weavers, and other craftspeople. The covenants, conditions and regulations (CC&Rs) of the building provide for a board of managers (Board), which has authority to make "necessary and appropriate rules." Board long ago established a rule against the sale within the building of items not created within the sellers' workshops.

3-yr lease

Artist accepted a three-year fellowship in Europe and leased the workshop to Weaver for that period. The lease prohibited an assignment of Weaver's rights. Weaver used the workshop to produce custom textiles.

A year into the term, Weaver transferred her right of occupancy to Sculptor for one year. Sculptor moved into the workshop with his cot, electric hotplate, and clothes. He also brought several works of art that he had created during a stay in South America and offered them for sale along with his current works. Sculptor mailed his rent checks every month to Artist, who accepted them. Both Weaver and Sculptor knew the terms of the CC&Rs and Board's rules when they acquired their interests in the workshop. *Waiver*

Three months after Sculptor moved in, Board told Sculptor to stop selling his South American pieces. He refused to do so and thereafter withheld his rent and complained that the regulation was unreasonable and that the building's heating was erratic.

1. What action, if any, may Board take against Artist to enforce the rule against the sale of Sculptor's South American pieces? Discuss.
2. Can Artist recover from Weaver the rent that Sculptor has refused to pay? Discuss.
3. Can Artist evict Sculptor from his occupancy? Discuss.

B v. A — Rule against Sale of Outside art

A v W — Breach of lease

A v. S — Eviction

JULY 2001, QUESTION 2

-- Written by Dennis P. Saccuzzo

Commentary:

The following question is a relatively modern version of a landlord-tenant fact pattern. The California Bar exam tests landlord-tenant (LT) issues periodically. Prior to this question, LT issues were tested in July 1999 and February 1997 or about every 2 – 2 ½ years between 1997 and 2001. Prior to February 1997, LT was tested in July 1993 and February 1989. Since this question, LT issues have not been tested as of July 2003, and can be expected soon.

The present fact pattern is divided into 3 distinct calls. As usual, when there are multiple calls it is essential to be responsive to the question and to answer the calls in the order given.

Here we have a condo owner (Artist) who leases his property for a 3-year period to Weaver. In spite of an anti-assignment clause, after one year Weaver subleases his leasehold estate for one year to Sculptor. Sculptor then violates a covenant of the building by selling items not made on the premises, and then refuses to pay rent. (T almost always refuses to pay rent in a landlord-tenant hypo – otherwise there wouldn't be much to talk about.)

The wrinkle in call 1 is that it asks what actions can be taken to enforce the rule against Sculptor's prohibited sale against Artist, the original owner. Many Bar candidates erred by trying to enforce the covenant against Sculptor, the one who violated the rule. That is not what the question asked. The model we provide shows a standard approach to real covenants and equitable servitudes. Notice that the big, arguable issue was whether the covenant touched and concerned the land.

Call 2 then asks whether Artist can recover from Weaver (the sublessor) for Sculptor's refusal to pay rent. Again, candidates erred by going directly after Sculptor. One problem in going after Artist is that he accepted rent directly from Sculptor, raising the issue of waiver. However, the bigger issues were sublease, assignment, anti-assignment clauses, and W's defenses (constructive eviction and warranty of habitability). Experience with LT questions on the California Bar exam is that one must always discuss both of these defenses, and not in general but by specific elements because almost always all the elements of only one of the defenses can be met.

Call 3 finally asks whether Artist can go directly after Sculptor. A precise understanding of sublease and assignment was necessary to successfully address the call, as illustrated in the following model.

Call 1. What action may Board take against Artist?

Covenants

Covenants are promises in a deed or lease that bind the promisor and promisee to act or refrain from certain conduct [p. 46].

Artist owns a workshop in a condominium (condo) with CC&Rs that grant a Board of Managers authority to make "necessary and appropriate rules." The Board has created a rule against the sale of items not created within the seller's workshops. Generally, CC&Rs are incorporated by reference into deeds or leases, and the present rule requires the parties to refrain from selling items not made in the condo. Therefore, a covenant exists and Board may attempt to enforce it against Artist in a court of law (real covenant) or a court of equity (equitable servitude).

Real Covenant

The covenant not to sell is a burden on Artist. For the burden to run to Artist, Board must show the following elements: (1) intent, (2) notice, (3) touch and concern the land, and (4) privity (both horizontal and vertical).

(1) Intent. To meet this element the parties must have intended the covenant to run with the land and to subsequent parties. The Board has authority to make necessary and appropriate rules, and established the sale ban long ago. Intent is strongly implied because the rule would be meaningless if it did not run with the land or bind successors. The court will likely find intent.

(2) Notice. Notice may be actual or constructive through recording of the CC&Rs and Board-adopted rules. Artist would have had actual notice if he had been told of the rules when he acquired his interest, or if he had been an owner when the rule was established. He would have constructive notice through the CC&Rs if the rule was already in place when he acquired his interest.

(3) Touch and Concern. To meet this element, the covenant generally must make the land more valuable or useful. Because the covenant in question merely prohibits sale of items not created in Condo, A will argue that the covenant merely protects residents of the Condo but does not affect the land. This argument will fail because in protecting residents against competition, the covenant makes the land more valuable to its occupants. Thus, this element will likely be met.

4 Privity. Privity must be both horizontal and vertical.

Horizontal Privity. This element requires that the original parties have an interest in land at the same time. Facts indicate that the CC&Rs go with the building. Thus, they were part of the original conditions of the grantor (seller), which were accepted by all of the original grantees (buyers of units). Therefore, horizontal privity exists because of the grantor-grantee relationship between the original parties.

Vertical Privity. For vertical privity to exist, the entire servient estate must be transferred to successors in interest. If A was the original owner, or if he acquired the entire interest held by each previous owner, then vertical privity exists.

Thus, it is likely that Board can enforce its covenant against A in a court of law. However, as indicated, the remedy would be damages against A. The Board may also seek a remedy in equity.

Equitable Servitude (ES)

An equitable servitude is an alternate remedy pursued in a court of equity in which the element of privity is replaced by notice. Board must meet the following elements: intent, notice, and touch & concern.

(1) Intent. Here the intent is to bind the land. As discussed above, intent is strongly implied by the powers granted to the Board, the duration of the covenant's existence, and its value to owners/occupants of the Condo.

(2) Notice. For an ES, notice may be actual, constructive, or inquiry. That A probably had at least constructive notice is discussed above, and is evident in the stipulated fact that both W and S had notice when they acquired their interests. However, even if A did not have actual or constructive notice, he would have been on inquiry notice given that the rule applied to all other workshops and sales counters in Condo and affected everyone's livelihood and interest in Condo.

(3) Touch and Concern. Discussed above, Board has the better argument because the covenant makes the land more valuable to its owner/occupants who use their workshops for commercial purposes. The covenant protects these commercial enterprises.

Defense: Laches

Because ES's are enforced in a court of equity, Artist may raise the equitable defense of laches. Laches are unreasonable delays that result in prejudice to the defendant. Although Board waited 3 months to enforce the covenant, this does not appear to be an unreasonable delay, and no facts indicate that A was prejudiced by this short delay.

Conclusion: Board will prevail on an equitable servitude. The court of equity can fashion a remedy against A. No doubt the threat of this action will move A to take action of his own. He can attempt to enforce the covenant on S through a real covenant or ES, or he can terminate his lease with W, sue W for damages, and oust S as discussed below.

Call 2. Can Artist recover from Weaver?

Assignment and Sublease

An assignment is a complete transfer of all interests; a sublease is a partial transfer. The issue is what is the relationship between A and W, given that A assigned his interest in Workshop to W for 3 years and W subleased her interest to S for 1 of those 3 years.

Privity

When a lessee signs a lease, the lessor and lessee are said to be in privity of contract, and the lessor can enforce the terms of the contract. When the lessee moves onto the land, the lessee is also in privity of estate with the lessor and the lessor can also bring an action under property law.

Facts stipulate a lease between A and W with an anti-assignment clause. Thus, W was in privity of contract with A and bound by the lease. When W moved on the premises, she was also in privity of estate with A.

Effect of Anti-Assignment Clause.

The A/W lease had an anti-assignment clause, which meant that W could not assign all of her interest to a successor. Under the modern law practiced in a majority of states, anti-assignment clauses are strictly construed, which means that such clauses will not bar a sublease agreement. W's sublease of her interest to S for 1 year is therefore valid.

Effect of Sublease on W

Even though W subleased her interest and vacated, she remained in privity of contract with A. As such, A could enforce the terms of the lease. W therefore had a duty to pay rent regardless of S's conduct. Therefore, when S failed to pay rent to A, A had a right to seek rent from W. A could take a number of actions including lawful detainer and suit for damages.

Effect of A Accepting Payment from S (Waiver)

A waiver is the relinquishment of a right. W will argue that A waived his right to collect rent from her when A accepted rent from S. This argument will fail because there was no novation (a new agreement between A and S), and even if A did waive he can retract it at any time as long as W did not detrimentally rely on the conduct. No facts indicate such reliance by W. A will prevail.

W's Defenses

Constructive Eviction

To succeed under the covenant of quiet use and enjoyment, W would have to meet the elements of constructive eviction: (1) L at fault, (2) interference substantial, and (3) T must vacate in a reasonable time. Under present facts, there is no compelling evidence that the erratic heat rose to the level of substantial interference. Even if it did, S, the sublessee, did not move out, and W moved out when she subleased the premises. Thus, this argument will fail.

Warranty of Habitability

Under this warranty L must provide property reasonably suited to residential use. In the majority of states, this warranty does not apply to commercial property.

Facts indicate that Condo is commercial. The building consists of workshops and sales counters of various artists and craftspeople. Even if the warranty did apply, W's case is weak, because no facts indicate the condo was not reasonably fit for human habitation. In fact, S moved into the workshop with his cot, electric hotplate and clothes, and neither he nor W appeared to have any problem living there until Board attempted to enforce its covenant.

Call 3. Can Artist evict Sculptor?

Effect of Sublease on S

For a sublease, there is neither privity of estate not privity of contract between the original landlord and the sublessee.

W had the right of possession to Workshop for 3 years. She subleased 1 year of that right to S, but did not give up her entire estate. There existed no privity of contract or estate between A and S. Instead, S is in both privity of estate and privity of contract with W. S's duties are to W, not A. Consequently, S is not personally liable to A. However, because of his failure to receive rent, A can oust S through an unlawful detainer action. He can also terminate his lease with W and, as discussed, sue W for damages.

JULY 2000 CALIFORNIA BAR EXAM -- QUESTION 2

1-Hour Essay

Sam and Paul entered into a written contract on September 1, 1999, for the sale by Sam to Paul of a mountain lakefront lot improved with a residence (the "parcel") for $100,000. The contract was silent as to the quality of title Sam would convey, but provided that a quitclaim deed would be used. Paul failed to tender the agreed-on price on the performance date. Sam sued Paul for specific performance on July 5, 2000. Paul defended the suit on the ground that Sam's title is not marketable.

Sam's claim of title goes back to Owen, who owned an unencumbered fee simple absolute in the parcel. The parcel, which was accessible only during the summer months, had been occupied by Owen and Owen's family as a summer vacation home since 1980. In 1984, Owen conveyed the parcel by recorded deed to "my daughter, Doris, and my son, George, so long as they both shall live, and then to the survivor of them."

Owen died testate in 1987, Owen's will made no specific reference to the parcel, but the residuary clause left to Doris "all my other property not specifically disposed of by this will." Doris and George and their families continued to use the vacation home each summer. Doris died testate in April 1988, her will "devising and bequeathing all my estate to my son, Ed."

George executed a deed in May 1988, purporting to convey a fee simple absolute in the parcel to Cain. Cain and his family occupied the parcel during the summers of 1988 through 1996. In May 1997, Cain conveyed the parcel to Sam. Sam's family occupied it during the summers of 1997 through 1999. *Adverse Possession*

The statute of limitations on actions to recover land in this jurisdiction is 10 years. There is no statute or decision by an appellate court either repudiating or affirming the common law doctrine of destructibility of contingent remainders.

Who should prevail in Sam's suit against Paul? Discuss.

Ed

Statute of Frauds

Sam and Paul entered into a written contract for the sale of land. Under the Statute of Frauds, contracts for land must be in writing. Here, the contract was written, so the Statute was satisfied.

Marketable Title and Quitclaim Deeds

Sam would convey by quitclaim deed. In such a deed, the seller makes no promises regarding warranties; he sells only that which he owned. However, a quitclaim deed does not obviate the general rule that at closing seller will give buyer marketable title, which means reasonably free of defects.

Here, Paul failed to tender the agreed upon price on performance date. He is defending on the grounds that Sam's title is not marketable. Because Sam must provide marketable title despite his purported conveyance by quitclaim deed, Paul will have a valid defense if he can prove that Sam's title was not marketable.

Was Sam's Title Marketable? The 1984 Conveyance

The first step in the analysis would be to examine the 1984 conveyance. Owen (O) conveyed by recorded deed to Doris (D) and George (G) "so long as they both shall live and then to the survivor of them."

Life Estate, Contingent Remainder, and Reversion

Doris and George each had a life estate (LE), which means their interests would terminate at death. Each also had a contingent remainder (CR) in Parcel. A remainder is a future interest in real property capable of becoming possessory immediately upon the natural termination of the preceding estate. Here, D's and G's contingent remainder is capable of becoming possessory immediately upon the death of either D or G, because the conveyance specified "and then to the survivor of them."

A remainder is contingent if either it contains a condition precedent or is to an unascertainable person. D and G are alive and therefore ascertainable. However, each has a condition precedent, namely to survive the other. Therefore they each have a contingent remainder in Parcel.

O has a reversion, which means that if both D's and G's CR fail, the property will revert back to him or to his estate.

Owen's Will

Owen died testate in 1987. Although he made no specific reference to Parcel, O devised all of his other property not specifically disposed of to Doris.

Thus, Doris inherited O's reversion. As indicated, a reversion is a future interest in a grantee. Reversions are transferable, devisable, and descendible, so D has a valid future interest in Parcel. A reversion is vested by law, and therefore is not subject to the Rule Against Perpetuities.

Effect of Doctrine of Destructibility of Contingent Remainders

At Common Law, a CR is destroyed if it fails to vest before or upon termination of the preceding estate. Here, Doris died, terminating her life estate and CR in Parcel and leaving George with a life estate and a CR in Parcel. The issue is whether George's CR vested, which would leave George with a Fee Simple Absolute (FSA) in Parcel.

Effect if George's (G's) CR is not Destroyed

If G's CR is not destroyed and his interest vests, he owns a fee simple absolute. Under this scenario, George executed a deed in May 88 conveying his FSA in Parcel to Cain. Cain then conveyed a FSA to Sam. Thus, Sam has marketable title because it is free of any encumbrances, and Paul's defense fails. Sam can specifically enforce the land sales contract.

Effect if G's CR is Destroyed

If George's CR is destroyed, then he owned only a life estate in Parcel; thus he could have conveyed only a life estate to Cain. Under this scenario, Cain did not convey marketable title and Paul can prevail unless Sam can claim title under an adverse possession theory.

Sam's Adverse Possession Claim

Adverse possession requires the following elements:

(1) Open: Sam occupied Parcel during the summer months. His occupation was open because it was visible and put any true owner on notice.

(2) Hostile: Sam took Parcel under color of title and believed he was the owner. His occupation was hostile because he intended to claim the land as his own, and because it was exclusive of any possible true owner.

(3) Actual: Sam used the property according to its character as a summer home, just as O had done. Thus, his possession was actual.

(4) Continuous through the Statutory Period (Tacking): The period in this jurisdiction is 10 years. Sam occupied for only 2 (1997-1999). However, the doctrine of tacking allows predecessors in interest to add on years if there is privity and no gaps.

Cain occupied the land during the summers of 1988-1996, or 8 years. There was a grantor-grantee relationship between Cain and Sam, establishing privity. Using tacking, Sam can satisfy this element.

Marketability, AP, and Time is of the Essence

Sam will succeed in an adverse possession claim. However, title by AP is not marketable. The owner must perfect title through a quiet title action. Under our facts, there is no time is of the essence clause, so failure to close at time of performance will not constitute a major breach. Sam will have time to cure the defect by perfecting his claim.

Conclusion: Under either scenario, Sam prevails and can enforce specific performance if he can meet the elements.

Specific Performance

(1) Inadequacy of Legal Remedy – Because land is unique, legal remedies are inadequate. Sam does not want money; he wants to sell his property according to the legally binding contract that Paul signed.

(2) Definite and Certain Terms – Here the land sale contract is written. Sam will convey Parcel by quitclaim deed for $100,000. Paul can argue that the contract is silent as to quality of title. However, Sam can argue that the parameters of this transaction are clear, or resolve the issue in Paul's favor by including a general warranty deed. Sam will prevail on this point.

(3) Feasibility of Enforcement – Sam will sue in a court encompassing Parcel, so the court will have subject matter jurisdiction. The court can assert personal jurisdiction over Paul because the transaction occurred in the jurisdiction and Paul is now in court defending on the merits.

(4) Mutuality – Not an issue because the court can create a constructive trust over Parcel to force Sam to convey Parcel if he refuses to perform after Paul tenders payment.

(5) Satisfaction of Conditions – As discussed, Sam can produce marketable title, and there is no time is of the essence clause. Thus, all conditions are satisfied.

(6) Defenses –As discussed, Paul's defense fails, and he has no other defenses.

Conclusion: Sam will prevail on his claim for specific performance.

JULY 1999 CALIFORNIA BAR EXAM – QUESTION 5

1-HOUR EXAM

Since the early 1960s, Artist has had a year-to-year lease of the third floor of a small loft building which, like most buildings in the area, has mixed commercial and light manufacturing uses. Artist has used her space, as other local craftspeople have used theirs, for both residential and studio purposes. She has enjoyed the serenity of her unit and the panoramic views of the distant hills and of the nearby park to which she has had easy access.

In July 1998, Landlord rented a lower floor of the building to Machinist, whose operations are extremely noisy. Artist's complaints about the noise to both Machinist and Landlord have been to no avail.

At about the same time, Developer began building a large office tower nearby which will block Artist's view when completed. The office building will provide needed employment for the community.

The State Power Department, a State governmental agency, has also begun construction of electric and communication lines for Developer's office building. For the next several years the State Power Department construction will block a path across an undeveloped lot which separates Artist's neighborhood from the park. The path has been regularly used for many years by Artist and other neighborhood residents because the only other access to the park is by a much longer circuitous street route.

1. What are Artist's rights and remedies, if any against landlord, Machinist and Developer? Discuss.

2. What are Artist's rights and remedies, if any, against State Power Department for blocking the path? Discuss.

PROPERTY
Question 5, July 1999 California Bar Exam
Written by Dennis P. Saccuzzo

Call 1. Artist's Rights and Duties

(a) Artist v. Landlord

Valid Periodic Tenancy

A periodic tenancy is a leasehold estate that continues for successive periods until terminated by notice.

Here, Artist rented year to year since the 1960's. She thus has a valid periodic tenancy along with the rights and duties associated with this leasehold estate.

Quiet Use and Enjoyment

Implied in every lease is a warranty of quiet use and enjoyment, which means the landlord has a duty not to disturb Artist in her use and enjoyment of the land. A breach of this warranty occurs when through an act or omission the landlord causes the property to become uninhabitable. The tenant may then sue under a constructive eviction theory. To prevail, T must show (1) L at fault and (2) substantial interference. T must then vacate within a reasonable time.

[handwritten margin note: Must be L who is at fault not another T]

Artist will claim that the extremely noisy operations of machinist pose a substantial interference, and that L was at fault for renting the lower floor to machinist. While the noise no doubt poses a substantial disruption to Artist, it is not L who is making the noise. Thus, L is not at fault. Even if L were at fault, Artist has not moved out within a reasonable time. She has remained in possession of the property since mechanist moved in during July 1998. Thus, Artist will not prevail under this theory.

Warranty of Habitability

A second right of Artist flows from the warranty of habitability, which means that L must provide property that is reasonably suitable to residential use. This warranty does not apply to commercial leases.

Artist's main problem in asserting this warranty is that her building has mixed commercial and manufacturing uses. While she, like other craftpersons, has used her space for both residential and studio purposes, she will likely have to persuade the court that her residential use satisfies the legal requirements for her to assert this warranty. Whether or not she could prevail would depend on case law and precedent in her jurisdiction.

Assuming she prevails by showing the warranty applies and that L breached because machinist's loud noise made the residence unsuitable for residential use, Artist has a variety of remedies including: (1) terminate the lease;

[handwritten note: If the warranty applies]

(2) a suit for damages, and (3) repair and deduct. Here, her remedy would be damages, which would be the difference between the fair market value of her lease now with the noise and its value before the noise.

Conclusion: Artist has a weak case against Landlord and will probably fail in her claim against Landlord. If she does prevail, she can get only damages for the reduced value of her rental because of noise.

(b) Artist v. Machinist

Private Nuisance

Artist can sue Machinist under a nuisance theory. A private nuisance is a substantial, unreasonable interference with another's use and enjoyment of property.

Substantial

Here, a tenant on the first floor has operations that are extremely noisy. Such noise constitutes a substantial interference because it would be annoying and irritating to a reasonable person.

Unreasonable

Artist can successfully argue that the noise is unreasonable if it is out of character with the mixed commercial and light manufacturing uses to which buildings in the area are placed. The facts indicate that Artist's building is used by craftspeople, so she has a good argument that an extremely noisy operation is unreasonable.

Non-Trespassory

The disturbance is noise; Machinist has not entered Artist's property, so it is non-trespassory.

Balance Utility versus Harm

The courts will balance the utility of Machinist's operation versus the harm to Artist. No facts indicate the value of Machinist's operation. He probably employs people and may produce a needed product. Nonetheless, because Artist has a mere year to year lease, she will have difficulty showing that the balance weighs in her favor.

Injunction

If Artist did prevail, she could get an injunction. An injunction requires the following:

(1) Inadequate Remedy at Law: Land is unique and this situation would require multiple lawsuits in a court of law. Artist can meet this element.

(2) Property Right: Artist has an interest in land; she has a leasehold as discussed above.

(3) <u>Feasibility</u>: The court could enjoin Machinist and use its power of contempt to enforce its decree.

(4) <u>Balance the Hardships</u>: As discussed above, despite the absence of facts, Artist's case is weak because her rights are limited to a year to year periodic tenancy in an area of mixed commercial and light manufacturing. Machinist will argue that she can easily move into a residential area and avoid the noise.

(5) <u>Defenses</u>: If Artist prevails on the above 4 elements, Machinist has no effective defenses. <u>Laches</u>, unreasonable delays that result in prejudice, won't work because Artist did not wait to take action; she complained to both Landlord and Machinist.

Conclusion: Machinist has the better argument. Artist will probably fail to prove nuisance, and even if she does, she is unlikely to get an injunction.

(c) Artist v. Developer

Negative Easement and Easement by Prescription

An easement is the right to enter land and either make limited use (affirmative easement) or restrain the use (negative easement).

Here, Developer will be blocking Artist's view. Artist would like to assert a prescriptive easement (discussed in greater detail below) because she has been openly enjoying the panoramic views since the 1960s (at least 30 years). Unfortunately, courts have limited negative easements to light, air, subjacent or lateral support, and flow of an artificial stream. None of these are impaired.

While it is possible to argue for a good faith change in the laws, here we do not have any special facts to support Artist. Developers build office buildings and block views all the time.

Conclusion: Artist has no case against Developer.

Call 2. Artist v. State

Prescriptive Easement by a Class

A prescriptive easement requires that the claimant meet the same elements as in adverse possession: open, hostile, actual, and continuous through the statutory period.

Open

Artist, along with other neighborhood residents, regularly used the path to the nearby park that State will now block. Her use was certainly visible. The land is undeveloped, so the owner was certainly put on notice. Had this been government land, Artist would have no rights because in general one may not adversely possess government land.

Hostile (Class Easement)

Hostile means intent to claim the land as one's own, exclusive of others. Here, the path has been used regularly by other neighborhood residents as well as Artist. However, Artist can claim a class easement. The courts recognize such easements, in which the hostile element is met by a class, such as in use of a road or path on private property to a beach or to a park, as in this case.

Actual

Artist and others in the class used the path consistently with its character – as a path. The only other access to the park is by a much longer circuitous street route.

Continuous

No statutory period is given, but the usual rule is 20 years. (In California it is 5 years). Artist has been using the path for many years.

Conclusion: Artist has a good case for a class easement by prescription and will probably prevail, especially if she can get the testimony of other adversely affected residents who can help persuade the jury of the merits of this claim.

Question asked for rights + remedies of Artist's. Not

FEBRUARY 1997 -- QUESTION 4

1-HOUR ESSAY

Tenant entered into a written lease of an apartment with Landlord on January 1, 1995. The lease provided that Tenant would pay $12,000 per year rent, payable in $1,000 per month installments, commencing immediately.

Tenant moved into the apartment. Soon thereafter Tenant was visited by Inspector, who told Tenant that Landlord had received numerous warnings over the years about the unsafe electrical wiring in the bathroom, and had been cited and fined once for it. Tenant called Landlord and asked him to fix the wiring. Landlord promised to send someone to fix the wiring, but when no one had come for several weeks, Tenant decided to fix the wiring himself. While he was doing the work, he also put mirrors on the ceiling and tore out the tub and replaced it with a whirlpool bath.

A few months later, a noxious slime began oozing from the fixtures in the kitchen sink. Tenant complained of this condition to Landlord, but Landlord refused to have it fixed. The ooze continued, and it became so bad that Tenant was forced to stop using the kitchen. Tenant reported the problem to Inspector, who caused Landlord to be cited and fined for the condition. Despite this, Landlord did not make the repairs and the kitchen remained unusable. Tenant has remained in the apartment but has stopped paying rent.

On December 1, 1995, Tenant received a registered letter from Landlord giving him notice to vacate the apartment on January 15, 1996. In a subsequent telephone conversation, Landlord told Tenant that the notice was given because he was tired of Tenant's demands for repairs and angry because of the fine.

What are Landlord's and Tenant's rights and obligations? Discuss.

Copyright © 2005 Applications of Psychology to Law, Inc.

Landlord's & Tenant's Rights & Obligations

Lease Terms

Landlord and Tenant entered into a written lease for an apartment on January 1, 1995 for the amount of $12,000 per year, payable in installments of $1,000 per month, commencing immediately. Inherent in every lease agreement are covenants and duties on the part of both landlords and tenants. Here Landlord will be required to **deliver possession** of the apartment to Tenant, and Tenant has the **duty to pay rent** in the amount of $1,000 per month to Landlord.

This lease may be characterized as a **periodic tenancy**. A periodic tenancy is a lease which continues for successive periods of time until it is terminated with notice. Since Landlord did not set a date for the lease to end, a periodic tenancy will be implied and the time period for this lease will be designated as **year-to-year**.

On the other hand, if Landlord had set a date for the lease to end, this would have been considered to be a **tenancy for years**. A tenancy for years is a lease which has a fixed duration. Due to the specified duration of a tenancy for years, no notice is required to terminate this type of lease because it will end automatically at the end of the lease term. Hence, since Landlord did not specify a date for the lease to end, the lease he entered into with Tenant will be characterized as a periodic tenancy. Note that leases which are greater in length than one year must be in writing in order to satisfy the **Statute of Frauds**. Here Landlord and Tenant entered into a **written** lease so that Statute of Frauds has been satisfied.

Proper notice must be given in order to terminate a periodic tenancy. With a year-to-year lease, six months notice must be given by the party seeking to terminate the lease. On December 1, 1995, Landlord gave Tenant notice that Tenant must vacate the apartment by January 15, 1996. This is improper notice because Landlord has not given Tenant six months notice to vacate the premises. Moreover, proper notice requires the correct **effective date of termination**. Since the due date for rent is the first of each month, then the effective date for terminating this lease would be the last day of the month following the six months notice. In sum, Landlord has acted improperly by failing to give Tenant proper notice to vacate the apartment.

Warranty of Habitability

All leases for residential property have an implied **warranty of habitability**. This means that a landlord must provide property that is reasonably suited for residential use. Landlord breached this duty when he failed to fix *unsafe electrical wiring* in Tenant's bathroom after being warned and cited for the problem.

When a Landlord breaches the warranty of habitability, a tenant may (1) **move out and terminate the lease**, (2) **stay and sue for damages**, or (3) **make repairs and offset the rent by the amount of the repairs**. Here Tenant chose to fix the wiring himself after waiting for several weeks for Landlord to send someone to repair the wiring. Although Tenant does have a duty to pay the $1,000 per month rent or else be in breach of the lease, he may offset the amount of money it cost him to fix the bathroom wiring from his rent since Landlord was in breach of the warranty of habitability.

Waste

Although tenants are permitted to cause ordinary wear and tear on a leasehold, tenants have a **duty not to commit waste**. Waste may be deemed as **affirmative** (intentional), **permissive** (tenant's failure to make ordinary minor repairs), or **ameliorating** (improvements).

When Tenant repaired the electrical wiring in the bathroom he decided to place mirrors on the bathroom ceiling and to tear out the tub and replace it with a whirlpool bath. By making such improvements to the property, Tenant has committed **ameliorative waste**. Even though such improvements may actually increase the value of the apartment, Tenant will be held liable to Landlord for the cost of returning the bathroom ceiling and tub to their original conditions.

Fixtures

However, Landlord may decide that he wants the bathroom to remain in its improved condition. When Tenant vacates the premises, Landlord may argue that the mirror on the ceiling and the whirlpool bath are **fixtures** and therefore cannot be removed from the apartment.

A fixture is chattel that becomes so affixed to real property that it actually becomes a part of the real property. The factors a court will consider in order to determine whether a piece is property is a fixture are (1) **the degree of attachment**, (2) **the harm to the premises if the chattel is removed**, and (3) **whether the chattel is customized to fit the real property**. Property that is used in a tenant's trade will not be deemed to be a fixture and generally may be removed. However, if a tenant is permitted to remove the chattel, the tenant must do so prior to vacating the premises and must repair damages.

Therefore, when Tenant moves out of the apartment a court will need to decide whether the mirrors on the ceiling and the whirlpool bath are fixtures, or whether Tenant may remove these items and return the bathroom to its original condition. Here it is likely that removing the mirrors from the ceiling and removing the whirlpool bath would cause considerable harm to the premises. In particular, the whirlpool bath would probably be considered a fixture since it has a great degree of attachment to the floor and the water pipes.

Covenant of Quiet Use and Enjoyment

Landlord made a second breach of the implied **warranty of habitability** when he failed to make repairs after a *noxious slime* began to ooze from the fixtures in the kitchen sink, rendering the kitchen unusable. (See discussion of the warranty of habitability *supra*.) In response, Tenant decided to remain in the apartment and stop paying rent. As stated above, Tenant has an obligation to pay his monthly rent or else be in breach of the lease.

However, Tenant may argue that Landlord is in breach of his duty not to interfere with Tenant's **quiet use and enjoyment** of the apartment. When a landlord substantially interferes with a tenant's quiet use and enjoyment of residential premises through a **total eviction, constructive eviction,** or **partial eviction** then a landlord will be found to be in breach of the covenant of quiet use and enjoyment.

Tenant will argue that Landlord's failure to repair the ooze from the kitchen fixtures amounted to a **constructive eviction**. A constructive eviction results when residential premises become uninhabitable through a landlord's own fault. Landlord's refusal to make repairs forced Tenant to stop using the kitchen. A kitchen is such an integral part of a residential unit that when a kitchen becomes unusable a tenant may argue that the premises are rendered uninhabitable. In such a situation a tenant has the option to stop paying rent, but the tenant **must vacate the premises** within a reasonable amount of time.

Although Tenant may stop paying rent due to Landlord's breach of the covenant of quiet use and enjoyment, Tenant must also vacate the premises. Because Tenant merely stopped paying rent without also vacating the premises, Tenant himself will be in breach of the lease agreement and Landlord may seek an **unlawful detainer action** against Tenant for his failure to pay rent.

Retaliatory Eviction

Although Landlord chose not to bring an unlawful detainer action against Tenant for Tenant's failure to pay rent, Landlord did send Tenant a letter on December 1, 1995 giving Tenant one and one-half months notice to vacate the apartment. Landlord subsequently telephoned Tenant and told Tenant the notice was given because Landlord was tired of Tenant's demand for repairs, and he was angry Tenant had reported the noxious slime problem to Inspector, resulting in a fine against Landlord.

Retaliatory eviction is generally presumed when a tenant is evicted within 3-6 months of reporting housing problems to inspectors or requesting a landlord to make necessary repairs. Here Landlord has engaged in retaliatory eviction since he specifically told Tenant that notice to vacate the premises was given because Landlord was irritated by Tenant's request for repairs and was angry that Inspector had levied a fine against Landlord for failure to make repairs. Retaliatory evictions by landlords are **prohibited**.

Conclusion

In sum, as stated earlier, a six-month notice for vacating the premise must be given in order to terminate the lease. Because Landlord has not provided proper notice, the lease will automatically be renewed and Tenant may continue to be in possession of the property for another year, provided he pays rent. Landlord will continue to be bound by the warranty of habitability and the covenant of quiet use and enjoyment.

However, if Tenant does not wish to be bound by another year in the lease, Tenant may move out of the premises due to Landlord's constructive eviction for failure to fix the ooze from the kitchen fixtures. Tenant may not simply remain in the apartment without paying rent or else Tenant will be in breach of the lease agreement. If Tenant chooses, he may pay for repairs to the kitchen and have the amount offset against his rent.

JULY 1996 BAR EXAM -- QUESTION 5

1-HOUR ESSAY

In 1980, Fred, a widower and the owner of Blackacre, a farm, died and by his will devised Blackacre to his three children, "Art, Bob and Carol as joint tenants with common law right of survivorship." Art, who had lived with his father on Blackacre, continued to occupy and farm it after Fred's death. Bob and Carol, although claiming equal rights to Blackacre, preferred to continue living in the cities in which they owned their homes and never went into possession of Blackacre.

Art lost money in his farming operations in each of the years 1980 to 1985. At the end of 1985, without consulting either Bob or Carol, Art conveyed by quitclaim deed all of his "right, title and interest in Blackacre to Dan and his heirs." Dan immediately took possession of Blackacre.

In 1990, Bob died intestate survived by Sam, his sole heir, and by Art, Carol and Dan. During the period from 1986 to 1995, the net profits resulting from Dan's operation of the farm amounted to $80,000. During the period from 1992 to 1995, Dan also received net rentals of $8,000 from a tenant renting a cottage on the farm.

Assume that there is a 10-year statute of limitations for the recovery of land and that no other statute of limitations applies.

1. What interest does each of the following have in Blackacre: Dan? Sam? Carol?. Discuss.

2. What rights do Sam and Carol have with respect to the profits in the years from 1986 – 1995 and the rents from 1992 – 1995? Discuss.

3. Is Carol liable to Art for any of the monetary losses suffered by Art from 1980 through 1986? Discuss.

1985 – Dan

Question 5, July 1996 California Bar Exam
Written by Dennis P. Saccuzzo & Nancy E. Johnson

Call 1: Interests in Blackacre – Dan, Sam & Carol

A. Dan's Interest

To determine Dan's interest, it is necessary to examine the original devise by Fred and the subsequent conveyance by Art to Dan.

1980 Devise – Joint Tenancy (JT)

In 1980, Fred devised BA by will to his three children, Art, Bob, and Carol, as joint tenants with right of survivorship. To form a joint tenancy requires the four unities of (1) time, (2) title, (3) interest, and (4) possession.

The three children took title together in 1980, meeting the time element. They all took title under the same instrument with equal rights of interest and possession. Thus the four unities are satisfied. Further, the instrument expressly stated with "right of survivorship." Therefore a joint tenancy was formed; each owned an undivided 1/3 interest in BA.

The effect of the right of survivorship is that at death, the interest of a joint tenant passes automatically to the surviving tenant(s) by operation of law.

1985 Conveyance – Severance of JT

A JT may be severed by conveyance by one of the joint tenants, partition, mortgage in a title theory state, lease under common law, or agreement.

Here, Art severed the JT when he conveyed by quitclaim deed all of his rights, title and interest in BA to Dan. A quitclaim deed conveys only what the owner had at the time of the conveyance and makes no promises concerning quality of title. Because Art owned only a 1/3 interest in BA, his deed conveyed only that 1/3 to Dan.

[handwritten margin note: Dan received 1/3 interest in quitclaim deed.]

The effect of the Art-Dan conveyance is to sever the JT with respect to Dan. Bob and Carol remain joint tenants, each with an undivided 1/3 interest and right of survivorship. Dan is a tenant in common, which means he also has an undivided 1/3 interest in BA but no right of survivorship.

Under the conveyance, Dan has a 1/3 interest in BA as a tenant in common with Bob and Carol.

Adverse Possession (AP)

Dan can claim all of BA under a theory of adverse possession if he can prove all of the elements: (1) open, (2) hostile, (3) actual, and (4) continuous through the statutory period.

Dan's occupation was certainly open. He farmed between 1986 and 1995, putting any true owner on clear notice. BA was a farm, so Dan's use was consistent with the character of the land, thus meeting the "actual" requirement. The statute of limitations is ten years and Dan was there from the end of 1985 to 1995, which is under ten years. Thus, Dan's possession based on the facts given was less than the 10-year statutory period.

Even if Dan had met the ten-year statute, however, he would fail under the "hostile" element. Dan no doubt intended to claim the land as his own. However, as discussed above he was a co-tenant with Bob and Carol. The general rule is no adverse possession among co-tenants unless there is an ouster, which requires the co-tenant in possession to deny possession to the other co-tenants. Although Bob and Carol never went into possession of BA, the facts indicate that they claimed equal rights to BA and no facts indicate that Dan ever attempted to deprive them of possession.

Dan's AP claim will fail; he owns only a 1/3 interest in BA.

B. Sam's Interest

In 1990 Bob died intestate, survived by his sole heir, Sam. Because Bob and Carol were joint tenants with right of survivorship as discussed above, Bob's 1/3 interest passed directly to Carol by operation of law at his death, leaving Carol with a 2/3 interest in BA and Sam with no interest in BA.

Conclusion: Sam has no interest in BA.

C. Carol's Interest

As discussed above, Carol acquired Bob's 1/3 interest by right of survivorship at Bob's death and now holds a 2/3 interest in BA as tenant in common with Dan.

Call 2: Rights of Sam and Carol with respect to profits and rents

A. Sam's Rights

As discussed above, Sam never had an interest in BA. Therefore he would have no rights to profits or rents unless those profits or rents were due to Bob and should have formed part of Bob's estate. The rule of law is co-tenants not in possession are not entitled to profits. The exceptions are ouster, agreement to share, lease to a third party, and depletion of natural resources, and none of these apply. Therefore Bob was due no profits. Bob died in 1990, 2 years before Dan rented BA in 1992; therefore no rents were due Bob either.
Sam has no right to profits or rents.

B. Carol's Rights

Carol is not entitled to profits because, as discussed above, co-tenants not in possession are not entitled to profits absent the enumerated exceptions, none of which apply here. Carol will be entitled to rents, however. As discussed, the general rule is that the co-tenant not in possession has no right to an accounting unless there is an ouster or an agreement to share or lease to a third party or depletion of the natural resources. Here, Dan rented a cottage on the farm to a

Co-tenants are entitled to rents.

third party and received a net of $8,000. Carol as a 2/3 owner would be entitled to 2/3 of the $8,000.

Call 3. Is Carol liable to Art?

Contribution refers to the right of one co-tenant to force the others to pay for expenditures on the property.

In general, the possessory co-tenant is not entitled to contribution for losses, improvements (except at sale/partition) or rents. There is symmetry in the law here: the nonpossessory tenant is not entitled to share the profits, therefore should not have to bear the burden of losses or costs to make the profit. The possessory co-tenant is entitled to a proportionate share of taxes and necessary repairs.

Here the issue is whether Carol is liable for losses suffered by Art. She is not, under the rule of law discussed above.

FEBRUARY 1994 CALIFORNIA BAR EXAM -- QUESTION 3

1-HOUR ESSAY

In 1950, Al properly executed and delivered a quitclaim deed granting his neighbor, Betty, an "easement of way, thirty feet wide" along the southern boundary of Al's five-acre residential parcel. Betty never recorded the deed. In 1951, Betty graded and graveled a twenty-foot wide road along the southern boundary of the five-acre parcel. Since then, Betty has used the road daily to reach her house and has maintained the road as needed.

In 1955, Al conveyed his entire parcel to Cal by a properly executed and delivered quitclaim deed. The deed to Cal made no mention of any easement. Cal paid Al $15,000 for the conveyance.

In September 1988, Cal and Dot signed the following contract concerning the five-acre parcel:

"Cal agrees to sell and Dot agrees to buy the following land [valid legal description]. Price, $90,000 cash, closing December 15, 1988."

On December 15, 1988, Dot paid Cal $90,000 cash, and Cal properly executed and delivered a warranty deed conveying the land to Dot. The deed contained no mention of the easement. Dot promptly recorded the deed. Betty has continued to use and maintain the road.

In June 1989, Dot built a fence blocking the road to Betty's house.

1. What right, if any, does Betty have to continue to use the road? Discuss.

2. What rights, if any, does Dot have against Cal based on the contract, the deed, or both? Discuss.

Question 3, February 1994 California Bar Exam
Written by Dennis P. Saccuzzo

Call 1. *Betty's Rights*

Express Easement by Grant

In 1950 Al executed and delivered a quitclaim deed granting Betty a 30-foot wide easement. An easement is the right to enter and make limited use of land. Betty's easement was created by a writing, thus satisfying the Statute of Frauds. It is called an easement by grant because it was specifically conveyed by the grantor, Al.

Characteristics of Betty's Easement

Betty's easement can be classified as appurtenant, which means it is tied to land. Betty holds the dominant tenement because her land benefits from the easement. Al's tenement is servient because it is hindered by the easement.

Easement Termination

A central issue is whether Betty's interest was terminated by either of the two conveyances.

Effect of Al-to-Cal Conveyance

The general rule is that the transfer of the servient estate subjects the new owner to an easement unless sold to a bonafide purchaser for value (BFP).

In 1955 Al conveyed his entire parcel by quitclaim deed to Cal. Such deeds convey only what the grantor actually owned, and make no promises or warranties concerning title. Al owned an estate burdened by Betty's easement, so the easement survived unless Cal was a BFP.

BFP

A BFP is a buyer who acts in good faith for valuable consideration, without notice of earlier interests or transactions. Notice may be actual, constructive, or inquiry.

Cal paid $15,000. Thus, he provided valuable consideration, and no facts indicate bad faith.

No one told Cal of Betty's easement, so he did not have actual notice. Betty did not record her deed, so Cal did not have constructive notice.

if deed recorded — constructive notice

The issue is whether Cal had inquiry notice, which means was it reasonable for Cal to inspect the premises for Betty's easement, and would a reasonable inspection have revealed it?

The facts indicate that though she never recorded, Betty graded and graveled a 20-foot wide road along the southern border of parcel, maintained the road as needed, and used the road every day to reach her house. Because a reasonable inspection would easily have revealed the road, if not Betty herself using the road, a court would hold that Cal had inquiry notice.

Conclusion: Cal does not qualify as a BFP because he had inquiry notice. Therefore, Betty's easement was not extinguished in 1955 by the Al-to-Cal conveyance.

Effect of the Cal-to-Dot Conveyance

In 1988 Dot purchased the land from Cal for $90,000. While Dot paid valuable consideration and appears to have acted in good faith, the issue is whether she had inquiry notice.

Because Betty's use of the road did not change, the analysis for Dot would be the same as for Cal. There was a 20-foot road being used every day. A reasonable person would have inspected the property and located the road. Like Cal, Dot does not qualify as a BFP, so the easement survived the second transfer of the servient estate.

Effect of the Recording Statute

Unlike Betty, Dot recorded her deed. The Common Law rule is 'first in time, first in right,' and under the facts discussed thus far, Dot would prevail. Similarly, in a race statute the first to record prevails, and Dot would win. Under a notice statute a subsequent BFP without notice prevails against a grantee who fails to record, while in a race-notice statute the first BFP without notice to record prevails. However, as discussed above, Dot had inquiry notice and therefore fails as a BFP.

Easement by Prescription

Even if Dot did prevail under a recording statute, Betty can assert an easement by prescription, the elements of which are the same as in adverse possession.

Open: Betty's use was visible. She paved a road and maintained and used it every day, putting any potential true owner on notice.

Hostile: Betty made exclusive use of her easement. Although she had Al's permission, no facts indicate that she had Cal's permission. Thus, between 1955 and 1988, she used the easement as her own, exclusive of Cal.

Actual: Her use was consistent with the character of the land. It was a road and Betty used it as a road.

Continuous: She used the road every day between 1950 and 1955, and between 1955 and 1985 during Cal's ownership. Her use exceeds the usual 20-year statue of limitations even omitting the five years she used the road with permission.

Conclusion: If Betty does not prevail under the recording acts, she will prevail under an easement by prescription theory, but she probably will be limited to the 20-foot road, rather than the 30 feet granted in the deed by Al, unless the courts accept her claim of color of title in spite of her failure to record.

Call 2: Dot v. Cal

The Contract and Warranty of Marketability

Cal and Dot entered into a land sales contract in Sept. 1988. Implied in every land sales contract is an implied warranty that at closing the seller will give buyer title that is reasonably free of defects. An easement is a defect.

Cal sold the land with an easement. Therefore he violated the warranty. However, according to the doctrine of merger, once a buyer accepts title, she waives all rights under the contract. Dot accepted title on Dec. 15; she waived all rights under the contract and must sue under the deed.

Covenants of Title

Cal executed a general warranty deed. Such deeds have 6 covenants – three present and three future.

Present Covenants

(1) Seisin – This covenant says the grantor has ownership. Because Betty had an easement (as discussed), Cal did not own what he purported to convey. He breached the warranty at closing.

(2) Convey – This covenant says the grantor has the right to convey. Cal purchased and owned the land, so he had a right to convey it, subject to Betty's easement.

(3) Encumbrances – This covenant says the grantor has given title that is free from encumbrances. As discussed, Betty's easement was an encumbrance. Cal therefore breached this warranty.

Conclusion: Cal breached at least two if not three present warranties, giving Dot the right to sue if she brings an action within the statute of limitations.

Future Covenants

(1) Quiet Enjoyment – Covenants that buyer will not be disturbed by a third party's claim of title. Betty has a lawful claim of title. This covenant will be breached when Betty sues Dot for building a fence that blocked Betty's road to her house.

(2) Warranty – Seller will defend buyer against any lawful claims. Cal will be required to defend Dot against any future claim Betty might bring.

(3) Further Assurances – Seller will do what is needed to perfect title. Cal must perfect title. He can do this by purchasing Betty's easement, or, more likely, paying Dot for the difference between the value of the land with the easement and without it.

JULY 1993 CALIFORNIA BAR EXAM -- QUESTION 5

1-HOUR ESSAY

Owner owns several apartment buildings. He uses a standard form agreement in leasing apartments in his building. The agreement includes the following relevant provisions: 1) the lease term is one year; 2) the tenant is not to disturb other tenants; and 3) the landlord's written permission is required before the tenant may sublease.

Lisa rented Apt. #1 from Owner on February 1. The same day, her friend, Mary, rented Apt. #2 in another Owner building. Each signed Owner's standard form lease agreement. In April, Mary learned that Lisa would be leaving the area in May, and asked Owner for permission to sublease Apt. #1 because Apt. #2 had flooded in recent rains. Owner denied permission because Mary was already a tenant. Lisa nevertheless made a written "assignment of all interest" in Apt. #1 to Mary, and Mary notified Owner on April 29 that she would leave Apt. #2 May 31, and occupy Apt. #1.

Mary moved into Apt. #1 on June 1 and paid the June rent on Apt. #1. Later that month, the police were called by neighboring tenants to Apt. #1 at 4:00 a.m. and asked to break up a very noisy party hosted by Mary.

On July 1, Mary informed Owner that she had paid out an amount equal to the entire July rent to replace an exposed, uninsulated electric wire which she had discovered in a closet within Apt. #1, and that she would not pay the July rent.

On July 12, Owner brought an action to repossess Apt. #1, to collect July rent from both Mary and Lisa for Apt. #1, and to collect June and July rent from Mary for Apt. #2, which he had not endeavored to re-rent because he had other unrented apartments.

1. Is Owner entitled to possession of Apt. #1? Discuss.

2. Is rent owed by Lisa or Mary on either apartment? Discuss.

Call 1. Is Owner (O) entitled to possession of Apt 1?

Tenancy for Years

A tenancy for years ends on a certain date. While it may be for more or less than one year, its beginning and end are fixed at the outset. It expires automatically without notice.

Lisa rented Apt 1 from O on Feb. 1. The lease agreement called for a 1-year term. Because the term is fixed at one year, the lease will end automatically on Jan. 31 of the following year. Lisa has a tenancy for one year that will end automatically without notice.

Lisa's Assignment

The lease agreement also required O's written permission before the tenant could sublease. A sublease is a partial transfer of the property. Lisa did not sublease. She assigned "all" of her interest in Apt 1 to Mary effective June 1. An assignment is a complete transfer of all interests. Therefore the transfer constituted an assignment. Because sublease and assignment clauses are strictly construed against the landlord, the anti-sublease clause will not bar Lisa's assignment.

Conclusion: There was a valid assignment of Apt 1 from Lisa to Mary, effective June 1.

Effect of Assignment

Following a valid assignment, the landlord and assignee are in privity of estate and are liable to each other for all covenants that run with the land. As of June 1, Mary was in privity of estate with O. Lisa remained in privity of contract with O because she signed a lease on Feb. 1.

Duty to Pay Rent

A tenant has a duty to pay rent. Mary paid the rent on Apt 1 in June, but did not in July. Her failure to pay rent would be grounds for eviction unless Mary has a valid defense.

Duty to Repair

A landlord (L) has a duty to make necessary repairs. Tenant (T) has a duty to give notice of needed repairs. If L fails to make repairs within a reasonable time following notice, T may make them and abate the expense from rents due.

Mary paid an amount equal to her entire July rent to replace an exposed, uninsulated electric wire in her closet in Apt 1. However, no facts indicate that she gave notice. She had no right to make these repairs and abate her rent because she failed to give notice. Thus, this defense will fail.

[handwritten margin note: Notice need be given before T can fix problem on their own.]

Quiet Use and Enjoyment

A constructive eviction occurs where the premises become uninhabitable. The interference with T's use of the premises must be substantial and T must vacate within a reasonable time.

Here, the interference was in a closet and Mary did not vacate. Thus, the defense will fail.

Warranty of Habitability

The rule is L must provide property that is reasonably suited to residential use.

Mary will argue that an uninsulated electric wire in a closet made the apartment unfit for residential use and probably was a violation of residential housing codes. Mary will prevail on this defense because an exposed wire in a closet poses a serious risk of an electrical fire, thus making the premises unsuitable.

Mary's remedies under this warranty include a suit for damages or repair and deduct. She chose to repair and deduct. Thus, Mary's actions were lawful and pose no grounds for O to take possession of Apt 1.

Can sue for damages or repair + deduct.

Effect of Noisy Party at 4 a.m.

Lisa, the assignor, signed a lease that included a covenant that a tenant is not to disturb other tenants. The issue is whether the covenant runs with the land and binds Mary, the assignee.

Covenants Running with the Land

A covenant is a promise in a lease or deed that binds the promisor and promisee to act or refrain from certain conduct.

Here, the provision in the lease requires T to refrain from disturbing other Ts. Thus, it is a covenant that burdens the tenant.

A burden will run with the land if there is intent, notice, it touches and concerns the land, and there is horizontal and vertical privity.

Intent: Intent can be implied here. The covenant benefits both the L and T. It is also a part of all leases in Apt. Therefore it is likely that L can successfully argue that the parties intended this covenant to run with the land, despite the absence of express language to that effect.

Notice: Mary had constructive notice. The covenant was written as part of the lease agreement. It can also be argued that she had actual notice because she signed an identical lease for Apt. 2.

Touch and Concern The covenant touches and concerns the land because it benefits all residents by giving them assurance that they will not be disturbed by noisy neighbors. It also makes the apt more desirable and hence more valuable.

Privity: Horizontal privity requires that the original parties have an interest in land at the same time. This is satisfied by the Landlord-Tenant relationship between Owner and Lisa, the original parties.

Vertical privity required that there be a transfer of the entire servient estate to a successor in interest. Here, Lisa transferred all her interests to Mary, thus this element is met.

Conclusion: the covenant runs with the land.

Effect of Breach: Mary breached the covenant in June when she had a noisy party that required the neighbors to call the police, who came at 4 a.m. to break it up. Because she breached the covenant, Mary violated the lease and O has a right to evict her and take possession unless Mary has a valid defense.

Defense – Retaliatory Eviction

A landlord may not evict a T where T exercises a legal right. As discussed above, Mary exercised her legal rights when she repaired the wire and abated her rent. Mary will argue that because L did not take action until well after the June breach, and within only 12 days after Mary exercised her legal right, there was a retaliatory eviction.

Conclusion: O is not entitled to possession.

Call 2. Is rent owed on either apartment?

Apartment 1

As indicated, Lisa is in privity of contract with O. If rents are due, O can seek them against either Lisa or Mary, who is in privity of estate.

As discussed above, Mary was in her legal right to make repairs and abate her rent. The cost of repairs equaled the July rent. Therefore, neither Lisa nor Mary owe rent on Apt 1 for July.

Apartment 2

Abandonment

Mary signed a 1-year lease for Apt 2 on Feb. 1. She paid rent only through May, then abandoned the property without permission.

An abandonment occurs when T leaves the property, as Mary did. When T abandons, L may sue for damages, treat it as a surrender in which case T's duties and liabilities end, or re-rent on T's account. Regardless of the remedy chosen, L has a duty to mitigate.

L has chosen to sue for rent for June and July as damages. Because Mary abandoned the property without permission before the end of the tenancy, she will be liable for damages unless she has a valid defense.

Warranty of Habitability

Defined supra, Mary's property may not have been reasonably suitable to residential use because it had been flooded by rain in April. If Mary prevails on this argument, she would have the right to stay and sue, repair and deduct, or move out and end the lease under a constructive eviction theory. She moved out.

Constructive Eviction (Quiet Use and Enjoyment)

To succeed on a constructive eviction theory Mary must show that (1) L was at fault, and (2) substantial interference. She must then (3) move out within a reasonable time. Her obligations to pay rent would then be excused.

L at Fault: The apt became flooded by rain. Since neither Mary nor any of the other tenants caused this flooding, the court will likely hold that L was at fault.

Interference Substantial: No facts indicate how much interference was actually caused by the flooding. The outcome of the suit will likely hinge on whether Mary can prove this element. We do know that Mary did in fact live in Apt 2 during May, so based on the available facts, O has the better argument.

Reasonable Time: Mary left at the end of May, 1-2 months after the flooding. It is arguable whether this is a reasonable time.

Conclusion: If Mary prevails in her constructive eviction defense, she will owe no rent. However, it appears as though O has the better argument.

Duty to Mitigate

Mary will argue that O has a duty to mitigate. However, there are other unrented apartments and O is only asking for 2 months' rent. He could have asked for rent through Jan 31.

Conclusion: Mary will be liable for rent in June and July on Apt 2.

EVIDENCE

Pure Evidence:

Crossover Questions:

Evidence + Crimes:

1-Hour Exam

Victor had been dating Daniel's estranged wife, Wilma. Several days after seeing Victor and Wilma together, Daniel asked Victor to help him work on his pickup truck at a nearby garage. While working under the truck, Victor saw Daniel nearby. Then Victor felt gasoline splash onto his upper body. He saw a flash and the gasoline ignited. He suffered second and third-degree burns. At the hospital, he talked to a police detective, who immediately thereafter searched the garage and found a cigarette lighter. Daniel was charged with attempted murder. At a jury trial, the following occurred:

a. Tom, an acquaintance of Daniel, testified for the prosecution that Daniel had complained to Tom that Victor had "burned" him several times and stated that he (Daniel) would "burn him one of these days." *Hearsay – Motive, Intent*

b. Victor testified for the prosecution that, while Victor was trying to douse the flames, Daniel laughed at him and ran out of the garage. *PSI, Admission*

c. At the request of the prosecutor, the judge took judicial notice of the properties of gasoline and its potential to cause serious bodily injury or death when placed on the body and ignited.

In his defense, Daniel testified that he was carrying a gasoline container, tripped, and spilled its contents. He denied possessing the lighter, and said that the fire must have started by accident. He said that he ran out of the garage because the flames frightened him.

d. On cross-examination, the prosecutor asked Daniel, "Isn't it true that the lighter found at the garage had your initials on it?" *Leading – Permitted on cross*

The prosecutor urged the jury to consider the improbability of Daniel's claim that he had accidentally spilled the gasoline.

e. During a break in deliberations, one juror commented to the other jurors on the low clearance under a pickup truck parked down the street from the courthouse. The juror measured the clearance with a piece of paper. Back in the jury room, the jurors tried to see whether Daniel could have spilled the gasoline in the way he claimed. One juror crouched under a table and another held a cup of water while simulating a fall. After the experiment, five jurors changed their votes and the jury returned a verdict of guilty.

Assume that, in each instance, all appropriate objections were made.

1. Should the court have admitted the evidence in item a? Discuss.
2. Should the court have admitted the evidence in item b? Discuss.
3. Should the court have taken judicial notice as requested in item c? Discuss.
4. Should the court have allowed the question asked in item d? Discuss.
5. Was the jury's conduct described in item e proper? Discuss.

Don't Forget to conclude each argument — "Therefore ..."

Call 1. Admissibility of item a.

Logical Relevance

Logical relevance is the tendency to make the existence of any fact of consequence more or less probable. Here 2 statements are at issue. First, that Daniel had complained to Tom that Victor had "burned" him; and that Daniel stated he would "burn him [Victor] one of these days." Both statements have a tendency to show the state of mind of Daniel, the defendant, as well as his intent. They have a tendency to make it more probable that Daniel attempted to kill Victor because he felt "burned" by Victor and "planned to burn him" at some point in the future. Therefore, the evidence is logically relevant.

Presentation – Witness Competent

A witness must be competent. This means the witness must have personal knowledge, must be able to understand and tell the truth, and must take an oath to "awaken" the witness' conscience.

Tom is an acquaintance of Daniel, testifying for the prosecution. As such, it can be assumed he took the proper oath and met the minimum standard of being able to understand and tell the truth. Tom is testifying as to what Daniel had communicated to him directly, thus Tom has personal knowledge because he is testifying as to his direct experience.

Hearsay

Hearsay is an out-of-court statement offered to prove the truth of the matter stated.

1. Tom testified that Daniel complained that Victor had "burned" him.

Daniel's statement "burned" was made to Tom in a setting other than the present court and therefore qualifies as an out-of-court statement. If the statement were being offered for its truth, it would be hearsay and inadmissible absent an exception or exemption. Whether or not Victor "burned" Daniel is not at issue. It is unlikely that it is being offered for its truth; therefore it would be excluded from the general inadmissibility of out-of-court statements.

Exclusion: State of mind of declarant to show intent, attitude, belief, knowledge, or insanity   "MIMIC"

Daniel's statement that Victor had "burned him" several times does show his attitude toward Victor, that is that Daniel was angry at Victor, and believed that Victor had hurt him. Therefore this statement is not being offered for its truth and it would be admissible as non-hearsay.

2. Tom testified that Daniel said he would "burn him one of these days."

Daniel's statement that he would "burn" Victor was made to Tom in a setting other than the present court and therefore qualifies as an out-of-court statement. This statement may be used either to show Daniel's state of mind reflecting intent, attitude, belief, or knowledge and thus not offered for its truth; or it may be offered for its truth to show Daniel's intent to burn Victor. If offered for its truth, the statement would be inadmissible absent an exemption or exception.

Exclusion: State of mind of declarant

— Exclusions - something other than TOMA

Defined above. Statements offered to show intent, attitude, belief, or knowledge of declarant that are not offered for their truth are admissible as non-hearsay. Daniel's statement that he intended to burn Victor could be offered to show Daniel's attitude, as discussed above. However, then the statement would not come in for its truth.

Exception: Present state of mind

This exception to the hearsay rule encompasses then-existing mental, emotional, or physical condition (intent, plan, motive, design, mental feeling, pain, health).

Daniel's statement that he intended to "burn" Victor one of these days shows his future intent to hurt or retaliate against Daniel. When combined with the statement that Daniel felt "burned" by Victor (as discussed above), it reflects that Daniel had a motive for dousing Victor with gasoline. As such, this statement falls under the state-of-mind exception to the hearsay rule and would therefore come in for its truth. There is no confrontation issue because the defendant is the one who purportedly made the out-of-court statement.

Conclusion: Both statements are admissible, the latter for its truth because it is excepted under the hearsay rule.

Exemption: Party Admission

Under the Federal Rules of Evidence, a party admission is exempted as non-hearsay. The admission must be the party's own statement and offered against the party. The statement need not be against interest when made.

Tom's testimony indicates Daniel himself made the statement that he intended to burn Victor. It is being used to show that Daniel did burn Victor and thus is being used against Daniel. That the admission may not have been against Daniel's interest at the time he made it is irrelevant. Thus the statement qualifies as a party admission. As non-hearsay, it is admissible.

Character Evidence

A prosecutor may not, in his case in chief, introduce evidence of defendant's bad character to show he acted in conformity on a particular occasion.

Tom is testifying for the prosecution and it can be assumed that Tom's testimony is being presented during the prosecutor's case in chief. Daniel's statement that he intended to burn Victor suggests that Daniel is resentful, hot-headed, and likely to be violent -- the type of person who would burn someone. As such, it is improper character evidence because the testimony suggests that because Daniel is the type of person who would burn someone, he was more likely to have burned Victor.

Exception: Offered to Show Intent

Evidence of one's character that is not offered to show the Defendant acted in conformity therewith but instead is offered for other purposes, such as to show motive, intent, mistake, identification, or common scheme, is admissible. As indicated, Daniel's statement shows his intent to burn Victor as well as his motive, that is revenge because he believed Victor had burned him several times. Because the statement is not being offered to show character conformity, it would be admissible to show Daniel's intent or motive.

Conclusion: Both statements are admissible, the first is admissible to show motive; the latter for its truth as non-hearsay and as an exception to the general prohibition against character conformity evidence.

Call 2. Admissibility of item b.

Logical Relevance

Daniel's laughter, presumably while Victor was on fire, has a tendency to show Daniel was pleased and was more likely to have committed the crime.

Presentation – Witness Competent

Victor is testifying as to what he heard while he was trying to douse the flames. He is therefore competent because he is testifying as to his own personal experience of hearing Daniel.

Hearsay

Defined above. The laughter occurred in the garage, so it was out of court. It is being offered to show Dan did in fact laugh and run away, so it is being offered for its truth.

Exception: Excited Utterance

This firmly rooted non-testimonial exception requires (1) a startling event, (2) the statement made under the stress of the event, and (3) the statement related to the event.

Victor was on fire, unquestionably a startling and stressful event. Daniel, observing the startling event, laughed. The laughter was related to seeing Victor on fire. Daniel's only counter-argument would be that he was not stressed, but that would be tantamount to an admission of his guilt. The statement qualifies as an excited utterance.

Non-Assertive Conduct

Under the Federal Rules, non-assertive conduct is considered non-hearsay. Arguably, Dan's laughter could be viewed as assertive (an expression of satisfaction) or as non-assertive as purely a nervous response to a disturbing sight. In either case, the statement would be admissible because if it was assertive it would come in as a party admission, as discussed above, and if non-assertive it is non-hearsay.

Call 3. Judicial Notice

In taking judicial notice, a court accepts facts as true without proof. A judicially noticed fact must be well established and not subject to reasonable dispute in that it is generally known within the territorial jurisdiction of the trial court or is capable of accurate and ready determination by resort to well established sources whose accuracy cannot be questioned.

The judge took judicial notice of the properties of gasoline. Gasoline is a manufactured substance whose chemical formula and properties can no doubt be determined by reference to established sources. However, the judge also took judicial notice of the potential of gasoline to cause serious bodily injury or death when placed on the body and ignited.

It is well known that gasoline is highly flammable and dangerous. Most gasoline pumps have clearly visible "no smoking" signs and signs stating that gasoline is flammable. Nevertheless, the potential of gasoline to cause death when placed on the body and ignited, or the seriousness of injuries, may depend on a number of factors such as the amount of gasoline and the surface area covered.

Daniel is being charged with attempted murder, which is a specific intent crime where intent to kill is an element. If the judge takes judicial notice of gasoline's potential to cause serious bodily injury or death when placed on the body and ignited, the judge has effectively relieved the burden of the prosecutor by creating a presumption of intent to kill. This would be improper, because the prosecution is required to prove each and every element of the crime. Because facts such as the amount of gasoline used and where on the body it was placed are missing, the taking of judicial notice is improper. In any case, because this is a criminal trial, the judge must instruct the jury that they can but need not accept any judicially noticed facts as conclusive, pursuant to Daniel's 6th Amendment right to confrontation.

Judicial notice was improper

Call 4: The cross-examination question ("Isn't it true that …")

Logical Relevance

If Daniel's initials are in fact on a lighter found in the garage at the scene of the crime after Victor was burned, it would make it more likely that Daniel set Victor on fire.

Leading Question

A leading question is one that suggests the answer. Leading questions are impermissible on direct. They are proper on cross-examination. The prosecutor's question asking "Isn't it true that the lighter . . . had your initials on it?" suggests the answer "yes," so it is leading. However, the question is being asked of Daniel on cross-examination and so is proper.

Presentation: Witness Competent

No facts indicate Daniel was ever shown the lighter to which the prosecutor referred in his cross-examination. In fact, Daniel denied possessing the lighter. Therefore, Daniel is not competent to testify because no facts indicate he has personal knowledge of the lighter.

Lack of Authentication

It is necessary to establish the authenticity of documentary evidence such as the lighter in this case. No facts indicate that a lighter containing Daniel's initials has been authenticated. The prosecutor could have authenticated the lighter either by showing it to Daniel and asking him if he recognized it or through the testimony of the police detective who searched the garage and found it. Because the lighter was not authenticated, the question is improper.

Assumes Facts not in Evidence

It is improper to imply the existence of a fact not in evidence. The prosecutor's question implies that the lighter found at the scene of the crime had Daniel's initials on it. No facts indicate that the lighter had Daniel's or anyone's initials on it. Therefore the question is improper because the prosecutor has not established the fact of the existence of initials on the lighter and has not, as indicated, authenticated the lighter to establish its existence in the court record.

Best Evidence Rule

Where the contents of a writing are at issue, it is necessary to use the original or show it is unavailable through no fault of the proponent. Whether Daniel's initials are on the lighter is at the heart of the issue. Therefore it would be necessary for the prosecutor to produce the original lighter in court or show it is unavailable through no fault of the prosecutor.

Hearsay

The initials purportedly are on the lighter found in the garage and therefore represent a writing (a statement) made out of court. The writing appears to be offered to show that the lighter did in fact have Daniel's initials on it and so is being offered for its truth. As such, it is hearsay and absent an exemption or exception would be inadmissible.

Exception: Party Admission

The statement is being offered against Daniel, but no facts indicate that Daniel caused the initials to be placed there. This exception is doubtful because it has not been established that the initials represent Daniel's own statement.

Exception: Statement Against Interest

Statement against interest will not work because Daniel is available and having one's initials on a lighter is not against one's financial or penal interest when made.

Impeachment

Because the statement appears to be hearsay without an exception, it cannot be offered for its truth. However, Daniel denied possessing the lighter. Statements offered for impeachment purposes are non-hearsay. Assuming the lighter had been properly authenticated and a proper foundation laid, the question about the lighter and Daniel's initials could be proper for impeachment purposes, as it tends to throw Daniel's credibility into question.

Conclusion: The question is improper because the lighter has not been properly authenticated, the prosecutor's question assumes facts not in evidence, the best evidence rule has been violated, and it has not been shown that Daniel is competent to testify.

Call 5: Jury's Conduct

The jury is the trier of fact. Its proper role is to evaluate evidence. Although it is proper for a jury to discuss evidence among the members, it is improper for a jury to produce evidence.

One juror commented to the other jurors about the low clearance under a pickup truck parked down the street from the courthouse. This was a proper discussion among the jurors. However, when the juror measured the clearance with a piece of paper, that juror was producing evidence beyond the scope of the juror's role. This measurement was therefore improper.

Back in the jury room, the jurors conducted an experiment, presumably to see whether Daniel could have spilled the gasoline in the way he claimed. Such experiments also involve the production of evidence and again are improper. Moreover, interpreting the results of such experiments requires an inference by a qualified expert. In spite of the absence of expert testimony, the jurors changed their vote following their own improper experiment. Therefore, with the possible exception of the discussion about the low clearance, the entire jury conduct described in (e) was improper.

JULY 2003 CALIFORNIA BAR EXAM -- QUESTION 3

1-HOUR ESSAY

Dan was charged with aggravated assault on Paul, an off-duty police officer, in a tavern. The prosecutor called Paul as the first witness at the criminal trial. Paul testified that he and Dan were at the tavern and that the incident arose when Dan became irate over their discussion about Dan's ex-girlfriend. Then the following questions were asked and answers given:

Q. What happened then?

[1] A: I went over to Dan and said to him, "Your ex-girlfriend Gina is living with me now."

Q: Did Dan say anything?

[2] A: He said, "Yeah, and my buddies tell me you're treating her like dirt."

[3] Q: Is that when he pulled the club out of his pocket?

A: He sure did. Then he just sat there tapping it against the bar.

[4] Q: Tell the jury everything that happened after that.

[5] A: I said that he was a fine one to be talking. I told him I'd read several police reports where Gina had called the police after he'd beaten her.

Q: Do you believe the substance of those reports?

[6] A: You bet I do. I know Gina to be a truthful person.

Q: How did Dan react to this statement about the police reports?

A: He hit me on the head with the club.

Q: What happened next?

[7] A: I heard somebody yell, "Watch out– he's gonna hit you again!" I ducked, but the club hit me on the top of my head. The last thing I remember, I saw a foot kicking at my face.

Q: What happened then?

[8] A: Dan must have kicked and hit me more after I passed out, because when I came to in the hospital, I had bruises all over my body.

At each of the eight points indicated by numbers, on what grounds could an objection or a motion to strike have properly been made, and how should the trial judge have ruled on each? Discuss.

Commentary

The key to evidence questions is having clearly in mind how the evidence is being presented. This includes whether the evidence is being presented by a witness or in the form of a document, whether it is coming in on direct or cross exam, and whether the examining attorney is the prosecutor/plaintiff or defense.

Generally it is a good idea to begin your response to the first call with a discussion of logical relevance. For each call, you should always keep in mind whether or not the proffered evidence is relevant and what it is being offered to show.

If testimony is being offered by a witness, then the witness must be competent, which means the witness had direct experience with the subject matter of his or her testimony. The exceptions would be expert testimony or lay opinions for common, everyday experiences. If the witness has not had direct experience, but is merely relying on what he or she has heard, then the proffered testimony is hearsay if it is being offered for its truth.

If the testimony is being offered as a document, 5 potential issues are raised: relevance, authentication, best evidence rule, hearsay, and privilege. In the present fact pattern, the mention of documents (police reports) in call #5 raised both the best evidence rule and hearsay.

Every full evidence fact pattern on the California Bar exam has one or more hearsay calls. In approaching such calls, you must first remember to prove that the statement is hearsay by demonstrating both that the statement was made out of court and that it is being offered for its truth. More importantly, if the proffered evidence is hearsay, you must always try to find at least 2 ways around the inadmissibility of the hearsay. Please note that exceptions and exemptions to hearsay must be discussed by applying the relevant facts to each element. If you can find no exception or exemption for which all elements can be met, then it is inadmissible hearsay.

In the present fact pattern, several out-of-court statements were made that were not being offered for their truth, but rather to show effect on the listener or state of mind of the declarant. Such statements are excluded from the general prohibition on out-of-court statements. The approach taken in the present model should be carefully studied as an illustration of how such statements should be handled, and of the distinction between effect on the listener and state of mind of the declarant.

It is also important to note that improper character evidence is a frequently occurring issue that is easy to overlook. There are 2 types of improper character evidence. One type goes to statements concerning traits, which are general dispositional tendencies. It's improper, for example, to say that someone was more likely to have started a fight just because he's an angry person. A second type goes to specific bad acts, and again it's improper to say that someone was more likely to start a fight just because he started a fight in the past. In the present fact pattern, call #5 proffers evidence that the defendant had beaten his ex-girlfriend Gina. This evidence is improper because it is offered to show that Dan, the defendant, was more likely to have been the perpetrator of an assault.

EVIDENCE

Paul, the alleged victim of an aggravated assault by defendant Dan, was called as the first witness by the prosecutor at Dan's criminal trial. The issue is on what grounds could an objection or motion to strike have been made at each of 8 points in Paul's testimony.

Two general issues apply to Paul's testimony:

Competence and Hearsay. Paul must be competent, which means he must have personal knowledge of the facts to which he is testifying. He will not be allowed to speculate or provide opinions unless excepted, and will not be allowed to testify on the basis of hearsay as defined below.

Logical Relevance
Paula's testimony must be logically relevant, which means it must have a tendency to make the existence of any fact of consequence more or less probable.

Point 1: "I went over to Don and said . . ."
Logical Relevance
Defined above, Paul's testimony that Dan's ex-girlfriend Gina is living with him supports the proposition that Dan may have become angered during the conversation that took place in the tavern, and has a tendency to show that Dan became angry and assaulted Paul as charged. Thus, the statement cannot be objected to or stricken as irrelevant.

Competence/Hearsay
Although Paul is competent to testify as to what he said to Dan because he has personal knowledge of what he said to Dan, his statement would be objectionable as hearsay.

Hearsay is an out-of-court statement offered for the truth of the matter asserted. Paul's statement was made in a tavern on the day of the alleged assault. Thus, the statement was made out of court. It is irrelevant that it was it was Paul himself who made the out-of-court statement.

Effect on the Listener
The issue is whether the statement is being offered for its truth. The prosecutor is not trying to show that Gina was in fact living with Paul, but rather to show the effect the statement may have had on Dan in provoking him to assault Paul.

Because the relevance of the statement goes to its effect on Paul, and the prosecutor would be offering the statement to show its effect on Paul rather than for its truth, the statement is not hearsay.

Conclusion: The court should overrule any objections based on relevance, competency, or hearsay. The testimony is admissible.

Point 2: "He said . . ."

Logical Relevance

    P's statement that Dan's buddies told Dan that Paul has been treating Gina like dirt is relevant to show Dan was angry or upset with Paul. Therefore it is logically relevant.

Hearsay

    The statement was made in the tavern, and therefore is an out-of-court statement.

State of Mind of Declarant

    It is well settled law that out-of-court statements offered to show the state of mind of the declarant reflecting intent, attitude, belief, knowledge, or insanity are excluded from the general prohibition against out-of-court statements because such statements are not being offered for their truth.

    Dan's alleged out-of-court statement reveals his belief or knowledge that Paul was mistreating his ex-girlfriend as well as his attitude of animosity for Paul. The prosecutor is not trying to show the truth of the out-of-court statement that Paul was treating Gina like dirt or that Dan's buddies told Dan this. Rather, the statement is being offered to show Dan's state of mind and hence is not hearsay.

Hearsay Within Hearsay

    Dan may argue that the statement is actually hearsay within hearsay because the proffered testimony by Paul is what Dan told Paul that Dan's buddies said to Dan.

    As indicated, what Dan told Paul reflects Dan's state of mind. For similar reasons, what Dan's buddies told Dan also reflects Dan's beliefs and attitudes, which is really what is at issue. Whether Dan's buddies actually made the statement is collateral to the prosecutor's case in chief.

Party Admission

    An admission by a party, offered against the party is non-hearsay under the Federal Rules of Evidence (FRE). It is non-hearsay even if the declarant's statement is in the form of an opinion or the declarant does not have personal knowledge.

    Dan's statement can be construed as an admission that he was angry with Paul for treating Gina like dirt. The fact that Dan's statement is not based on personal knowledge, but rather on what his buddies told him, is irrelevant, and the statement is being offered against Dan, who is the defendant (a party). Therefore, Paul's statement is also admissible as a party admission, in which case it could be offered for its truth.

Conclusion: The court should over-rule any objections based on relevance or hearsay, and there are no other reasonable grounds to object. The statement is admissible.

Point 3: "Is that when . . . "

Assuming Facts Not in Evidence

    It is impermissible to ask a question that implies a fact not in evidence. Such questions lack foundation, and are tantamount to making an argument to the jury in the form of a question.

The prosecutor's question assumes that Dan pulled a club out of his pocket. There is no foundation or basis for this assertion, so the question is objectionable. The prosecutor must lay a proper foundation and Paul's answer should be stricken.

Leading Question on Direct

Leading questions may not be used in a direct exam unless the question is to a hostile witness or adverse party, or there is another exception such as for foundational purposes, to refresh recollection, handicapped witness, or expert testimony.

Paul is the prosecutor's first witness. The prosecutor always has the burden of production, so this must be a direct exam. Paul is not hostile or adverse because he is the victim being willingly examined by the prosecutor, and none of the other exceptions apply.

A leading question is one that suggests an answer. Here, the prosecutor's statement suggests the answer "yes." Therefore it is leading.

Conclusion: An objection should be sustained on either of the grounds indicated above.

Point 4: "Tell the jury . . ."
Calls for a Narrative

Questions that are excessively broad are objectionable because they jeopardize the court's ability to exercise control to make the interrogation effective for the ascertainment of truth and avoid needless consumption of time. Direct examinations are controlled through how, what, where, when, and why questions.

Prosecutor's instruction to tell everything is excessively broad and Dan's objection should be sustained. The court should have admonished Prosecutor to rephrase.

Point 5: "I said. . ."

Because Paul's response was to an improper question, his response should be stricken, and a motion to strike should be sustained. In addition, Dan may object on other grounds.

(a) "I said he was a fine one to be talking"
Irrelevant

Whether Dan had a right to be talking is not relevant to the charge of assault. It reflects Paul's attitude and Paul is not on trial.

Hearsay

The statement was made in the tavern, and therefore it is out of court. Arguably, however, it is being offered to show the effect on the listener because it is combative and confrontational, and may have provoked Dan.

Prejudicial Impact

Evidence may be excluded if its probative value is substantially outweighed by unfair prejudice, confusion of the issue, misleading the jury, and for considerations of undue delay, waste of time, and cumulative evidence.

As indicated, the statement is of little relevance to a material issue. Even if it is relevant to show Dan's state of mind, its probative value is slight because Dan's state of mind has been well established. Moreover, as discussed, the initial question was impermissible.

The statement is objectionable and should be stricken.

(b) "I told him I read several reports. . ."
<u>Improper Character Evidence</u>

Evidence of character is inadmissible to show that Dan acted in conformity therewith. In a criminal case, the prosecutor may not, in his case in chief, introduce evidence of Dan's bad character to show that he acted in conformity on a particular occasion.

The statement that Police had indicated that Dan had beaten Gina would suggest that Dan has a violent character. As such, it would be more likely that Dan was violent in the tavern and assaulted Paul. Such evidence is highly prejudicial and impermissible because the prosecutor has the burden of proving that Dan committed the charged offense, not that he had a character trait that made him more likely to do so.

The court should sustain Dan's objection based on improper character evidence and the statement should be stricken.

Best Evidence Rule

Where the contents of a writing are at issue, it is necessary to produce an original or show that it is unavailable through no fault of the proponent.

Paul's testimony appears to be relying on police documents. Dan should object and the objection should be sustained.

<u>Hearsay</u>

Paul's statement is hearsay within hearsay. Paul is testifying as to what he told Dan in the tavern that had been written in a police report made out of court.

Even if what Paul said to Dan can be admissible as nonhearsay to show its effect on Dan being provoked (a weak argument), the police report would be inadmissible as hearsay without an exception. It does not fit under the business record exception because it very arguably was made in anticipation of litigation and hence is not dependable. It violates Paul's 6th Amendment right to confront adverse witnesses.

Conclusion: The entire testimony in Point 5 is objectionable on several grounds and should be stricken.

Point 6: "You bet . . ."
<u>Improper Character Evidence: Bolstering</u>

A witness' credibility may not be supported until her creditability is attacked. Paul is the first witness. Gina's character has not been attacked. The bolstering of her character is improper and impermissible. The objection should be sustained and the testimony stricken.

Point 7: (a) "Watch out . . ."

The statement was made out of court in the tavern and is being offered for its truth, which is that Dan was about to hit Paul again. It is therefore hearsay.

Excited Utterance

A statement made after a startling event, made under the stress of the event, and related to the event is excepted under the hearsay rule.

If Dan was going to hit Paul "again," an observer would be startled and under the stress because someone is about to be hit, so the statement qualifies as an excited utterance.

Present Sense Impression

Statements describing or explaining an event while perceiving an event or immediately thereafter are also excepted. Here, observer appears be describing his current perception that Dan has hit Paul and is about to do so again.

The statement is admissible as an exception to hearsay.

(b) "I ducked . . ."

Witness Competent

The remainder of Paul's statement merely describes his direct personal experience: he ducked, got hit by a club, and remembers a foot kicking him in the face. Because it is based on Paul's personal knowledge, it is admissible.

Conclusion: The entire testimony in Point 7 is admissible. Any objection should be overruled.

Point 8: "Dan must have. . ."

Speculation/Competency

Witnesses are not allowed to speculate. Here, P is speculating that Dan must have kicked him. He has no direct knowledge of this, only that he had bruises. Anyone could have kicked him. However, the fact that Paul had bruises is based on personal knowledge and is admissible.

Conclusion: Paul's speculation should be stricken, but not the testimony about bruises.

Phil sued Dirk, a barber, seeking damages for personal injuries resulting from a hair treatment Dirk performed on Phil. The complaint alleged that most of Phil's hair fell out as a result of the treatment. At a jury trial, the following occurred:

A. Phil's attorney called Wit to testify that the type of hair loss suffered by Phil was abnormal. Before Wit could testify, the judge stated that he had been a trained barber prior to going to law school. He took judicial notice that this type of hair loss was not normal and instructed the jury accordingly. *No!*

B. Phil testified that, right after he discovered his hair loss, he called Dirk and told Dirk what had happened. Phil testified that Dirk then said: (1) "I knew I put too many chemicals in the solution I used on you, so won't you take $1,000 in settlement?" (2) "I fixed the solution and now have it corrected." (3) "Don't worry because Insco, my insurance company, told me that it will take care of everything."  *Admission, but settlement negotiation*

C. Phil produced a letter at trial addressed to him bearing the signature "Dirk." The letter states that Dirk used an improper solution containing too many chemicals on Phil for his hair treatment. Phil testified that he received this letter through the mail about a week after the incident at the barbershop. The court admitted the letter into evidence.

Expert

D. In his defense, Dirk called Chemist, who testified as an expert witness that he applied to his own hair the same solution that had been used on Phil and that he suffered no loss of hair. *Qualified?* *Lay*

Assume that, in each instance, all appropriate objections were made. Did the court err in:

1. Taking judicial notice and instructing the jury on hair loss? Discuss.

2. Admitting Phil's testimony regarding Dirk's statements? Discuss.

3. Admitting the letter produced by Phil? Discuss.

4. Admitting Chemist's testimony? Discuss.

FEBRUARY 2002, QUESTION 6
EVIDENCE

-- Written by Dennis P. Saccuzzo & Nancy E. Johnson

Commentary:

All evidence questions on the California Bar exam are racehorses. This question is no exception. It contains four separate calls, but what a lot of people missed was that call #1 had two parts. Because evidence questions have so many issues, Bar candidates who adhere to a rigid or formulaic outline tend to get low scores and miss important issues. A second thing to remember about evidence questions on the California Bar is that hearsay is always an issue. More importantly, whenever hearsay is present, the Bar expects candidates to attempt to apply two exceptions/exemptions/exclusions. One of the biggest mistakes made by Bar candidates in applying them is the failure to discuss the individual elements. Often a superficial analysis will give the appearance that some way out of the hearsay rule can be found. A more careful application of the facts to the individual elements will show this is not always the case.

Hearsay is usually pretty easy to spot. One clue is that the statement is in quotes. Another is that a witness offers to testify as to what she was told or what someone said. The California Bar rarely hides hearsay issues. A common trap, however, is to be conclusory when discussing hearsay. A typical conclusory response states the hearsay rule and then asserts that the statement is hearsay without providing any of the facts that would demonstrate that it is in fact hearsay. You must first show that the statement was made in a forum outside of the court in which the witness is now testifying. Next analyze whether the statement is being offered for its truth. In other words, prove that it is hearsay, as opposed to asserting it is hearsay. Then attempt to find more than one way out of the hearsay rule so that the statement will be admissible and therefore not offend the 6th Amendment right to confrontation. Never conclude that a statement is inadmissible hearsay without at least attempting to apply the facts to find a way out of the rule.

The present fact pattern was very complicated in that each of the 3 statements in paragraph B were both hearsay (with possible exceptions) and policy exclusions. This complexity created an organizational problem. The present model, after discussing the relevance of each statement, begins with hearsay and only then discusses the policy exclusions because, for 2 out of 3 of the statements there was a way out of the hearsay rule but the statement was inadmissible for policy reasons. It would have been illogical to exclude the statement for policy reasons and then analyze hearsay to find it admissible.

In approaching evidence questions, it is essential to remember that testifying witnesses other than experts must have personal knowledge in order to give admissible testimony. That means they must have experienced or directly perceived the subject of their testimony.

Call 1: Taking judicial notice and instructing the jury

Judicial Notice

In taking judicial notice, a court accepts facts as true without proof. A judicially noticed fact must be well established and not subject to reasonable dispute in that it is generally known within the territorial jurisdiction of the trial court or it is capable of accurate and ready determination by resort to well-established sources whose accuracy cannot be questioned.

The judge took judicial notice that a certain type of hair loss was not normal. He made this determination based on his training as a barber. What is normal and abnormal loss of hair cannot be something generally known if it is based on technical training as a barber. That an expert was called and prepared to testify indicates that the abnormality of such hair loss is not a well-established fact that can be verified by sources whose accuracy cannot be questioned. Therefore, the judge erred in taking judicial notice. The judge also erred in that he testified based on personal experience, and the judge's role is to hear the case, not act as a witness. In fact, it is generally unprofessional for judges or lawyers to act as witnesses.

Instructing the Jury

In instructing the jury on judicial notice, for civil cases the court must instruct to accept as conclusive any judicially noticed fact. In a criminal case the court must instruct the jury that it may, but is not required to accept the judicially noticed fact as conclusive.

[handwritten margin note: Civil - must accept. Criminal may accept.]

Phil is suing Dirk for damages. Therefore, this is a civil case. As such, the judge should have instructed the jury to accept the judicially noticed fact as conclusive. He did not, and so erred again.

Call 2: Phil's Testimony

Phil made three statements pertaining to his conversation with Dirk.

Statement 1: "I knew I put too many chemicals . . . "
Relevance

To be admissible, a statement must be logically relevant, which means it has the tendency to make any fact of consequence more or less probable. This statement is relevant to show that Dirk was negligent in that he put in too many chemicals.

Hearsay

Hearsay is an out of court statement offered for the truth of the matter asserted. Dirk's statement was made out of court, in a telephone conversation. It is being offered to show that Dirk was negligent because he put in too many chemicals. Therefore, it is hearsay, and absent an exception or exemption will be inadmissible.

Exemption: Party Admission

A party's own admission offered against him is exempted from the hearsay rule. Dirk admitted that he used too many chemicals. The admission is being used against him. Therefore, because the statement would be exempted from the hearsay rule it would be admissible.

Exception: Declaration Against Interest
This exception will not work because the witness must be unavailable. Here, Dirk is being sued and is available.

Policy Exclusions: Settlement Offer
Although relevant and otherwise admissible, certain statements may be excluded for policy reasons. Offers of compromise to settle a dispute as to validity or amount of a claim are not admissible to prove liability or amount of damages. The policy is to encourage settlement. Here, Dirk said "won't you take $1,000 in settlement?" Although there may have been no dispute as to liability, Dirk's offer suggests that there was no agreement about amount. Phil's refusal to accept the offer demonstrated that there was a dispute as to amount, so Dirk's statement cannot be used to prove his liability or amount owed.

Conclusion: Even though the statement is exempted from the hearsay rule and would be admissible on that basis, it will be excluded for policy reasons as a part of a settlement offer.

Statement 2: "I fixed the solution . . . "
Relevance
The statement is relevant to show the solution wasn't made right and that Dirk is negligent.

Hearsay and Exemptions
Like Statement 1, this statement was made out of court in a telephone conservation and is being offered for its truth, namely to show the original solution was defective and needed correcting. As with Statement 1, Dirk is making an admission, which is being used against him, so the statement would be exempted from the hearsay rule. Declaration against interest will again not work because Dirk is available as the defendant.

Policy Exclusion: Subsequent Remedial Measures
Subsequent remedial measures are not admissible to prove negligence. The policy is to encourage repairs without such repairs being used as evidence against a defendant. Dirk's statement that he fixed the solution and now has it corrected is a measure taken after Phil was damaged. As a subsequent remedial measure, this statement would be inadmissible to show that Dirk was negligent.

Conclusion: The statement is inadmissible to show negligence for policy reasons, as a subsequent remedial measure.

Statement 3: "Don't worry . . . "
Relevance
Having insurance could be used to show that Dirk was less careful than he might otherwise have been.

Hearsay Within Hearsay

Phil is testifying as to what Dirk told Phil about what Dirk's insurance company told Dirk. Both statements were made on the phone and are being offered for their truth. To be admissible, there must be an exception for each level of hearsay.

Exceptions to Hearsay
Dirk's statement to Phil ("Don't worry ...")

As with the two previous statements, this statement may be exempted from the hearsay rule as an admission used against Dirk. It may also come in under the state of mind exception, to show Dirk's intent to make sure Phil gets compensated.

Insurance company's statement to Dirk

This statement is problematic as there is no clear exclusion, exemption, or exception to the hearsay rule. It would not qualify as a statement by an agent of Dirk's, as this exemption requires an employee-employer relationship and insurance company is not employed by Dirk. Instead, his relationship with the insurance company is a contractual one to cover Dirk's liability within the coverage of the policy. The state of mind exception is also doubtful, as the insurance company representative may have simply been operating under his belief about the coverage. Declaration against interest won't work because insurance has a duty to defend and indemnify and saying that they will cover things would not be contrary to their pecuniary interest.

Policy Exclusions: Liability Insurance

Statements pertaining to liability insurance are inadmissible to prove negligence. The policy is to encourage people to get insurance without fear that this can be used against them in a civil case.

Dirk's statement that he had insurance that would take care of everything is inadmissible to show Dirk was negligent.

Conclusion: The statement is inadmissible for policy reasons and as hearsay without an exception.

Call 3: Phil's Letter

The letter must be relevant, authenticated, comply with the best evidence rule, and not be hearsay or privileged.

Relevance

The letter is relevant to show that Dirk was negligent and liable because he used an improper solution.

Authentication

The letter could be authenticated by anyone familiar with Dirk's handwriting, as it contained his signature.

Best Evidence Rule

When the contents of a writing are at issue, it is necessary to use the original or show that the original is unavailable through no fault of the proponent. Contents are at issue when W's testimony depends on its contents.

The letter my introduced thus the BER is met

The letter is apparently being introduced as direct evidence of an admission by Dirk that he used an improper solution containing too many chemicals. Consequently, its contents are at issue, and Phil must produce the original. No facts indicate the letter produced is not the original, so the Best Evidence Rule is met.

Hearsay

The letter was written out of court and Phil received it about a week after the barbershop incident. It is being offered for its truth, namely that Dirk used an improper solution. Thus, it is hearsay and absent an exception, exemption or exclusion will be inadmissible.

Exceptions: Party Admission and Declaration Against Interest

As with prior statements, those in the letter qualify as an admission by Dirk that he used too many chemicals. It is being used against Dirk, so this admission will be exempted from the hearsay rule and therefore is admissible.

Admitting that he used too many chemicals is quite contrary to Dirk's pecuniary interest because it subjects him to liability. Because a reasonable person in Dirk's shoes would not make such a statement unless he believed it to be true, the statement is against his interest. However, because he is not unavailable, this exception to the hearsay rule will not work.

Privilege

No facts indicate a privilege.

Conclusion: The letter is admissible and the court did not err in admitting it.

Call 4: The Chemist's Testimony

Expert Opinion

Experts are witnesses who, because of specialized knowledge, are able to assist the trier of fact. They must be qualified and use techniques and evidence reasonably relied on by other experts in the field.

An expert chemist would us scientific techniques and experiments similar to those that other chemists might use, such as analyzing the chemical composition of the solution or testing it in a controlled fashion. Instead, Chemist used the solution on his own hair. This is not what other experts in this field would do to test the solution.

Further, experts provide opinion testimony based on their expertise and techniques. Chemist did not provide an opinion. He testified as to his own personal experience. Chemist acted as a fact witness and not as an expert. The court erred in admitting his testimony.

JULY 2001 CALIFORNIA BAR EXAM -- QUESTION 3

1-HOUR ESSAY

Walker sued Truck Co. for personal injuries. Walker alleged that Dan, Truck Co.'s driver, negligently ran a red light and struck him as he was crossing the street in the crosswalk with the "Walk" signal. Truck Co. claimed that Dan had the green light and that Walker was outside the crosswalk. At trial, Walker called George Clerk and the following questions were asked and answers given:

Q. Would you tell the jury your name and spell your last name for the record, please?

A. George Clerk. C-l-e-r-k.

[1] Q: Where were you when you saw the truck hit Walker? *When you saw*

A: I was standing behind the counter in the pharmacy where I work.

[2] Q: What were the weather conditions just before the accident?

[3] A: Well, some people had their umbrellas up, so I'm pretty sure it must have been raining.

[4] Q: Tell me everything that happened.

[5] A: This guy rushed into my store and shouted, "Call an ambulance! A truck just ran a red light and hit someone."

Q: What happened next?

[6] A: I walked over to the window and looked out. I said, "That truck must have been going way over the speed limit." Then I called an ambulance.

Q: Then what happened?

[7] A: I walked out to where this guy was lying in the street. Dan, the driver for Truck Co., was kneeling over him. A woman was kneeling there too. She spoke calmly to Dan and said, "It's all your fault," and Dan said nothing in response.

At each of the seven indicated points, what objection or objections, if any, should have been made, and how should the court have ruled on each objection? Discuss.

JULY 2001, QUESTION 3
EVIDENCE

-- Written by Dennis P. Saccuzzo & Nancy E. Johnson

Commentary:

This evidence fact pattern has seven calls and required candidates to raise as many objections as possible. *In making objections it is important to consider both the form of the question (e.g., compound, argumentative, calls for a narrative) and whether an objection can be raised based on admissibility (e.g., relevance, hearsay, improper opinion).* The larger issues will always be those related to admissibility (e.g., objection, hearsay), rather than mere improper form (e.g., leading question on direct). In fact, on the California Bar exam, hearsay is always an issue on evidence fact patterns. Whenever hearsay is found, it is usually necessary to discuss two ways to admit the hearsay (e.g., one exception and one exemption). Importantly, exceptions and exemptions must be discussed by *element*. Candidates often go astray when they spot an exception or exemption but do not apply the facts to the elements. Consequently, they wind up admitting evidence that should be excluded and vice versa.

With 7 calls, it was necessary to pace oneself. Most people who failed the question simply didn't finish. The final calls were richer and more complex than the earlier ones, so spending too much time on the earlier calls was devastating. To make matters worse, this was question #3(the last question in the 3-hour Tuesday morning session), a common tactic used by the Bar examiners to defeat Bar candidates.

Many people were short of time even before they started this question, having spent an extra 5 to 10 minutes on Essays 1 and 2. Fifty minutes was simply not enough time to answer this one. Call 5 had a hearsay issue with 2 exceptions that, as indicated, had to be discussed by element. Call 6 had 4 issues, including *inadmissible hearsay*. Call 7 was also hearsay with the party's adoptive admission exemption as a major issue. Candidates who got to call 7 and did a good job of discussing the exemptions generally received very good scores. The moral: pace yourself throughout the exam; *never spend more than one hour per question,* and never forget that all evidence fact patterns on the California Bar exam are racehorses.

Pace was especially important for this question. Some of the richer parts came at the end.

Model Answer

Point 1 – *Where were you standing…*

Lack of Foundation/Witness Competence

To be competent, a witness must have personal knowledge.

Walker's (W's) Lawyer (L) fails to lay the proper foundation that Witness Clerk actually saw the accident, and therefore is competent to testify. The objection should be sustained.

Assumes Facts not in Evidence

A question may not imply a fact.

L's question implies two facts: (1) that W actually saw the accident and (2) that W saw the truck hit Walker. The objection is sustainable on either of the two assumed facts.

Argumentative

Counsel may not make an argument in the form of a question.

L's question makes the argument that the truck hit W. In fact, this is merely part of W's allegations. The objection is sustainable.

Point 2 – *What were the weather conditions…*

Relevance

To be admissible, all evidence must be logically relevant, which means that it has a tendency to make the existence of any fact of consequence more or less probable.

Trucker may argue that weather conditions are irrelevant to the main issue, namely whether Dan had a green light. However, to be relevant the evidence merely has to make a fact of consequence more or less probable.

Here, the ability of either of the parties and of the testifying witness to see the light is of consequence. Because the weather conditions can affect visibility, this question could be relevant to show that the light was difficult to see. It can also be relevant to show that the testifying witness is not competent because lack of visibility impaired his ability to see the light, or to impeach the testifying witness on the basis of lack of perception. Thus, the objection should be overruled.

Lack of Foundation/Witness Competence

Discussed *supra*, the statement implies that Clerk had an opportunity to observe the weather conditions. The objection should be sustained, and counsel should be required to lay a proper foundation.

Opinion Testimony

As a general rule, a lay witness may not offer an opinion. Here, Clerk is being asked to give an opinion on the weather, and no foundation has been laid to show that Clerk is an expert.

An exception to the general rule concerns sensory opinions with common experience plus an opportunity to observe. Weather conditions are common sensory experiences. Assuming that a proper foundation is laid showing that Clerk had an opportunity to observe the weather conditions, this objection should be overruled.

Point 3 – *Some people had umbrellas up...*

Witness Incompetent

Discussed *supra*, a witness must have personal knowledge.

When clerk said some people had their umbrellas up, he was testifying based on his personal observations, and this testimony is not objectionable. However, when clerk said "I'm pretty sure . . . " it is clear that he did not have personal knowledge, and instead was drawing an inference. Opposing counsel's objection as well as his or her motion to strike the second part of the statement should be sustained.

Calls for Speculation

Witnesses should not be required to guess.

When Clerk said, "I'm pretty sure," he was speculating about what the weather conditions were. Because Clerk was merely guessing, the objection should be sustained and, as discussed above, the speculation should be stricken.

Point 4 – *Tell me everything. . .*

Calls for a Narrative

A question may not be excessively broad, and under the Federal Rules of Evidence the court shall exercise control to make the interrogation effective for the ascertainment of truth and avoid needless consumption of time.

An open-ended statement such as 'tell me everything that happened' is excessively broad because it sets no limits on what the witness might say. It is also an ineffective method for ascertaining the truth because an unguided witness may introduce testimony that is inadmissible. Such questions may also waste time because the witness has no guidance or direction. Instead, the L on direct should ask how, what, why, who, when, and where questions to develop a clear record of the facts.

The objection should be sustained, and counsel should be instructed by the judge to rephrase the question.

Point 5 – *"This guy rushed into my store."*

Hearsay
   Hearsay is an out of court statement offered to prove the truth of the matter asserted. As a general rule, hearsay is inadmissible.

   Clerk is testifying as to what some guy said in his store. Thus, the statement was made out of court. The second part of the statement, "a truck just ran a red light and hit someone" is being offered for its truth, as this is the very allegation Walker is trying to establish. As an out of court statement offered for its truth, the statement is hearsay and inadmissible absent an appropriate exception, exclusion, or exemption.

Exception to Hearsay – Excited Utterance
   An excited utterance is an exception to the general inadmissibility of hearsay. It requires a statement relating to a startling event or condition, made while the declarant was under the stress of the event, and related to the event.

   Startling event. Assuming the truth of the declarant's statement, he had just witnessed a truck run a red light and cause injuries. Thus, there was a startling event.

   Made under stress of event. The declarant rushed into the store and shouted, "Call an ambulance!" His actions and exclamatory words indicate he was under the stress of the accident.

   Related to the event. The declarant's statement was related to the accident, which is the event in question.

Conclusion: The entire statement comes in as an excited utterance.

Exception to Hearsay – Present Sense Impression
   A statement which (1) describes or explains (2) an event or condition made while perceiving or shortly thereafter is also a reliable exception to the hearsay rule that does not offend the confrontation clause.

   The first statement "Call an ambulance," would not qualify under this exception because it does not describe the event, but instead is the declarant's reaction to the event.

   The second statement, "A truck just ran a red light and hit someone," does indeed describe an event. That the declarant rushed into the store and shouted for an ambulance suggests that the statement was indeed made shortly after perceiving. However, the court may require counsel to lay a better foundation for this exception.

Conclusion: Excited utterance is the better exception because it does not require additional foundation and permits both statements to come in.

Point 6 – *I walked over…*

Clerk's statements that he walked over to the window and looked out, and that he then called an ambulance are both admissible because they are relevant to show there had been an injury accident, are based on Clerk's personal knowledge, and are not hearsay.

However, the statement that the truck must have been going over the speed limit is inadmissible for a number of reasons.

Incompetent Witness

Clerk is not testifying based on personal knowledge. He is merely drawing an inference about the speed of the truck.

Speculation

Clerk is guessing as to what must have happened. His testimony is speculative.

Improper Opinion

How fast a truck must have been going following an accident is not a matter of common, everyday experience but rather would require a qualified expert. Thus, Clerk is offering improper opinion testimony.

Hearsay "That truck must have been going way over the speed limit)"

Defined *supra*, the statement was made in Clerk's store, and therefore was out of court. It is being offered to show the truck was going over the speed limit and thus is being offered for its truth. Therefore it is hearsay.

Walker may try to argue that the statement should come in under the present state of mind exception, to show Clerk's then-existing state of mind. This argument will fail, however, because Clerk is testifying as to his memory of what he said.

Clerk's statement is inadmissible hearsay.

Conclusion: The statement about the truck exceeding the speed limit is inadmissible and the objection should be sustained on all of the above grounds.

Point 7 – *"I walked out…"*

Clerk's statement that he walked out to where the guy was lying in the street and saw the truck driver and a woman kneeling over him are admissible because they are relevant to show Walker was hit and injured and are based on Clerk's personal knowledge, and are not hearsay or otherwise inadmissible.

However, the woman's statement to Dan, "It's all your fault," is objectionable for a number of reasons.

Hearsay

Defined above, Clerk is testifying as to what a woman at the scene of the accident said to Dan. The statement was therefore made out of court and is being offered for its truth to prove Walker's allegations that the accident was the truck driver's fault. Absent an exception, exemption, or exclusion, the statement is inadmissible.

Exceptions: Excited Utterance and Present Sense Impression

Both of these exceptions were defined above. Excited utterance will fail because facts stipulate that the woman spoke calmly. Thus, she was not under the stress of the event. Present sense is questionable because no facts suggest that the woman's statement was made while perceiving or shortly thereafter. In fact, her calm demeanor indicates a time lapse that would exclude this exception.

Exemption: Party's Adoptive Admission

An expressed or implied adoption by silence is an exemption to the hearsay rule. Facts stipulate that Dan said nothing. Walker must show (1) that Dan heard and understood the woman's statement; (2) that Dan was physically and mentally capable of denying the accusation; (3) a reasonable person would have denied the accusation; and (4) that the statement is being offered against a party.

This exemption will cause Walker problems. We can assume that Dan heard the woman, given that Dan and the woman were both kneeling over Victim and thus were in close proximity. However, Dan had just been in an accident, and may have been mentally incapable of responding. Further, it is arguable whether a reasonable person would speak in this situation, given that everyone knows that what he says may be used against him in a court of law. Finally, there are no facts to indicate that Dan is a party. The suit is Walker v. Truck Company, apparently on a respondeat superior theory.

The statement is hearsay without an exception, and the objection should be sustained.

1-HOUR ESSAY

Dan was arrested and charged with possession of heroin with intent to sell. Dan allegedly sold a small bag of heroin to Peters, an undercover officer, at Guy's Bar and Grill. In his opening statement, Dan's lawyer said the evidence would show that Dan was entrapped. The following incidents occurred at trial:

1. The prosecutor called Wolf, a patron at Guy's, who testified over defense objections that Dan told him the night before the alleged sale that Dan intended to "sell some baggies" to Peters the next night. *Hearsay — Admission*

2. The prosecutor called Peters, who testified that she was working as an undercover officer and received information that Dan was selling heroin at Guy's. She testified she went to Guy's two nights before the date of the arrest. Over defense objections, Peters testified she talked to Bob, another bar patron, who told her that he had bought marijuana from Dan at Guy's the night before.

3. Peters testified she found out that Dan used e-mail. Over defense objections, she testified that she had e-mailed Dan a message to meet her at Guy's with a small bag of heroin on the night in question. Peters preserved a paper copy of her e-mail message, which, over defense objections, was introduced into evidence.

4. The defense called Dan as a witness. Dan testified that Peters had begged and pleaded with him to get heroin for her because she was suffering from withdrawal and needed a fix. On cross-examination, the prosecutor asked Dan, over defense objections: "Isn't it true that you were arrested by the police for selling marijuana in 1994?" Dan answered "Yes, but they didn't have any evidence to make the charge stick." The prosecutor moved to strike Dan's answer.

5. The defense called Cal, Dan's employer, as a character witness. The defense laid a foundation showing that Cal had known Dan for ten years. Over the prosecutor's objection, Dan's lawyer asked Cal if he had an opinion on Dan's good moral character. Cal answered: "Yes, I and everyone else who have known Dan for many years know that he always tells the truth." The prosecutor moved to strike Cal's answer.

Assume all appropriate objections were made. Was the objected-to evidence in items 1 through 4 properly admitted, and should the motion to strike in items 4 and 5 have been granted? Discuss.

Evidence
Question 1 From July, 2000 California Bar Exam

Answer Written by Dennis P. Saccuzzo

Item 1 – Dan's statement to Wolf that he intended to sell baggies

Logical Relevance

To be admissible, evidence must be logically relevant, which means that the evidence tends to make the existence of any fact of consequence more or less probable.

The statement that Dan intended to "sell some baggies" the next night to Peters tends to make it more likely that Dan sold a controlled substance to Peters. Therefore, it is logically relevant.

Hearsay

Hearsay is an out of court statement offered to prove the truth of the matter asserted. As a general rule, hearsay is inadmissible.

Wolf testified about what Dan told him the night before. Dan's statement was an out of court statement because it is Wolf, not Dan, who testified. The statement is being offered to show that Dan did in fact sell heroin to Peters. Therefore it is hearsay. Absent an exclusion, exemption, or exception, Wolf's statement will be inadmissible.

Exception to Hearsay – Party Admission

An Admission by a Party is exempted from the hearsay rule under the FRE as long as it is offered against the party.

Here, Dan made the admission that he intended to sell baggies, and this statement is being offered against Dan. Therefore, the statement will be exempted from the general prohibition against hearsay.

Exception to Hearsay – Present State of Mind

An individual's then existing mental, emotional, or physical condition, or state of mind (such as intent, plan, motive, design, mental feeling, etc.) is excluded from the hearsay rule.

Dan's statement about selling baggies indicated his future plan to do so. Therefore, it shows his future intent and qualifies as a state of mind exception to the hearsay rule.

Conclusion

Although it is hearsay, Wolf's statement is admissible as either an admission or state of mind exception. Therefore the evidence was properly admitted.

Item 2 – Peters Testified He Talked to Bob

Logical Relevance

Defined supra, Bob's statement to Peters that he had bought marijuana from Dan is logically relevant because it provides circumstantial evidence that Dan intended to sell drugs to Peters and contradicts Dan's entrapment defense.

Improper Character Evidence

Dan will further argue that the proffered evidence is inadmissible character evidence. Under the FRE, evidence of a defendant's character is inadmissible to show that he acted in conformity therewith on a particular occasion. However, when one offers an entrapment defense, one's relevant character is at issue because one of the elements of an entrapment defense is that the defendant was not predisposed to commit the crime.

If the prosecution plans to use the evidence that Dan sold marijuana as evidence that he subsequently sold heroin to Peters, it would likely be inadmissible as character evidence due to its highly prejudicial impact on Dan. However, if the purpose of the evidence is to contradict Dan's entrapment defense by showing that he was predisposed to commit the crime, then the evidence would be admissible.

Hearsay

Defined supra, Bob's statement is also hearsay because it was made out of court by Bob two nights ago, and is offered by Peters for its truth to show that Bob bought marijuana from Dan.

Statement Against Interest (Unavailability Required)

A statement against financial or penal interest, against interest when made, and which a reasonable person would not make unless he believed it to be true is an exception to the hearsay rule, but only if the witness is unavailable.

While saying he bought marijuana from Dan is against Bob's penal interest, there are no facts to show that Bob is unavailable. Therefore, Peters' testimony is hearsay, without an exception.

Conclusion

Peters' testimony is probably inadmissible hearsay.

Item 3 – The e-Mail

The e-mail evidence is a document and as such, must be relevant, authenticated, comply with the best evidence rule, and not be hearsay or privileged.

Relevance and Authentication

The e-mail is relevant because it tends to show that Dan intended to sell heroin. It is authenticated by Peters' first hand knowledge.

Best Evidence Rule

Where the contents of a writing are at issue, the original is generally required.

Because Peters is testifying about the contents of the e-mail, the contents are at issue. Therefore, an original would be required. However, a duplicate is admissible to the same extent as an original unless a genuine question is raised as to the authenticity of the original or it would be unfair to admit the duplicate.

Here, we have a paper copy of the e-mail message. As a duplicate, it should be admissible, and there are no facts to indicate that Dan has questioned its fairness or authenticity.

Hearsay

The e-mail is an out of court statement; it is a statement on a document collected by Peters out of court on her computer, and is being offered for its truth.

Effect on Listener

Under the FRE, a statement offered to show its effect on the listener is not hearsay. Here, the purpose of the e-mail is to show its effect on Dan, namely, that he would bring a small bag of heroin to Peters. Thus, the e-mail is nonhearsay.

Privilege

No facts suggest a privilege.

Conclusion

The e-mail was properly admitted.

Item 4 – Dan's Prior Arrest

The prior arrest is relevant to disprove entrapment. As such, it would be an exception to the rule against character conformity evidence. However, it is highly prejudicial.

Impeachment

The evidence of prior arrest is also improper impeachment. The prosecution is questioning Dan on cross about a prior arrest. This is permissible as long as she has a reasonable basis to believe Dan was in fact arrested and the question goes to truth or veracity. Being arrested for drugs does not speak to Dan's character for truthfulness.

The prosecution is questioning Dan on cross about a prior arrest. This is permissible as long as she has a reasonable basis to believe Dan was in fact arrested and the question goes to truth or veracity. Being arrested for drugs does not speak to Dan's character for truthfulness.

Therefore, the impeachment is improper and was improperly admitted. The entire question should be stricken. Further, Dan's statement should be stricken not only because the question has been stricken, but also because it was nonresponsive in that it went beyond the scope of the question asked.

Item 5 – Dan's Employer Opinion Testimony

Under the mercy rule, a defendant can introduce evidence as to his own relevant good character using reputation or opinion testimony.

Here, the defense laid a proper foundation for Cal to offer an opinion about Dan's relevant good moral character. However, Cal would only be allowed to state his opinion concerning Dan's character.

Cal's statement went beyond the scope of the question and was unresponsive.

Thus, the motion to strike should be sustained.

JULY 1999 CALIFORNIA BAR EXAM -- QUESTION 4

1-HOUR ESSAY

Mary Smith sued Dr. Jones, alleging that Jones negligently performed surgery on her back, leaving her partly paralyzed. In her case-in-chief, Mary called the defendant, Dr. Jones, as her witness. The following questions were asked and answers given:

[1] Q. Now, you did not test the drill before you used it on Mary Smith's vertebrae, did you? *Leading*

[2] A. No. That's not part of our procedure. We don't ordinarily do that. *Non-Responsive + answering to improper question*

[3] Q. Well, since Mary's operation, you now test these drills immediately before using them, don't you? *SRM*

    A. Yes.

[4] Q. Just before you inserted the drill into my client's spine, you heard Nurse Clark say "The drill looks wobbly," didn't you? *Leading, Hearsay,*

    A. No. I did not.

    Q. Let me show what has been marked as plaintiff's exhibit number 10. [Tendering document] This is the surgical report written by Nurse Clark, isn't it? *Doc, Authentication, BER*

    A. Yes.

[5] Q. In her report she wrote: "At time of insertion I said the drill bit looked wobbly," didn't she? *Hearsay, Bus. Record*

    A. Yes. That's her opinion.

    Q. Okay, speaking of opinions, you are familiar with the book, General Surgical Techniques by Tompkins, aren't you? *Learned Treatise*

    A. Yes.

    Q. And it is authoritative, isn't it?

    A. Some people think so.

[6] Q. And this book says, at page 255, "Always test drill bits before using them in spinal surgery," doesn't it? *Present Recollection Recorded*

    A. I guess so, but again that's his opinion.

    Q. Now, you've had some trouble yourself in the past?

    A. What do you mean?

[7] Q. Well, you were accused by two patients of having sexually abused them, weren't you? *Relevance?*

    A. That was all a lot of nonsense.

[8] Q. But you do admit that in two other operations which you performed in 1993 the drill bit which you were using slipped during back surgery, causing injury to your patients?

    A. Accidents do happen.

What objection or objections could Dr. Jones' attorney reasonably have made to the question or answer at each of the places indicated above by the numbers in the left-hand margin, and how should the court have ruled in each instance? Discuss.

EVIDENCE

July 1999 California Bar – Question 4

Model Answer Written by Dennis P. Saccuzzo

CALL 1 – Did you test the drill?

Objection – Leading Question

The general rule is that leading questions should not be used on direct examination. A leading question is one which tends to suggest an answer. Here, Mary's probe "did you" suggests Jones did not; therefore it is leading. Further, it is Mary who is questioning Jones as part of her case in chief. Therefore, this is a direct examination, and the leading question would normally be objectionable.

Exception – Adverse Party

When a party calls a hostile witness, an adversarial party, or a witness identified with an adverse party, leading questions are permitted.

Jones is the defendant. Thus, he falls under the adverse party exception and the leading question is permissible.

Objection – Argumentative/Badgering the Witness

The court shall exercise reasonable control over the mode of questioning so as to protect the witness from harassment.

Jones has a good argument that Mary's question is combative and argumentative.

Objection – Ambiguous

The court shall exercise reasonable control over the mode of questioning so as to make the interrogation and presentation effective for the ascertainment of the truth.

Mary's statement, "you did not, . . . did you" is confusing.

Conclusion: Jones' objections based on argumentative and ambiguous should be sustained. Mary should re-phrase her question.

CALL 2 – Not part of our procedure

Objection – Non-responsive/Motion to Strike

A nonresponsive answer includes testimony not called for by the question. Such answers are especially applicable to a voluntary response by an adverse witness, such as Jones.

Jones was merely asked if he tested the drill. Further, the form of the question only called for a yes-no response. Jones said no, then proceeded to discuss the ordinary procedure. Because his response includes testimony not called for, it is nonresponsive.

Jones' attorney can and should make a motion to strike everything after "no."

Conclusion: Objection sustained; motion to strike granted.

CALL 3 – Since Mary's Operation

Objection – Prejudice Outweighs Probative Value (Legal Relevance/Policy Exclusions)

Subsequent remedial measures are actions taken after an event which would have made the event less likely to occur. Such measures are not admissible to prove negligence or culpable conduct except when offered for another purpose such as to prove ownership, control, or feasibility of the precautionary measures.

Here, Mary is asking Jones if he now tests drills, which of course is a subsequent remedial measure because it would make operations such as Mary's safer. There are no apparent exceptions, so Mary's statement is not admissible.

Conclusion: Objection sustained.

Call 4 – Nurse Clark's Statement

Objection – Hearsay

Hearsay is an out of court statement offered to prove the truth of the matter asserted. In general, hearsay is inadmissible.

Nurse Clark's statement "the drill looked wobbly" was made out of court, during the operation just before Jones inserted the drill. If it is being offered for its truth, namely that the drill was wobbly, then the statement would be hearsay and absent an exclusion, exception, or exemption will be inadmissible.

Exception 1 – Party's Adopted Statement (by silence)

A party's adopted statement may be express or implied. Such adopted statements are exempted from the hearsay rule if it can be shown that (1) the party heard and understood the statement; (2) the party was physically and mentally capable of denying the accusation; and (3) a reasonable person would have denied the accusation.

While Nurse Clark's statement is being used against Jones, and he certainly was physically and mentally capable of denying an accusation (he was conducting surgery), it is unclear whether he actually heard the statement. Indeed, in his answer, Jones denies ever hearing the statement. Thus, it is unlikely that this exception will apply.

Exception 2 – Statement by Party's Agent

A statement by a party's agent is also exempted under the federal rules if the statement is used against a party, was a matter within the scope of agency, and made during the existence of the relationship.

Again, Clark's statement is being used against Jones. Mary's attorney will argue that as a nurse assisting Jones during the operation, Clark was Jones' agent. This argument is weak. Even if Clark was a hospital employee, there are no facts to indicate that Clark was Jones' agent. Thus, Jones will probably successfully argue that Clark's statement was not within the scope of agency and that no such relationship existed.

Exception 3 – Present Sense Impression

A statement which (1) describes or explains (2) an event or condition made while perceiving the event or shortly thereafter is a reliable exception to the hearsay rule that does not offend the confrontation clause.

Jones has denied hearing Clark's statement. However, this should not affect admissibility because it is valid for Mary to introduce evidence that Jones had notice, regardless of his denial.

Here, Mary is describing her experience that the drill looks wobbly while perceiving the drill just before Jones inserted it. Thus, the elements of the exception are satisfied.

Non-Hearsay – Effect on Listener: To Show Notice

A statement offered to show its effect on the listener is not hearsay because it is not offered for its truth.

Mary will argue that Clark's statement should be admitted because it is merely being used to show that Jones had notice that the drill was wobbly.

Conclusion: Objection overruled based on the present sense exception to the hearsay and the argument that it is non-hearsay because offered to show the effect on the listener.

CALL 5 – Clark's Report

Objection – Hearsay

The evidence in question is double hearsay. First, Clark's statement "At the time of insertion the drill looked wobbly" was made out of court and is being offered to show Clark said the drill looked wobbly. Thus, the statement is hearsay. Second, the statement is contained in a report made out of court which again is being offered for its truth. To be admissible, there will have to be an exception for each level of hearsay.

Level 1 – Clark's Statement

Discussed supra, this statement is admissible as a present sense impression.

Level 2 – The Report: Business Record

Business records are excepted from the hearsay rule if (1) the record is made at or near the time, (2) from a person with knowledge, (3) kept in the course of regularly conducted business, where (4) it was a regular practice of the business to make that memo, and (5) the record is authenticated.

Here, while Jones authenticated the report by his personal knowledge, Mary has failed to lay a foundation to show that any of the other elements of this exception are met.

Conclusion: Objection sustained.

CALL 6 – The Book

Objection – Hearsay

 Mary is attempting to use a statement in a book for its truth.

Exception – Learned Treatise

 Treatises are excepted to the extent called to the attention of an expert upon cross examination or relied upon by the expert in direct examination. The treatise must be established as reliable by testimony or admission of the witness (or by another expert or by judicial notice). If admitted, the statements may be read into evidence but may not be received as exhibits.

 At this trial, Jones may have established the reliability of the treatise, though "some people think so" could leave room for doubt. Further, there is no evidence to suggest that Jones "relied on it," and he isn't being cross-examined.

Conclusion: Objection sustained.

CALL 7 – The Accusation of Abuse

Objection – Irrelevant

 To be admissible, evidence must be logically relevant, which means it has a tendency to make the existence of any act of consequence more or less probable.

 Mary will be unable to convince the judge that the accusation of abuse is materially relevant to any fact of consequence in this negligence action.

Objection – Prejudice Outweighs Probative Value

 Evidence may be excluded if its probative value is substantially outweighed by the danger of unfair prejudice.

 Even if relevant, the accusation of abuse is of little probative value and extremely prejudicial.

Objection – Improper Impeachment

 While the prosecutor in a criminal trial is allowed to inquire into specific bad acts on cross-examination to impeach a witness, Jones is being questioned on direct exam. The question is improper.

Objection – Improper Character Evidence

 Evidence of a defendant's character is inadmissible to show he acted in conformity on a particular occasion.

 It is improper to imply that because Jones may have abused patients, that he is the type of person who would be careless.

Conclusion: Objection sustained on all of the above grounds.

CALL 8 – Two Other Operations

Objection – Improper Character Evidence
    Discussed supra, it is impermissible for Mary to imply that because Jones' drill slipped on two prior occasions that it slipped on this occasion.

Objection – Irrelevant
    Prior accidents or claims are not relevant unless to show fraud or past damage. Neither of these exceptions apply.

Conclusion: Objections sustained.

JULY 1998 CALIFORNIA BAR EXAM -- QUESTION 6

1-HOUR ESSAY

A car driven by Dunn collided with Empire Trucking Co.'s truck driven by Kemper. Kemper died at the scene. Dunn and Dunn's passenger, Paul, were seriously injured. Paul sued Empire for personal injuries. Paul attempted to serve Sigel, an Empire mechanic who was on duty the day of the collision, with a subpoena to appear at the trial, but the process server could not locate Sigel. The following occurred at the jury trial.

3. Paul called the investigating police officer, Oliver, who testified that he talked to Wit at the scene a half hour after the collision. Oliver wrote down Wit's statement and attached it to his report. Oliver testified that Wit told him that he ran over to the scene from the curb and spoke to the driver of the car, Dunn, who told Wit: 'I'm not going to make it and I want you to know the truth-the truck ran a red light.'

4. Paul called a court reporter who properly authenticated the trial transcript of Sigel's testimony in *People v. Dunn,* a reckless homicide case relating to the same incident, in which Sigel testified that on the morning of the incident he warned Kemper that the brakes on the truck were defective, but Kemper drove the truck anyway. The transcript was admitted into evidence.

5. Paul called Dunn who testified that she had a green light and was driving below the speed limit when defendant's truck struck her car.

6. Empire offered into evidence a properly authenticated copy of the conviction of Dunn for reckless homicide based on this incident. Paul's objections to this offer were sustained.

7. Empire asked Dunn on cross examination: "Q. Isn't it true your insurance carrier reached a settlement with Paul and as part of that written agreement, you agreed to testify on Paul's behalf today?" Paul's objections to this question were sustained.

Assume that all appropriate objections were made. Was the evidence in items (1), (2), and (3), properly admitted, and were the objections in (4) and (5) properly sustained? Discuss.

Call 1. Oliver's Testimony

Logical Relevance

To be admissible all evidence must be logically relevant, which means it has a tendency to make the existence of any fact of consequence more or less probable.

Dunn's statement that the truck ran the red light is relevant to prove that Kemper, the truck driver, was negligent. Therefore it is logically relevant.

Legal Relevance

Although logically relevant, evidence may be excluded if its probative value is substantially outweighed by the danger of unfair prejudice, confusion of the issues, misleading the jury; or on considerations of undue delay, waste of time, or cumulative evidence.

Dunn's statement, if admissible, would be highly probative of negligence, and therefore will not be excluded on grounds of legal relevance.

Hearsay

Hearsay is an out-of-court statement offered for the truth of the matter asserted. In general, hearsay is inadmissible.

Dunn's statement was made out of court, at the accident scene. It is being offered for its truth, namely that Kemper did in fact run the red light.

Hearsay Within Hearsay

Dunn's statement is hearsay within hearsay. Oliver is testifying as to what Wit told him Dunn said to Wit at the scene. For Dunn's statement to be admissible, there must be an exclusion, exemption, or exception for each level: (1) "Dunn told Wit" and (2) "Wit told Oliver."

Level 1: Dunn told Wit

Dying Declaration

A statement made under the belief of impending death is excepted from the hearsay rule when: (1) the statement is made while the declarant believed death was imminent; (2) concerning the cause or circumstances of impending death, (3) the testimony is offered in a prosecution for homicide or in a civil case, and (4) the witness is unavailable.

Dunn told Wit that "I'm not going to make it because the truck ran the red light," so the statement was made under the belief of impending death, and concerned the cause of death. In addition, this is a civil case. However, plaintiff has failed to provide any facts that Dunn is unavailable. Indeed, Dunn testifies in this case. Therefore, the exception will not work.

Excited Utterance

An excited utterance is a statement relating to a startling event or condition made while declarant was under the stress of excitement caused by the event or condition.

Dunn was seriously injured following an auto collision. The collision was the startling event that caused her stress. Her statement that the truck did it was related to the collision, and because Wit ran over to the scene from the curb, it can be assumed that Dunn was still under the stress of the collision.

Dunn's statement qualifies as an excited utterance and is an exception to hearsay.

Level 2: Wit told Oliver

Excited Utterance

Defined supra, it is unlikely that Wit was under the stress of the accident because he did not report to Oliver until ½ hour after the accident.

Present Sense Impression

This is a statement describing or explaining an event while perceiving or immediately thereafter. Again, Wit talked to Oliver ½ hour after the collision. This exception does not apply.

Business Record

This exception does not apply because Oliver's report is in anticipation of litigation and therefore not a reliable exception to the hearsay rule.

Conclusion: The evidence was not properly admitted because there is no valid exception to the hearsay rule for Wit's statement to Oliver.

Call 2. Trial Transcript of Sigel's Testimony

Logical Relevance

Defined supra, Sigel's warning to Kemper that the brakes were unsafe is relevant to show Kemper had notice and therefore was more likely to be negligent. The statement is logically relevant.

Authentication

The court reporter properly authenticated the trial transcript.

Hearsay

Defined supra, Sigel's statement was made in the separate case of People v. Dunn, and is therefore out of court. If it is being offered for its truth to show that on the morning of the incident Sigel warned Kemper that the brakes were defective, then the statement is hearsay and will generally not be admissible.

Hearsay Exception: Former Testimony

To qualify under this exception (1) the witness must be unavailable; (2) the party against whom testimony is being offered was a party or privy with a party; (3) same subject matter; (4) under oath; (5) opportunity to develop.

Although Sigel is unavailable because the process server could not locate him and he was under oath, the statement in the prior action was not against Kemper. Paul is now using the statement against Kemper. Because Kemper was not a party in the prior action this exception will not apply.

Hearsay Exception: Statement by Party's Agent

A statement (1) by a party's servant (2) concerning a matter within the scope of employment and (3) made during the existence of the relationship is exempted from the hearsay rule.

Sigel is an Empire mechanic. Empire is the party and Sigel is a servant of Empire. The matter concerned the brakes, which is certainly within the scope of a mechanic's duties. Finally, the statement was made while Sigel was on duty on the day of the collision. Therefore, the statement qualifies as an exemption to the hearsay rule and can be admitted for its truth.

Effect on the Listener

Even if the statement could not come in for its truth, it would be admissible to show that Kemper had notice. However, then Empire's attorney should have objected and asked for a limiting instruction to preserve their appeal rights.

Conclusion: The statement is admissible for its truth as a statement by party's agent and therefore was properly admitted.

Call 3. Dunn's Testimony

Logical Relevance

Dunn's statement tends to show that she was driving safely and did not contribute to the accident. It is also gives an inference that the accident was caused by Kemper's negligence. Therefore it is logically relevant.

Presentation

Dunn was competent to testify; she had personal knowledge.

Lay Opinion Testimony

Driving speed is considered to be within the experience of the lay witness and does not require expert testimony. It was therefore proper to admit lay testimony about the speed of the car.

Conclusion: Dunn's statement was properly admitted.

Call 4. Copy of Dunn's Conviction

Logical Relevance

The conviction is relevant to show Dunn was the one at fault, which would exonerate Empire.

Legal Relevance

Although prejudicial, it is highly probative of the fact that Dunn was at fault. It will not be excluded on grounds of legal relevance.

Character Evidence

Evidence of character is generally inadmissible to show that the defendant acted in conformity therewith.

Paul will argue that this evidence is being offered to show that Dunn has a character of recklessness, and should be excluded under the ban against character conformity evidence. However, the conviction does not relate to a past act, but pertains to the conduct at issue in Paul v. Empire.

Best Evidence Rule

Where the contents of a writing are at issue, the proponent must produce the original. Here the contents are at issue. However, an authenticated copy will be allowed as long as there are no objections or questions concerning its authenticity.

Hearsay

The copy is an out of court statement being offered for its truth. It is hearsay without an exception and therefore inadmissible.

Impeachment

Extrinsic evidence of conviction of crime is nonhearsay if offered for impeachment purposes.

Because the crime is a felony not involving dishonesty, the probative value of the evidence must not be substantially outweighed by the danger of unfair prejudice when a witness other than the accused is on the stand. As discussed, the statement is highly probative of the fact that Dunn was at fault and will not be excluded on grounds of prejudice.

Here, the conviction impeaches Dunn's implicit claim that she was driving safely. The conviction is admissible as proper impeachment.

Conclusion: Paul's objection was improperly sustained. The statement is admissible to impeach Dunn..

Call 5. Cross of Dunn

Objection: Leading Question

A leading question is one that suggests an answer. Leading questions are proper on cross so Empire's leading question is okay.

Objection: Policy Exclusion

Settlement offers are inadmissible to prove liability, but can be used to show bias. Here the question goes to bias and is proper for that purpose.

Objection: Compound Question

A compound question contains more than one question. Empire is asking 2 questions. It is objectionable.

Conclusion: The statement is objectionable because it is compound. Paul's objection was properly sustained.

FEBRUARY 1998 CALIFORNIA BAR EXAM -- QUESTION 3

1-HOUR ESSAY

Don is being prosecuted criminally for committing an armed assault against Victor. The evidentiary issues presented in his jury trial are based upon the following chronology of events:

1. June 5, 1985: Don was convicted of bribery and received a three-year sentence which he served in full without parole;

2. June 1, 1997: Victor was assaulted, allegedly by Don;

3. June 4, 1997: Victor identified Don from a lineup as the person who assaulted him (Victor);

4. June 6, 1997: Don was arrested and charged with the assault of Victor;

5. August 1, 1997: Don confessed privately to his long-time fiancée, Bernice, that he (Don) is the one who assaulted Victor;

6. August 15, 1997: Detective Phillips, who had been present at the June 4 lineup, testified at a preliminary hearing that Victor identified Don at the June 4 lineup, and Phillips was cross-examined by Don's attorney;

7. September 1, 1997: Don and Bernice were married;

8. September 15, 1997: Detective Phillips was shot and killed in a hunting accident;

9. October 1, 1997: Don, again privately, confessed to Bernice that he (Don) is the one who assaulted Victor;

10. November 1, 1997: Don and Bernice were divorced;

11. December 1, 1997: The case against Don comes to trial;

12. December 1, 1997: Victor testifies at trial, remembers making a lineup identification, but cannot make an in-court identification;

13. **December 3, 1997: The prosecution seeks to introduce a certified transcript of the preliminary hearing testimony of Detective Phillips;**

14. **December 4, 1997: The prosecution calls Bernice, seeking to have her testify to the August 1 and October 1 confessions of Don, and both Bernice and Don raise marital privilege objections;**

15. **December 8, 1997: The prosecution calls a witness, seeking testimony as to Victor's reputation for peacefulness in the community;** *Victim's peacefulness*

16. December 9, 1997: The prosecution rests; and

17. **December 10, 1997: Don testifies in his own defense, and on cross-examination the prosecution seeks to impeach Don with his 1985 bribery conviction.**

Assuming that all appropriate objections were made, should the court admit the evidence offered by the prosecution in numbers 13, 14, 15, and 17, as specified above? Discuss.

February 1998 California Bar – Question 3
Model Answer
Written by Dennis P. Saccuzzo

CALL 1 – Certified Transcript

For a document, such as a certified transcript, to be admissible it must be <u>logically relevant</u>, <u>authenticated</u>, comply with the <u>best evidence rule</u>, and <u>not</u> be <u>hearsay</u> or privileged.

Logical Relevance

To be admissible all evidence must be logically relevant, which means it has a tendency to make the existence of any fact of consequence more or less probably.

The transcript is relevant to prove that Victor, the victim, had identified Don at a June 4 line-up. It gives an inference that Don was in fact the assailant. Therefore, it is logically relevant.

Authenticated

A certified document is an official public record, and therefore self-authenticating under the Federal Rules of Evidence (FRE).

Best Evidence

Where the contents of a writing are at issue, it is necessary to use the original or show unavailability through no fault of the proponent.

Here, there are no facts to indicate that anything other than the original certified transcript is being used. A certified copy would also meet the rule as long as there are no challenges to its authenticity. The rule is satisfied.

Hearsay

Hearsay is an out of court statement offered to prove the truth of the matter stated. The certified transcript is actually double hearsay (hearsay within hearsay) because it contains Detective Phillips' testimony as to Victor's out of court statement and because the transcript itself reflects Phillips' out of court testimony. It is being offered for its truth, that is, to show that Victor did in fact identify Don at the June 4 line up.

Therefore the transcript is double hearsay, and unless an exception can be found for each level of hearsay, it will be inadmissible.

Since <u>Crawford</u>, in a criminal case testimonial hearsay is inadmissible unless the defendant had or gets the right to confrontation. Testimonial hearsay includes prior testimony from a preliminary hearing, prior trial, or grand jury proceeding, as well as statements elicited by police interrogation. Victor is a testifying witness and is available for confrontation. However, Phillips, who testified at a preliminary hearing (which is per se testimonial under <u>Crawford</u>), is dead and therefore unavailable. Unless D had the right to confront Phillips at the preliminary hearing and the stakes were the same, the testimony will be excluded as a violation of the 6th Amendment right to confrontation under the ruling in Crawford.

Phillips was in fact cross-examined at the preliminary hearing in the same case in which Don was the defendant. Because the charge was the same, the stakes were the same and Don had a full and fair opportunity to confront. Don's 6th Amendment rights have not been compromised, so Phillips' testimony could come in if there is a valid exception or exemption for both Phillips' statement and Victor's identification.

Phillips' out of court Statement: Former Testimony
    Former testimony is an exception to hearsay if
        (1) The witness is unavailable
        (2) The party against whom testimony is being offered was a party or privy in the previous action
        (3) Former action was of the same subject matter
        (4) Testimony was given under oath
        (5) The party against whom the evidence is being used had an opportunity to develop (cross-examine)

Here, Phillips is unavailable; he was shot and killed in a hunting accident.
Don was the party in the former and in the present action.
The subject matter is identical, namely Victor's prior identification.
Phillips "testified" at a preliminary hearing and therefore was under oath.
Finally, the stakes are the same in the preliminary and present actions and Phillips was cross-examined by Don's attorney.

Thus, the former testimony will be excepted from the hearsay rule.

Victor's out of court Identification: Prior Identification
    A prior identification of a person after perceiving the person is exempted from the general prohibition against hearsay if the declarant is available for cross-examination.

Victor is a testifying witness, available for cross-examination. Therefore Don's 6th Amendment rights are intact. Moreover, because Phillips is testifying as to Victor's prior identification of Don after perceiving him at a line up, the statement will be exempted as non-hearsay.

Privileged
    No facts indicate a privilege.

Conclusion: The transcript is admissible.

CALL 2 – Confessions

August 1 Confession
    The August 1 confession was made prior to marriage. Therefore, the testimonial (spousal) privilege applies. This privilege applies to all communications made before or during the marriage. It applies to all adverse testimony; the holder is the witness spouse; and it ends with the marriage.

Both Don and Bernice raised the marital privilege. However, only Bernice, as holder, has a right to assert it. Because Don and Bernice were divorced on Nov. 1, the privilege ended prior to Don's trial. Therefore, the August 1 confession is admissible because there is no privilege.

October 1 Confession

The marital privilege applies to communications between spouses while husband and wife; either spouse is the holder; it lasts forever, and must be confidential.

Don and Bernice were married on Sept. 1, 1997, so the Oct. 1 communication was made while they were husband and wife. Either has a right to assert the privilege and both have here. Because it lasts forever, the divorce is irrelevant. Don confessed privately, so the communication is confidential. Thus, the Oct. 1 confession is inadmissible because all elements of the marital privilege are met.

Conclusion: The Aug. 1 confession is admissible; the Oct. 1 confession is not.

CALL 3 – Victor's Reputation for Peacefulness

Logical Relevance

Defined supra, Victor's reputation for peacefulness would be relevant to negate a self-defense claim by Don. No facts indicate Don has made such a claim; therefore, this evidence is irrelevant.

Improper Character Evidence

Evidence of a person's character or disposition is generally inadmissible to show that he/she acted in conformity on a particular occasion.

The prosecution is trying to show that because Victor has a peaceful disposition, he acted as such on June 1, when he was assaulted. Absent an exception, this evidence would be inadmissible.

Victim's Exception

Except for rape, where a criminal defendant raises self-defense the prosecutor may rebut with evidence of a pertinent trait of the victim using reputation or opinion evidence.

There are no facts to show Don raised self-defense. If he did, the testimony would be admissible (and relevant).

Don did not raise self-defense, therefore the testimony is inadmissible character evidence as well as irrelevant.

CALL 4 – Impeachment of Don Based on Past Conviction

A witness may be impeached with evidence of a past conviction. Extrinsic evidence may be used. Admissibility is based on the type of crime.

For felonies not involving dishonesty, where the witness is the accused as here, the probative value of the evidence must outweigh the unfair prejudice.

However, for any crime involving dishonesty, the generally is no balancing and no discretion.

For remote crimes (more than 10 years old, since date of conviction or release, whichever is later), the probative value must substantially outweigh the prejudicial effect.

Here, Don was convicted in 1985, but not released until June 5, 1988. The relevant date is June 5, 1988. Don is being tried on Dec. 10, 1997. Therefore, the crime is less than 10 years old. Bribery is a crime of dishonesty. Thus, there will be no balancing.

Even if the crime was more than 10 years ago, bribery is highly probative, and therefore would probably come in.

The evidence is admissible.

CONSTITUTIONAL LAW

Pure Constitutional Law:

Crossover Questions:

Constitutional Law + Criminal Procedure

JULY 2004 CALIFORNIA BAR EXAM -- QUESTION 2

1-HOUR ESSAY

State X amended its anti-loitering statute by adding a new section 4, which reads as follows:

> A person is guilty of loitering when the person loiters, remains, or wanders about in a public place, or on that part of private property that is open to the public, for the purpose of begging. *Vague*

Alice, Bob, and Mac were separately convicted in a State X court of violating section 4. Alice was convicted of loitering for the purpose of begging on a sidewalk located outside the City's Public Center for the Performing Arts in violation of section 4. *Public Forum*

Bob was convicted of loitering for the purpose of begging on a waiting platform at a stop on City's subway system in violation of section 4.

Mac was convicted of loitering for the purpose of begging in the lobby of the privately owned Downtown Lawyers Building located in the business district of City in violation of section 4.

Alice, Bob, and Mac have each appealed their convictions, and their appeals have been consolidated in the State X appellate court. It has been stipulated that Alice, Bob, and Mac are indigent, that section 4 is not void for vagueness, and that the only issue on appeal concerns the validity of section 4 under the First Amendment to the United States Constitution.

How should the appellate court decide the three appeals, and why? Discuss.

Procedural Issues

To bring a first Amendment claim, the plaintiff must have standing and show state action. Given that all three cases have been consolidated in the State X appellate court and the only issue on appeal concerns the validity of section 4 under the first Amendment, it can be assumed that all three appellants, Alice, Bob, and Mack had standing. Moreover, they were prosecuted and convicted under a state statute, therefore there was state action.

First Amendment

The first Amendment, applicable to the states via the fourteenth Amendment, prohibits government from certain regulation of speech and other forms of expression.

Facts stipulate that the only issue concerns the validity of Section 4 under the first Amendment. The State X statute itself appears to limit begging, which is a form of expression, therefore the first Amendment is triggered.

Facial Attacks

Facts also stipulate that Section 4 is not void for vagueness. In addition, the statute cannot be attacked on its face as a prior restraint because there is no prohibition of expression or conduct prior to the prohibited act. This is a law that punishes conduct or speech after it has occurred, rather than a court order (injunction) that prohibits specific content under penalty of contempt. Arguably the statute is overbroad because it does not criminalize begging itself, but rather a host of poorly defined activities such as loitering, remaining, or wandering about for the "purpose" of begging. For example, someone may be loitering for the purpose of waiting for a friend and could be arrested based on this statute if the officer believed the loitering was for the purpose of begging.

Conduct Regulation

All three appellants may attack the state statute as an invalid conduct regulation. The general rule is that the government can regulate conduct that communicated if it has an important interest unrelated to the suppression of the message and if the impact on communication is no greater than necessary to achieve the government's purpose. If the government has the power to regulate the conduct in question (here, begging) the time, place and manner in which the government does so is irrelevant, so the specific fora would not be an issue.

Begging may be in the form of speech, or may be done exclusively in the form of conduct in gestures such as holding out a hand or putting out a container. The first issue then is whether State X can suppress that aspect of begging that involves only conduct.

Elements for Conduct Regulation:

Furthers an important or substantial government interest

Presumably the purpose of the State X statute is to preserve the health, safety and welfare of State X citizens by preventing begging. Theoretically, a beggar may pose a threat to a citizen by impeding the flow of foot or automobile traffic, or by threatened or implied coercion. Hence the government appears to be protecting an important or substantial interest.

Government interest unrelated to the suppression of speech

The statute does not merely prohibit loitering, remaining, or wandering. It prohibits such activities "for the purposes of begging." The government is therefore attempting to prohibit a specific message, begging. It does not prohibit other kinds of messages such as preaching or voicing political opinions. Therefore, the government interest is related to a particular form of expression and the government would fail under this particular element of the test for conduct regulation.

related to suppression of speech

Incidental restrictions no greater than necessary to further the government interest

As indicated, the statute not only prohibits begging, but also all of those activities that presumable lead to and are for the purpose of begging. Even though the statute, by stipulation, is not void for vagueness, the language of the statute is very likely to lead to numerous incidental restrictions unrelated to the government interest. Based on the language of the statute, a police officer might arrest an indigent, or even one appearing to be indigent, for a whole host of activities that have nothing to do with begging if the officer believed those activities were for the purpose of begging. For example, an indigent merely walking slowly in one of the prohibited places might be viewed as "loitering for the purpose of begging" and be arrested. Therefore, the incidental restrictions appear to be far greater than necessary and the government would fail on this element as well.

Conclusion: All 3 appellants would succeed in striking down any conviction based on the conduct aspect of their begging as unconstitutional conduct regulation by the state. The next issue is whether any or all of the 3 could have their convictions reversed based on the verbal aspect of their begging.

Time, Place and Manner (TPM) Restrictions

The government has a legitimate interest to regulate TPM of speech or expression as long as standards are specifically defined and unrelated to the content of expression. The government will argue that the statute is merely a TPM restriction. If so, the test used depends on the specific forum in which the restriction occurs, so each appellant's case must be analyzed separately.

Alice's Appeal – Public Forum

Public fora are government properties that the government is constitutionally required to make available for speech, such as parks and streets. Alice's conviction was for loitering for the purpose of begging on a sidewalk outside the City's Public Center for the Performing Arts. Public sidewalks such as the sidewalk outside a city-owned building are such traditionally public fora. Therefore, public forum doctrine will apply in Alice's case.

In a public forum, the government may restrict time, place and manner of speech only if the regulation is content neutral, narrowly tailored, serves an important government interest, and leaves open alternate means of expression. As discussed above, the State X statute regulates loitering only for the purpose of begging and not for the purpose of other forms of expression such as political viewpoints. It is regulation based on content. In addition, as discussed above, it is not narrowly tailored because its prohibition on all loitering for the purpose of begging could subject indigent people to prosecution for a host of actions that are unrelated to the government interest in keeping its citizens safe from foot traffic congestion and coercion. Finally, the statute is a total ban that leaves open no alternate means for its indigent citizens to beg for help without trespassing on private property.

Because the statute is a content-based regulation that is not narrowly tailored and does not leave open alternate channels for the same message, the statute is unconstitutional as applied to Alice's activities in a public forum. Alice's conviction will be overturned.

Bob's Appeal – Non-Public Forum

Non-public fora include public property with limited or controlled use, such as military bases, airport, areas outside jails, and ad space on buses. Bob was convicted of loitering for the purpose of begging on a waiting platform at a stop on City's subway system. A waiting platform is like an airport or the area outside a jail in that it is open for public use for a limited purpose with a need for security and controlled flow of traffic. Because a subway waiting platform is a non-public forum, the state will argue that Bob's conviction should be reviewed under a more deferential standard.

The government may restrict the time, place and manner of speech in a non-public forum as long as the restriction is viewpoint neutral and reasonably related to a legitimate government purpose. Although restricting loitering in a congested, limited area such as the waiting platform of a subway stop is reasonably related to the state's legitimate interest in public safety, the problem for State X is that their statute is, as discussed above, related to the content of the expression, namely begging. Because it is content-related, the court will not apply the more deferential standard. Instead, the court will apply a strict scrutiny analysis for content-related restrictions and Bob's conviction will be overturned, as analyzed below.

Mac's Appeal – Private Forum

In general, there is no constitutional right to access private property for speech purposes. Mac was convicted of loitering for the purpose of begging in the lobby of the privately owned Downtown Lawyer's Building located in the business district. Mac accessed private property for speech purposes but was not charged with trespass, so it can be assumed he was legally on the premises. Therefore, Mac will prevail unless the state can meet a strict scrutiny test for content-based regulation of speech.

Content Regulation

Because this statute is content-based, the forum is irrelevant. Content-based restrictions on speech must meet strict scrutiny, regardless of the forum being regulated. That means the regulation must be necessary to promote a compelling government interest. It must be narrowly tailored to achieve that interest. Even assuming the government interest in health and safety is compelling, the government means (that is, the law in question) is hardly necessary to promote this interest because there are numerous less restrictive alternatives the government can use to protect the public. For example, the State could allow begging in limited designated areas clear of traffic flow, provide greater police protection, or prohibit any direct solicitation while allowing passive means such as placing a container in a non-traffic area. The statute is unconstitutional. Alice, Bob and Mac will succeed in appealing their convictions.

FEB 2004 CALIFORNIA BAR EXAM -- QUESTION 5

1-HOUR ESSAY

The National Highway Transportation and Safety Administration (NHTSA), a federal agency, after appropriate hearings and investigation, made the following finding of fact: "The NHTSA finds that, while motor vehicle radar detectors have some beneficial purpose in keeping drivers alert to the speed of their vehicles, most are used to avoid highway speed-control traps and lawful apprehension by law enforcement officials for violations of speed-control laws." On the basis of this finding, the NHTSA promulgated regulations banning the use of radar detectors in trucks with a gross weight of five tons or more on all roads and highways within the United States.

State X subsequently enacted a statute prohibiting the use of radar detectors in any motor vehicle on any road or highway within State X. The State X Highway Department (Department) enforces the statute.

The American Car Association (ACA) is an association comprised of automobile motorists residing throughout the United States. One of ACA's purposes is to promote free and unimpeded automobile travel. ACA has received numerous complaints about the State X statute from its members who drive vehicles there.

In response to such complaints, ACA has filed suit against the Department in federal district court in State X, seeking a declaration that the State X statute is invalid under the Commerce Clause and the Supremacy Clause of the United States Constitution. The Department has moved to dismiss ACA's complaint on the ground that ACA lacks standing.

1. How should the court rule on the Department's motion to dismiss on the ground of ACA's lack of standing? Discuss.

2. On the assumption that ACA has standing, how should the court decide ACA's claim that the State X statute is invalid under the Commerce Clause and the Supremacy Clause of the United States Constitution? Discuss.

Commentary

The key to mastering the California Bar exam is studying the past essays and model answers. This is because the California Bar recurrently tests the same issues and issue clusters. The following fact pattern is a case in point. A similar hypothetical was tested in February 1991. One of the differences between Feb 1991 and Feb 2004 is that the issue of association standing was specifically called in Feb 2004, whereas in Feb 1991 call #2 asked if The National Association of Waste Truckers had standing, but did not specifically call association standing. The California Bar became more explicit in 2004 in insisting on a discussion of association standing by calling the question. Perhaps this is because in February 1991 and 2002, when the state was given the opportunity to write about association standing, very few did. Nevertheless, anyone familiar with model answers to Feb 1991 and Feb 2002 would have had a marked advantage in responding to this Feb 2004 call on association standing.

The Feb 2004 fact pattern was also much more specific and insular than the Feb 1991 fact pattern. In 1991 there was a general call, "What challenges, if any, under the Constitution, may be brought . . .." Students had to figure out for themselves that the Supremacy Clause, Dormant Commerce Clause, and Privileges and Immunities Clause were at issue. In Feb 2004, the Bar examiners specifically called the Supremacy Clause and the Commerce Clause.

The problem in responding to the Commerce Clause call was that the issue concerned a state law statute. Usually when the Commerce Clause is called, the issue is whether Congress had the authority to pass the law at issue. Here the issue was whether State X has the authority to pass a law that regulated in the area of interstate commerce.

The Commerce Clause grants legislative powers only to Congress. However, as indicated in the following model, neither the Commerce Clause nor anything else in the Constitution prohibits the states from legislating in the area of interstate commerce. The relevant law and the various tests that should have been used are illustrated in the model, which follows.

Model Answer

Call 1. ACA's Standing

The American Car Association (ACA), an association of automobile motorists, has brought suit in Federal District Court under the Commerce and Supremacy clauses of the U.S. Constitution. The issue is whether ACA lacks standing to bring the claim.

Association Standing

To have standing, a plaintiff must have a personal stake in the outcome under the Constitution. To qualify for association standing, (1) the members must have standing, (2) the interest asserted must be germane to the association's purpose, and (3) individual membership in the lawsuit must not be required.

Members have standing. For individual members of ACA to have standing, they must show injury in fact, causation, and redressibility.

Injury in Fact: As a result of the State X statute, motorists who drive their vehicles in State X are prohibited from using radar detectors on any road or highway within State X. Findings from NHTSA have indicated that radar detectors have some beneficial effects, including in keeping drivers alert to the speed of their vehicles. Because of the State X law, ACA members are now deprived of the benefit of radar detectors and therefore have suffered injury in fact.

Causation: To find causation, the injury must be traceable to the defendant. State X, the defendant, passed the law that bars drivers from using radar detectors. But for the law, the members would not be deprived of the benefit of radar detectors. The injury is traceable to State X.

Redressibility: ACA has requested that the statute be declared invalid. If they are successful, members will not be barred from the use and benefits of radar detectors. Therefore, the injury is redressable by the requested relief because if the statute is invalidated, members will have the benefit of the detectors.

Conclusion: The individual members have standing.

Interest asserted is germane to association's purpose. The interest asserted is the members' right to use radar detectors. Assembly's purpose is to promote free and unimpeded automobile travel. Radar detectors facilitate unimpeded automobile travel by keeping drivers alert to the speed of their vehicles. Moreover, fewer drivers may go through State X because of the law, which would conflict with ACA's purpose to promote free and unimpeded travel. Because State's attempt to prohibit the use of detectors is an impediment, the right to use detectors is germane to ACA's purpose.

Individual membership not required. Individual membership would be required if any of ACA's members were uniquely damaged and were requesting specific relief. Their presence would then be needed to determine whether and how each was uniquely damaged. In this case, ACA is merely attempting to invalidate State X's statute, and no facts indicate that any single member has been uniquely damaged or is making a claim. Therefore, individual membership is not required.

Conclusion. ACA has association standing. The court should deny Department's motion to dismiss on the grounds that ACA lacks standing.

Call 2. ACA's Claims under Commerce Clause and Supremacy Clause

State Action

establish state action

The Constitution applies only to government action. Private conduct need not comply with the Constitution. To invalidate the statute under either theory, ACA will have to show state action. The State X highway Department enforces the statute, therefore there is state action.

A. Commerce Clause

All legislative powers are vested in Congress by Article I Section 1. Article I Section 8 gives Congress broad powers to regulate commerce among the several states. There is no express grant of power in the Constitution giving the states similar power over ISC; neither does the Constitution expressly prohibit the states from passing laws that affect ISC.

State X has enacted a statute prohibiting the use of radar detectors in any motor vehicle on any road or highway within its state. Because radar detectors are legally manufactured and sold outside of State X pursuant to federal law (which prohibits their use only on trucks of 5 tons or more), they are articles of interstate commerce. Moreover, the law affects all vehicles entering or leaving the state. Therefore, the state law affects ISC.

Dormant Commerce Clause

Under the 10th amendment, powers not granted to the United States by the Constitution or prohibited by it are reserved to the states. It is through the 10th Amendment that the states have police power to protect the health, safety and welfare of their citizens. Under this 10th Amendment power, states may pass laws even if they affect interstate commerce, subject to certain limitations. This is known as the Dormant Commerce Clause or negative Commerce Clause.

In general, state and local laws that affect interstate commerce are unconstitutional if they (1) discriminate against or (2) unduly burden interstate commerce. The test used to determine the constitutionality of such laws depends on whether the state law discriminates against out-of-state businesses or is facially neutral and regulates evenhandedly.

(1) Discriminates

The State X statute prohibits the use of detectors in any motor vehicle. It does not, on its face, discriminate against out-of-state businesses or individuals. Therefore it is facially neutral, and the regulation is evenhanded because it does not advantage in-state businesses.

Where the law is facially neutral and regulates evenhandedly, it must be rationally related to a legitimate state interest and must not unduly burden interstate commerce. A legitimate interest would be one related to the health, safety or welfare of its citizens. The State X law arguably was enacted to prevent drivers from using detectors to speed indiscriminately and without detection. As such, the law is legitimately related to the state interest in protecting the safety of its citizens from speeding vehicles. Therefore it meets the rational basis requirement because the law serves a legitimate local purpose.

(2) Undue Burden

Where a state or local law is facially neutral and rationally related to a legitimate state interest, as here, the court will use the undue burden test (a balancing test) to determine if the state or local law is constitutional. Under this test, a facially neutral state law with a legitimate local interest will be held unconstitutional where the burden on ISC is excessive in relation to the nature of the local interest involved.

The state has a strong interest in maintaining the safety of its citizens. It is widely known that speeding is a major factor in traffic fatalities and injuries. By preventing motorists from evading state speed laws, the State X statute protects the safety of its citizens.

Although, as indicated, the statute affects ISC, the burden might best be described as an inconvenience at most. Out-of-state motorists might have to disable their detectors when traveling through X. The argument that the detectors will make drivers more alert to the speed rings hollow, given the findings of fact by the federal agency (NHTSA) that most detectors are really used to avoid compliance with speed laws.

The court should rule that the State X statute does not violate the Commerce Clause because it promotes the legitimate local purpose of protecting the safety of its citizens and its burden on ISC is not excessive relative to the local purpose.

B. Supremacy Clause

In general, federal law preempts conflicting state law when federal and state laws are mutually exclusive, state law impedes a federal objective, or Congress has a clear intent to occupy the field.

1. Mutually Exclusive

Federal law bans the use of detectors in trucks with a gross weight of 5 tons or more. State X law bans detectors on all vehicles. The laws are not mutually exclusive because anyone in compliance with State X law would also be in compliance with federal law.

2. State Law Impedes a Federal Objective

The objective of the federal law is to control highway speed by banning radar detectors in trucks with a gross weight of 5 tons or more so that truck drivers cannot avoid law enforcement. The State X ban includes such trucks and thus does not impede the federal objective.

3. Congressional Intent to Occupy the Field

To determine whether the intent of the federal law is to occupy the field, the court will balance the federal interest versus that of the state. In addition, the court will require the federal law to demonstrate a "clear and manifest purpose" to occupy the field or require actual conflict.

As indicated, there is no actual conflict because the federal and state laws are not mutually exclusive. Moreover, as shown above under the Commerce Clause, the balancing of interests favors State X.

No facts indicate a clear and manifest intent by NHTSA to preempt state law. The federal law regulation merely bans the use of detectors in trucks weighing 5 tons or more on all roads and highways within the United States. Even if the phrase "all roads and highways within the United States" did reflect an attempt to occupy the field, State X may still prevail under a general exception to preemption.

General Exception to Preemption

States may prevail in spite of the Supremacy Clause where (1) the field is traditionally left to the states, such as for issues relating to schools, health, safety and welfare; (2) where the state law focuses on a different aspect (*e.g.*, the federal purpose is economic, but the state focuses on health and safety); or (3) the state law sets a higher standard.

Here, the issue relates to safety, which is traditionally left to the states; State X law is for the purpose of preventing speeding. In addition, State X bans detectors in all vehicles whereas the federal law bans only certain vehicles (trucks weighing 5 tons or more). Therefore, the state law would not be unconstitutional under the Supremacy Clause not only because it regulates in an area traditionally left to the states, but also because it sets a higher standard.

The court should rule that the State X law does not violate the Supremacy Clause. There is no clear and manifest purpose to preempt state law, no actual conflict, and the state law sets a higher standard.

The court should decide in favor of State X; ACA's claims under both the Commerce Clause and the Supremacy Clause are invalid and do not provide grounds for invalidating the State X statute.

1-HOUR EXAM

Paul, a student at Rural State University ("Rural"), wishes to sue Rural, a public school, for violation of his rights under the U.S. Constitution because Rural refused to select him for its cheerleading squad solely on the basis that he is a male. Paul is indigent, however, and cannot afford to pay the costs of suit, including filing and service of process fees.

Gender

State law permits court commissioners to grant a prospective state court litigant permission to proceed *in forma pauperis*, which exempts the litigant from any requirement to pay filing and service of process fees. Paul applied for permission to proceed *in forma pauperis*. At a hearing, the state court commissioner conceded that Rural's refusal to select Paul was constitutionally discriminatory, but nevertheless denied Paul's application on the ground that Paul's prospective lawsuit "involves merely cheerleading."

What arguments could Paul reasonably make that the denial of his *in forma pauperis* application violated his rights under the U.S. Constitution, and what is the likely outcome? Discuss.

-- Written by Dennis P. Saccuzzo & Nancy E. Johnson

Commentary:

Bar candidates found the following fact pattern puzzling, and many went astray. The question involves a case within a case. (Finding a "case-within-a-case" is not uncommon on Bar exams. One simple example is a malpractice lawsuit against an attorney, in which one must show that the client had a valid claim for damages that was lost because of attorney negligence.) Plaintiff Paul was discriminated against by Rural University. His application to proceed in forma pauperis against Rural was denied by a state commissioner. The call of the questions was what arguments could Paul reasonably make that the denial of his application by the commissioner violated his rights under the U.S. Constitution.

One of the most fundamental principles of responding to essay exams is to be responsive to the call of the question. The call of the question went to Paul's case against the commissioner, not Rural. A surprising number of Bar candidates found that Paul had standing because he was injured by Rural, and proceeded to discuss the discrimination claim. This fact pattern is difficult because it is very easy to lose track of which claim you're discussing – the one against the commissioner or the underlying discrimination claim. True, it was necessary to discuss the underlying discrimination claim, but one had to find a way to do that while being responsive to the question and not shifting in midstream from the case against the commissioner to the case against Rural. It is necessary to remain aware of the call of the question throughout your answer.

It took some creativity to realize that Paul had a first amendment claim. Included in the first amendment is the fundamental right to petition the government for redress of grievances, and this right is separate from the right to freedom of expression. Right to petition for redress includes the right to access the courts to pursue a lawsuit, as long as the claim pursued is colorable and not baseless. Most Bar review programs do not cover this right, which perhaps explains why neither of the Bar's selected answers covered it. By contrast, conduct regulation is covered extensively and appeared in the Bar's selected answers

Another important point about the call is that it asks about reasonable arguments Paul can make. This was the Bar's way of asking candidates to think of colorable claims, rather than just slam-dunk claims in which all the elements can be met. Indeed, on the California Bar exam with its hour-long essays, it is important to raise as many colorable claims as possible. A common mistake is to think of an issue but then reject it because one or more element cannot be met. A good rule of thumb is that if an issue crosses your mind because facts raise it and go to at least element, it probably should be discussed.

Model Answer

The issue is what arguments can Paul reasonably make that the State Commissioner's denial of his application denied his rights under the U.S. Constitution. To exercise his rights under the Constitution, Paul must first have standing and demonstrate state action.

Standing to sue the State Commissioner

To have standing, Paul must have a personal stake in the outcome. He must show injury in fact, causation, and redressibility.

Injury in Fact: Paul applied for permission to proceed *in forma pauperis*, because he is indigent and cannot afford to pay the costs to file a suit against Rural for denying him his rights under the U.S. Constitution. The State Commissioner denied Paul's application, even though the Commissioner acknowledged that Rural's refusal to select him was constitutionally discriminatory. Because his application was denied, Paul will not be able to pursue his constitutionally valid claim. Therefore he has suffered injury in fact.

Causation: To show causation, Paul must demonstrate that his injury is traceable to the defendant. Paul's application was inappropriately denied by the State Commissioner. But for this denial, Paul would have been able to proceed *in forma pauperis*. Therefore his injury is traceable to the State Commissioner.

Redressibility: Paul must show that his injury would be redressed by his requested relief. Here, Paul would request an injunction declaring his application was unconstitutionally denied. If this is granted, Paul would be able to proceed and defend his constitutional rights against Rural.

Conclusion: Paul has standing to pursue a constitutional claim against State Commissioner.

State Action

Paul will be pursuing claims that his due process rights as well as his rights under the First and Fourteenth Amendments have been violated. To pursue these rights, he must show state action. The Constitution applies only to government action. Here, the state court Commissioner is an agent of the state acting pursuant to state law that permits the Commissioner to grant prospective state court litigants permission to proceed *in forma pauperis*. Thus, there is state action.

Eleventh Amendment

The Eleventh Amendment bars citizens from suing a state in federal court without the state's consent. It is unclear whether Paul will pursue his claim against State Commissioner in state or federal court. However, an exception to the Eleventh Amendment bar is an action in federal court to enjoin a state officer from unconstitutional conduct. Because Paul will request such an injunction, the Eleventh Amendment will not be a bar to his claim against Commissioner.

Validity of Underlying Claim

Due to the public policies pertaining to judicial economy, to apply for *in forma pauperis* status, one needs a valid underlying claim. As a threshold to pursuing his claim against Commissioner, Paul must show that his claim against Rural is not frivolous. Paul will have to show standing and state action in relation to Rural as well as that his discrimination claim is valid.

Standing Against Rural. Paul was injured by Rural because Rural refused to select him for its cheerleading squad solely on the basis that he is male. But for this refusal, Paul could have been eligible to be a cheerleader. A court order (injunction) to allow him an equal opportunity to be eligible would redress his problem. Therefore Paul has standing against Rural.

State Action. Rural is a public school and as such is an agent of the city government. Thus there is state action.

Eleventh Amendment: As with his action against Commissioner, Paul's action to enjoin Rural for its unconstitutional conduct will not be barred by the Eleventh Amendment.

Paul's Underlying Claims Against Rural:

Gender Discrimination

Where government actions discriminate on the basis of gender, the courts will apply an intermediate scrutiny test, which means the government must show that the action in substantially related to an important government interest. Based on the facts, Rural does not have a leg to stand on. They assert no interest; Paul was denied solely on the basis that he was male. Moreover, the State Commissioner conceded that Rural's refusal to select Paul was constitutionally discriminatory. Therefore, Paul's underlying claim is valid and he can proceed against State Commissioner.

First Amendment Rights

Paul also has a number of first amendment claims based on his right of association and, as will be discussed, his right to express himself through conduct.

Denial of *In Forma Pauperis* Status: First Amendment Right – Freedom of Speech

Conduct Regulation

Paul can reasonably argue that his desire to be heard in court is to express his views that men can appropriately serve as cheerleaders at state universities. As such, he can bring an argument that his First Amendment right to freedom of speech has been violated.

The First Amendment, applicable to the state via the 14th Amendment, prohibits government from certain regulation of speech and other forms of expression. The relevant Supreme Court rule is that government can regulate conduct that communicates only if it has an important interest unrelated to the suppression of the message and the impact on communication is no greater than necessary to achieve the government purpose.

State Commissioner asserts no government interest for denying Paul's application other than that the prospective lawsuit "involves mere cheerleading." While the state may have an interest in saving money and denying frivolous lawsuits, as already discussed, Paul has a valid claim that Rural has violated his 14th Amendment equal protection rights. Even Commissioner has acknowledged that Rural's conduct was discriminatory. Therefore, if the court believes that Paul's intent was to express his views through conduct, he would succeed in his action against Commissioner because Paul's First Amendment rights were denied for no valid reason; in fact, the denial was arbitrary and capricious. (*Note that Paul can make a similar claim against Rural on the basis of Rural's refusal to select him solely because of his gender.*)

Unfettered Discretion

Although the state may regulate the time, place, and manner of expression where it has a legitimate interest and specifically defined standards unrelated to the content of expression, it is unconstitutional for state officials to have unfettered discretion in such regulations.

It is unclear whether State Commissioner was guided or constrained by any standards. Even if Commissioner was so guided, the denial of Paul's application was on the grounds that Paul's suit merely involved cheerleading. As such, the denial appears arbitrary and capricious and Paul has a reasonable argument that the denial was unconstitutional because Commissioner had unfettered discretion.

Prior Restraint on Speech

The courts are particularly suspicious of prior restraints on speech, and Paul has a reasonable argument that Commissioner's denial was a prior restraint on Paul's freedom to express his views through conduct.

Prior restraints are judged by a strict scrutiny test, which means the government conduct must be necessary to a compelling interest and there are no less burdensome alternatives. Commissioner's action won't even come close to meeting a strict scrutiny test. As indicated, no government interest was asserted, let alone a compelling interest. Paul will succeed in his claim against Commissioner if a strict scrutiny test is applied.

Denial of a Fundamental Right based on Speech

First Amendment rights are protected as fundamental rights. If Paul asserts that his right to freedom of expression has been violated, he can reasonably assert that he has been denied a fundamental right. Where a government action infringes on a fundamental right, it will be subjected to a strict scrutiny test. As discussed above, Paul will succeed on a strict scrutiny test because Commissioner has stated no compelling interest. Moreover, denial of Paul's application would not be necessary in any case, as government already has a less burdensome alternative, namely, the requirement that the claim not be frivolous.

Denial of a Fundamental Right based on Right to Petition Government

The right to petition the government for redress of grievances is also a first amendment right, and states may make no laws which abridge that right. Paul's lawsuit against Rural is his petition for redress of his grievance and is therefore constitutionally protected. *In forma pauperis* status is the mechanism by which indigent individuals such as Paul are able to petition. In being denied this status by the commissioner, Paul is being denied his fundamental right to petition the government for redress. Because a fundamental right is implicated the commissioner's decision would be subject to a strict scrutiny test and the analysis would be similar to that above, in that the state will be unable to meet its burden of showing compelling interest and no less burdensome alternative.

Procedural Due Process

The Fifth and Fourteenth Amendments protect against deprivation of life, liberty, or property interests without due process (notice and opportunity to be heard). To argue that his due process rights have been violated, Paul would have to argue that his application to proceed *in forma pauperis* was a property or liberty interest. If he could show this, the issue would be what procedures would be required. The courts analyze this issue in a three-part test that looks at (1) the importance of the interest to the individual; (2) the government interest, and (3) the ability of additional procedures to increase the accuracy of fact-finding.

A property right occurs if there is an entitlement and that entitlement is not fulfilled. State law did not appear to create an entitlement. It merely permits the Commissioner to grant applications such as Paul's.

A deprivation of a liberty interest occurs if there is loss of a significant freedom provided by the Constitution or a statute. Paul has a much better, and far more reasonable, argument that Commissioner's denial deprives him of a liberty interest because it prevents him from pursuing his Fourteenth Amendment equal protection rights (and possibly free speech and fundamental rights) against Rural.

Assuming Paul was deprived of a liberty interest, it must be acknowledged that he was afforded the opportunity to be heard by Commissioner pursuant to state law. The issue is whether the hearing was sufficient to protect Paul's due process rights under the 3-part test defined above.

Importance of the Interest to the Individual. As indicated, Paul's interests may include several constitutionally guaranteed rights, including substantive due process, First Amendment, and 14th Amendment rights. Therefore, the interests at stake are very important.

Government Interest: The government interest is in fiscal and administrative efficiency. However, as indicated, Paul was denied because his application involved "merely cheerleading." His underlying claim was valid; his claim was not frivolous. The government's argument that the denial was in the service of efficiency is weak.

Ability of Additional Procedures. Additional procedures, such as an appeal or an administrative panel that would oversee biased, discriminatory, or arbitrary state actors like Commissioner would have been very helpful in allowing Paul to demonstrate the validity of his claim and that more than cheerleading was at stake.

On the balance, Paul's procedural due process rights were also violated.

In sum, Paul has a number of good arguments against Commissioner's denial and, ultimately, against Rural.

FEBRUARY 2002 CALIFORNIA BAR EXAM -- QUESTION 5

1-HOUR ESSAY

The growth of City has recently accelerated, putting stress on municipal infrastructure. City's water supply, roads, sewers, and schools are all operating in excess of designed capacity.

The Assembly of Future Life was organized in City not long ago. Its members adhere to certain unpopular religious beliefs. City gave the Assembly preliminary zoning approval for plans to build a worship center on a one-acre parcel of real property the Assembly owned within City's borders. The Assembly's plans incorporated a dwelling for its minister. Soon after the preliminary zoning approval, newspapers in City featured articles about the Assembly and its members' beliefs.

After these newspaper articles appeared, City adopted a "slow growth" ordinance providing for an annual lottery to allocate up to 50 building permits, with applicants for certain "priority status" dwellings entitled to participate first. Priority status dwellings were defined as: (1) affordable housing; (2) housing on five-acre lots with available sewer and water connections; or (3) housing with final zoning approval as of the date the ordinance was adopted. Only after all applicants for priority status dwellings had received permits in the lottery could other applicants participate.

Over 500 applicants for priority status dwellings participated in the first annual lottery. Realizing that its opportunity to participate in a lottery could be years away, the Assembly submitted an application for retroactive final zoning approval and a building permit. City denied the application. *Association Standing*

The Assembly brought suit in federal district court against City, alleging that: (1) City's ordinance was invalid under the due process, equal protection, and takings clauses of the U.S. Constitution; and (2) City's denial of the Assembly's application was invalid under the due process clause of the U.S. Constitution.

What arguments can the Assembly reasonably make in support of its allegations and is each argument likely to succeed? Discuss.

FEBRUARY 2002, QUESTION 5
CONSTITUTIONAL LAW

-- Written by Dennis P. Saccuzzo & Nancy E. Johnson

Commentary:

This Con. Law fact pattern has two calls and in both the candidate is asked to invalidate an ordinance under the due process clause of the U.S. Constitution. When the Bar asks you to invalidate under the due process clause, they are referring to substantive due process unless otherwise indicated. When the due process clause is brought up a second time, it then refers to procedural due process. A call concerning the due process clause could consider both substantive and procedural due process. Then, in considering procedural due process one must first determine whether there is a property or liberty interest before moving on to the 3-part test, as explicated in the Bar Secrets: The Multistate Subjects book.

An important feature of the present fact pattern was determining whether first amendment religious freedoms were implicated at all. Even though a religious organization was the central character, what was really at stake was a zoning permit. Call #1 expressly asked candidates to discuss due process, equal protection and takings, but a lot of Bar candidates immediately went to the free exercise and establishment clauses of the first amendment. They were not only non-responsive, but missed the point of the question. Another common error was to immediately go into a strict scrutiny analysis based on a fundamental right (freedom of religion) without even considering the counter-argument that this was a mere economic regulation.

In dealing with a substantive due process question, it is important to realize that there are always two sides. The government is always going to argue it is a mere economic or social regulation and apply a rational basis test. The plaintiff, by contrast, will argue fundamental right and apply a strict scrutiny test. It is important to do both tests. Further, one must make a clear argument that a fundamental right is involved and expressly articulate the right that is implicated, as illustrated in the following model.

This was one of the few times the Bar gave candidates an opportunity to discuss association standing. Both association standing and third party standing require one to establish individual standing and then have additional elements to prove. By addressing these additional elements, Bar candidates are able to demonstrate their knowledge and understanding of the law.

In conducting the equal protection analysis, again notice that it is necessary to discuss both rational basis and strict scrutiny. Further, the strict scrutiny analysis under equal protection requires the two additional elements of discriminatory impact and discriminatory intent. Finally, the model that follows demonstrates a complete procedural due process analysis.

- 232 -

Model Answer

Call 1: Assembly's Arguments

Assembly has brought suit in Federal District Court under the due process, equal protection, and takings clauses of the U.S. Constitution. To bring these claims, Assembly must have standing and the case must otherwise be justiciable.

Association Standing

To have standing, a plaintiff must have a personal stake in the outcome under the Constitution. Assembly, rather than any of its individual members, appears to be the plaintiff. Therefore, they must meet the elements of association standing.

To qualify for association standing, (1) the members must have standing, (2) the interest asserted must be germane to the association's purpose, and (3) individual membership in the lawsuit must not be required.

Members have standing. For individual members of the association to have standing, they must show injury in fact, causation, and redressibility. The members can show injury in fact because City's "slow growth" ordinance will prevent them from proceeding with their plan to build both a place of worship and a dwelling for their minister. Their application for retroactive final zoning approval and a building permit was denied. They can argue economic loss in that they can no longer use their land as originally planned. They can also argue loss of first amendment rights because their ability to assemble and practice their religion will be impaired. Causation will be found because but for the slow growth ordinance, the members could have built their place of worship, given that City had already granted preliminary approval. The requested relief is to invalidate the ordinance, which would remove the blocks to Assembly's plans. The injury therefore is redressable by the requested relief.

Conclusion: The individual members have standing.

Interest asserted is germane to association's purpose. The interest asserted is Assembly's desire for zoning approval to allow them to build a place of worship and a dwelling for their minister. Having a place of worship and housing for a minister is germane to Assembly because it is a religious organization.

Individual membership not required. Individual membership would be required if any of Assembly's members were uniquely damaged and were requesting specific relief. Their presence would then be needed to determine whether and how each was uniquely damaged. In this case, Assembly is merely attempting to invalidate City's slow growth ordinance, and no single member has been uniquely damaged or is making a claim. Therefore, individual membership is not required.

Conclusion: Assembly has association standing

Ripeness

A genuine and immediate threat of harm must exist. The court will consider the hardship to the plaintiff if the decision is withheld.

City's attorney will argue that the case is not ripe because Assembly can still participate in the lottery. This argument will fail because City's slow growth lottery allows only 50 permits annually, with stringent requirements for participation that Assembly does not meet. Already, 5000 applicants have qualified and participated. In effect, under the ordinance Assembly will likely never get its permit. The hardship to Assembly is great because of the possibility it may be effectively prevented from practicing its unpopular religious beliefs in City. Therefore, the case will not be denied for lack of ripeness.

State Action

State action is required for due process claims (substantive and procedural), equal protection, takings, and first Amendment protections. The Constitution applies only to government action; private conduct generally need not comply with the Constitution. City is a subdivision of the government and has passed an ordinance that affects Assembly. Therefore there is state action.

Assembly's Due Process Claim

The issue is whether A's due process claim involves an economic/social regulation or a fundamental right.

Economic & Social Regulation

City will argue that the slow growth ordinance limits growth and that it is a mere economic and social regulation needed because of the stress on municipal infrastructure. Economic and social regulations are subject to a rational basis test, which means that to prevail City must show that the ordinance is rationally related to a legitimate government purpose.

City will allege that its purpose is to slow the recently accelerated growth that has City's water supplies, roads, sewers and schools all operating at excess of designated capacity. The lottery system is rationally related to City's plan to slow growth because it limits construction of new dwellings.

Assembly will argue that City's categorization of priority status is arbitrary and capricious. However, this argument likely will fail because at a minimum priority statuses 2 and 3 (for 5-acre lots with sewer and water hook-ups and housing with final zoning approval) appear rational.

Conclusion: If the ordinance is interpreted as an economic/social regulation, it will be upheld under a rational basis review and Assembly will fail in this claim.

Fundamental Right

When a governmental regulation infringes on a fundamental right, it is subjected to a strict scrutiny review, which means it will be found invalid unless necessary to promote a compelling state interest where there is no less burdensome means to accomplish the state's interest. All 1st Amendment rights (association, speech, and religion) are fundamental rights.

Assembly will argue that the ordinance infringes on their 1st Amendment rights (association and religion) on the grounds that the ordinance hinders their ability to lawfully meet and worship according to their beliefs. If a strict scrutiny test is used, City's effort to slow growth may be considered a compelling interest to protect City's infrastructure for the health, safety, and welfare of its citizens. That City's means of protecting this interest through a lottery is necessary, however, is far less compelling. City can use less burdensome means, such as increasing taxes or floating bonds to pay for expanded infrastructure or perhaps purchasing surrounding land.

Assembly's argument is unlikely to succeed, because its members are still free to associate and to worship as they always have. They are simply prevented from building as they had planned, with a dwelling for their minister. It is unclear whether the ordinance prevents final approval for a worship center alone, or simply restricts the building of new dwellings. If the former, Assembly would still have the option of worshipping where they do now. If the latter, Assembly may get approval for modified plans, without the dwelling, and assemble and worship in their new worship center.

Conclusion: Assembly would prevail under the due process clause if the court agrees Ordinance infringes on its 1st Amendment rights, but the court is unlikely to do so.

Equal Protection
The 14th Amendment prohibits states from depriving anyone of equal protection under the law. Government regulations cannot discriminate. Discrimination based on race, national origin, or a fundamental right are reviewed under a strict scrutiny test. Discrimination based on economic matters, such as the approval of zoning permits and priority status, are reviewed under a rational basis test.

Rational Basis Review.
If the discrimination is based on "priority status" versus "nonpriority status." Or upon "preliminarily approved permits" versus housing with final approval, it will be subject to a rational basis test. The analysis would be similar to that for an economic regulation as discussed above, and City will prevail because the distinctions between priority/nonpriority and approved/non-approved are rationally related to the legitimate goal of slowing growth.

Strict Scrutiny Analysis under Equal Protection
If the discrimination is based on those with popular religious beliefs versus those with unpopular beliefs, it implicates Assembly's fundamental religious rights and will be subject to a strict scrutiny test under equal protection.

The analysis would be similar to that discussed above for a fundamental right except that under an equal protection analysis, where a statute or ordinance is facially neutral there must be both discriminatory impact and discriminatory intent in order for plaintiff to prevail.

City's ordinance provides for an annual lottery. It does not apply specifically to any particular religious group and is facially neutral as to the 1st Amendment.

Therefore, to succeed on its equal protection claim, Assembly will have to show discriminatory impact and intent.

Discriminatory Impact. City will argue that there is no discriminatory impact because the ordinance affects any religious group that wants to build a residence of any kind within city limits, as well as any secular group or individual. Assembly's argument is that in being new and having unpopular religious beliefs, they are uniquely affected. Both arguments have validity.

Discriminatory Intent. This will be more problematic. City will argue that its intent is not discriminatory at all, and that its goal is simply to save City's infrastructure. Assembly will point to the fact that its religious beliefs are unpopular and to a rather suspicious (circumstantial) connection between disparaging articles in City's newspapers and the passage of the slow growth ordinance. Given the importance of freedom of religion and the apparent resentment in City against Assembly and its members' beliefs, it is more likely than not that the court will find discriminatory intent.

Conclusion: Assembly will fail in its equal protection claim, either as an economic/social regulation or if the discrimination is held to be based on popular versus unpopular religious beliefs and no discriminatory impact is found.

Takings Clause

The 5th Amendment provides that private property may not be taken for public use without just compensation.

To qualify as a taking, there must be government confiscation or physical occupation. Where a land use regulation is involved, as in Assembly's case, there must be either denial of all economic value or decreased economic value based on a balancing test. In the case of land use regulation, the burden on the plaintiff is high.

Assembly's land was not confiscated or physically occupied. At issue is a land use regulation. The regulation did not deprive Assembly of all economic value. For example, they still own the land, can meet there as a group, and perhaps build a worship center but not a dwelling on it. Therefore, it will be necessary to conduct a balancing test.

Where there is decreased economic value, the court will consider social goals, diminution in value, and the owner's expectation. Here, City's zoning goals are to protect its infrastructure; Assembly's to worship according to their own religious beliefs. The diminution in value is great, unless Assembly is allowed to build a worship center, but not the dwelling prohibited by the slow-growth ordinance. Assembly's expectation, based preliminary zoning approval, was to build a place of worship and a home for its minister.

On balance, City has the better argument, and the ordinance does not qualify as a taking.

Call 2: Denial of Due Process

The 5th and 14th Amendments protect against deprivation of life, liberty, or property interests without due process (notice and opportunity to be heard).

Property Interest

The first step in the analysis is to determine whether there has been deprivation of a protected interest.

Assembly had preliminary approval to build a worship center on a one-acre parcel of real property within City's borders. Assembly will argue that this created an expectation because they had already had plans to build to which City had preliminarily approved. Usually, once such approval is given, final approval is a formality. Therefore, Assembly has a good argument.

City will counter that preliminary approval does not confer the right to build and is not a property right. Although City probably has the better argument, it is a close question.

What procedures are required?

Assuming Assembly had a protected interest, the next step in the analysis is a three-part test to determine what type of notice and opportunity to be heard Assembly is entitled to, as follows:

First, the court will examine the importance of the interest to Assembly. Here, having a place of worship, especially where one holds unpopular beliefs, is a very important interest. However, it is not a matter of life and death, such as welfare benefits where the courts have held that notice and hearing are required before termination.

Second, the court will examine the government interest. Here, assuming City does not have a hidden agenda to discriminate against Assembly, its interest in protecting its infrastructure is, as indicated, very strong.

Third, the court will evaluate the extent to which additional procedures are needed to increase the accuracy of fact finding. As indicated, the issue for Assembly is not a matter of life and death. The members can still meet and practice their beliefs, though not in a newly built worship center within City's limits.

On the balance, Assembly should have been given notice of the Ordinance. It is a close call as to whether City should have been required to give Assembly a chance to oppose the ordinance before it was enacted, or simply given Assembly a right to plead its case for permanent approval (*e.g.*, a variance) after ordinance was passed. In either case, Assembly was denied its right to notice and opportunity to be heard, and City violated its rights to procedural due process.

JULY 2001 CALIFORNIA BAR EXAM -- QUESTION 4

1-HOUR ESSAY

To prepare herself for a spiritual calling to serve as a pastor at City's jail, Ada enrolled in a nondenominational bible school. After graduating, Ada advised the pastor of her own church that she was ready to commence a ministry and asked that her church ordain her. While sympathetic to her ambition, Ada's pastor accurately advised her that their church did not ordain women.

Ada began going to City's jail during visiting hours and developed an effective ministry with prisoners, particularly women inmates who increasingly sought her counsel. Ada noticed that ordained ministers who visited the jail received special privileges denied to her.

Dan, the jail supervisor, told Ada that ministers who were ordained and endorsed by a recognized religious group were designated "jail chaplains" and, as such, were permitted access to the jail during nonvisiting hours. He told Ada that she too could be designated a jail chaplain if she obtained a letter from a recognized religious group stating that it had ordained her as a minister and had endorsed her for such work.

Ada replied that her church was not part of any recognized religious group and would not ordain her anyway because she was a woman. She asked Dan nonetheless to designate her a jail chaplain because of the effectiveness of her work.

Dan refused to designate Ada a jail chaplain or to allow her the access enjoyed by jail chaplains. He acted pursuant to jail regulations adopted to avoid security risks and staff involvement in making determinations as to who was really a "minister."

Ada has brought suit in federal court to obtain an injunction requiring that she be designated a jail chaplain or be granted access to City's jail equivalent to those who have been designated jail chaplains. Ada's complaint is based on the grounds that the refusal to designate her a jail chaplain violates rights guaranteed to her and the prisoners by the First Amendment to the U.S. Constitution and also violates rights guaranteed to her by the equal protection clause of the Fourteenth Amendment to the U.S. Constitution.

How should Ada's suit be decided? Discuss.

JULY 2001, QUESTION 4
CONSTITUTIONAL LAW

-- Written by Dennis P. Saccuzzo

Commentary:

This fact pattern was the first con. law question that tested the establishment and free exercise clauses of the First Amendment since 1983. Ada, a woman graduate of a nondenominational Bible school, was not allowed to become a minister of her church because she was a woman. Nevertheless, she developed an effective ministry with prisoners, particularly women, in a local jail. However, Ada was denied privileges by prison officials that were afforded other ministers on the grounds that she was not an ordained minister from a recognized religion.

The existence of regulations enforced by a state actor (jail) that appeared to favor one religious group over another implicated the Establishment clause. Because the state actor recognized certain religions but not others, the Free Exercise clause was implicated. Equal protection was also implicated because the jail appeared to be discriminating on the basis of religious affiliation and gender (because women are less likely to be ordained than men). The first form of discrimination (recognized vs. non-recognized religion) required a rational basis test; the gender discrimination an intermediate scrutiny test. Finally, because of the discrimination based on a fundamental right (all First Amendment rights are fundamental rights), strict scrutiny analysis was required.

In sum, it was necessary to discuss the Establishment and Free Exercise clauses as well as all three levels of scrutiny in an equal protection context. In addition, it was necessary to discuss state action and standing.

Please notice that Ada's complaint is based on a violation of her own rights as well as a violation of rights guaranteed to the prisoners who were receiving counseling from her. In raising Constitutional issues on behalf of the prisoners, Ada was bringing a third party lawsuit, which required an analysis of third party standing. Many candidates missed this point, and lost points. The lesson is that every phrase on a fact pattern can be significant, particularly one containing connectors like "and."

Bar exam fact patterns are designed to allow you to show the breadth as well as depth of your knowledge and understanding of the law by applying facts to a wide variety of issues. In Constitutional law essays, the fact pattern will give you the opportunity to apply different standards of review, and you must find a way to apply at least two standards. In this essay, because you were given the opportunity to apply all 3 (rational basis, intermediate scrutiny and strict scrutiny) and needed to cover so many other issues, the analysis needed to be concise.

Ada has brought suit in federal court alleging a violation of her and City prisoners' First and 14th Amendment rights. To bring this case, she must first show that she has standing.

Standing

To have standing, a plaintiff (P) must have a personal stake in the outcome under the Constitution. She must show injury in fact, causation, and redressibility.

Injury in Fact. Ada must show she has been or will be injured. Facts indicate that Ada has been denied special privileges available only to ministers ordained and endorsed by a recognized religious group. This denial may infringe on her First and 14th Amendment rights. Because she has been denied access afforded to others of "recognized religions," Ada has suffered injury in fact.

Causation. But for City Jail's regulation, Ada, who has developed an effective ministry with prisoners, would not have been injured. Therefore Ada's injury is traceable to the regulation.

Redressibility. Ada is requesting an injunction that would grant her access equivalent to those who have been designated as jail chaplains. Her requested relief would redress her injury.

Conclusion: Ada has standing.

Third Party Standing

Ada is also claiming that prisoners' rights have been violated. To bring a suit on behalf of the prisoners, Ada must have third party standing. To do so, she must not only have standing herself, but also show a special relationship with the third party and a special hindrance to them.

Claimant has Standing. As discussed above, Ada has standing, and therefore is within the "zone of interest".

Special Relationship. Ada is a minister, and has, in fact, developed an effective ministry with prisoners, particularly women inmates who increasingly seek her counsel. Her pastor-penitent relationship should qualify as a special relationship.

Special Hindrance. Prisoners have limited resources and arguably would be handicapped here in asserting their rights. *[Note that the Bar examiners did not care which position you took here, as long as you argued it well.]*

Conclusion: Ada has standing to assert a third party claim on behalf of the prisoners.

Eleventh Amendment

The 11th Amendment bars citizens from suing a state in federal court without its consent. However, Ada is suing City's jail, and the 11th Amendment does not apply to local government. Even if it did, an injunction against state officers is an exception to the 11th Amendment bar. Because Ada is merely requesting an injunction that would compel Dan to allow her comparable access, her suit would not be barred even if she were suing a state.

State Action

The Constitution applies only to government action. City is a branch of the state government. Therefore, there is state action.

First Amendment

The First Amendment, applicable to the states via the 14th Amendment, prohibits government from infringing on religious freedom. Ada is being denied privileges offered to others because her religion is not recognized and refuses to ordain her. Therefore her First Amendment rights are implicated. Ada may bring an action under both the Establishment Clause and the Free Expression Clause of the First Amendment.

Exercise

Establishment Clause

The government may neither aid nor formally establish religion. Here, City appears to be aiding what it believes to be a recognized religious group. For City to defend this regulation, it must show (1) a secular purpose for the law; (2) that the primary effect neither advances nor hinders religion; and (3) no excessive government entanglement.

Secular Purpose, The purpose of the regulation is to avoid security risks and staff involvement as to who was really a minister. Maintaining security is of utmost concern to a prison, as is conserving staff time. Therefore the law has a secular purpose.

Primary Effect. The primary effect of the regulation is that "recognized" religions have greater access to prisoners than groups that are not recognized. The law therefore appears to advance certain religious beliefs at the expense of others and as such, the government will lose on this element.

Entanglement. That there is excessive government entanglement is demonstrated by the fact that Dan must deal with Ada as well as others who may not enjoy recognition by City's jail. The regulation precluding Dan from making a personal decision does not save the government, because somebody in city's jail administration must ultimately make the decision about what groups to recognize.

Conclusion: Ada will prevail under the Establishment Clause.

Free Exercise Clause

The government may not punish religious beliefs. Nor can it test the validity of beliefs or gauge the reasonableness or logic of beliefs. If the government is intentionally interfering with one's free exercise of religion, the law will be invalid unless it is narrowly tailored to advance a compelling state interest (strict scrutiny test). However, the Free Exercise Clause cannot be used to challenge a law of general applicability unless the laws are motivated by a desire to interfere with religion.

The City will successfully argue that jail security is a compelling interest. However, it will fail to show that its regulation is narrowly tailored to meet that interest because there are many equally effective alternatives. For example, rather than attempt to ascertain what is a recognized religion and then rely on a letter, City could perhaps more effectively conduct background checks and/or in-jail monitoring of religious representatives.

City's argument that the regulation is of general applicability will also fail. The regulation has a specific negative effect on religious groups that are not recognized and on those who follow these beliefs. Thus, the regulation is not neutral, with only an incidental effect on religion. Instead, it directly interferes with the religious beliefs of religions not recognized, and appears to be questioning the legitimacy of those beliefs by not granting its ministers the privileges it affords recognized groups.

Conclusion: Ada will also prevail under the Free Exercise Clause.

Equal Protection
The 14th Amendment prohibits states from depriving anyone of equal protection under the law. This means that government regulations cannot discriminate [see step 3, p. 85 of the schema].

City's regulation discriminates between ordained ministers and those not ordained and between "recognized" groups and those not recognized. It also appears to discriminate against women, because Ada's church, like many, ordains men but not women. Finally, because City's regulation involves disparate treatment based on freedom of religion, it relates to a fundamental right.

Classification based on ordained and recognized: Rational Basis Test
Classifications that are not based on race, national origin, alienage, gender, or nonmarital children are judged by the Rational Basis Test. The law or regulation merely must be rationally related to a legitimate government objective.

City's classification based on ordained versus not ordained and recognized versus not recognized is rationally related to the legitimate interest of jail security. The regulation arguably reduces the probability that an imposter will be allowed special jail access and ensures security. Thus, Ada's claims will fail based on these classifications.

Classification based on gender: Intermediate Scrutiny
Classifications based on gender are judged by an intermediate scrutiny test, which means the regulation must be substantially related to an important government interest (and under the modern test, the justification must be "exceedingly persuasive").

City will have a more difficult task defending its regulation as substantially related to its security goals. As indicated, there are many less restrictive alternatives that would maintain jail security, and no apparent reasons why men should be favored over women.

However, when a law or regulation is facially neutral, it is necessary to show both discriminatory impact as well as intent. Ada will probably have little difficulty showing discriminatory impact, given that her church, like many churches, does not ordain women. Thus, relatively fewer women ministers would be afforded the opportunity for the jail's special privileges. However, no facts indicate that City's jail had any discriminatory intent when they required ordained ministers. Because the regulation is facially neutral (it does not discriminate against women on its face) with no evidence of discriminatory intent, Ada will fail on this claim.

Discrimination based on a fundamental right: Strict Scrutiny

Where disparate treatment occurs in relation to a fundamental right, the court will apply a strict scrutiny test. This means the regulation must be necessary to promote a compelling state interest where there is no less burdensome alternative means to accomplish the state interest.

As discussed above under the Free Exercise Clause, Ada will prevail under a strict scrutiny test because there are less burdensome alternatives such as background checks.

Conclusion: Ada will prevail in her First Amendment claims and on her claim of discrimination based on a fundamental right.

JULY 2000 CALIFORNIA BAR EXAM -- QUESTION 4

1-HOUR EXAM

State law makes it a felony to either promote a dogfight or knowingly attend a dogfight where admission is charged. Ruth, a reporter for the *Dispatch*, City's only newspaper, observed a staged dogfight by posing as a patron and paying the admission fee. She took over 30 photographs of the event with a concealed camera. Later, she wrote an article about the event in the *Dispatch* that did not identify anyone else present, but which was accompanied by one of her photographs showing two dogs in bloody mortal combat.

The City police then asked Ruth if she knew the names of any persons at the illegal dogfight and requested all of her unpublished photographs in order to try to identify the fight promoters and attendees. With the backing of the *Dispatch*, Ruth flatly refused the police requests.

When Ruth's refusal came to the attention of the city council, several councilmembers stated publicly that the *Dispatch* was guilty of "bad citizenship." The council then unanimously enacted an ordinance banning all coin-operated newsracks from City's public sidewalks and any other public property in order to "improve public safety." The ordinance left unaffected those other newsracks on public property, far fewer in number, that dispensed several kinds of free publications (commercial, political, religious, etc.).

The state prosecutor in City commenced a grand jury investigation of illegal dogfighting in City. The grand jury subpoenaed Ruth to testify and answer questions about the dogfight she had attended and to produce all her unpublished photos of the event. Ruth brought an appropriate action in state court seeking an order quashing the grand jury subpoena.

The *Dispatch* sells about half of its daily editions from coin-operated newsracks located on City's sidewalks. The *Dispatch* commenced an action against the city council in the local federal district court, seeking a declaration that the ordinance banning coin-operated newsracks violates rights guaranteed under the U.S. Constitution.

1. What arguments based on rights guaranteed by the U.S. Constitution could Ruth reasonably make in support of her action for an order quashing the grand jury subpoena, and how should the court rule on each? Discuss.

2. What arguments could the *Dispatch* reasonably make in support of its claim that the city ordinance violates rights guaranteed under the U.S. Constitution, and how should the court rule on each? Discuss.

July 2000 California Bar – Question 4
Model Answer Written by Professor Dennis P. Saccuzzo

CALL 1 – Constitutional Arguments for Ruth's Action for an Order Quashing the Subpoena.

Ruth is being subpoenaed to testify and to produce her unpublished photographs. A subpoena is a judicial order that would require Ruth to give the requested testimony and documents. The issue is whether Ruth can quash, that is void or set aside, the subpoena under her First Amendment and Fifth Amendment rights.

First Amendment: Freedom of Press and Reporter's Privilege

The First Amendment, applicable to the states via the Due Process Clause of the Fourteenth Amendment, prohibits the government from certain regulation of speech and other forms of expression. While the First Amendment makes direct reference to freedom of the press, it is well settled that the press has no greater privilege than ordinary citizens.

Ruth's argument that she is privileged not to testify or produce her photographs will fail under a First Amendment challenge. Members of the press, just like ordinary citizens, have no privilege to refuse to disclose confidential sources to a grand jury. Although states may enact shield laws to afford such protection, no facts indicate the existence of any such laws in Ruth's state.

Fifth Amendment: Ruth's Testimony

The Fifth Amendment, applicable to the states via the Due Process Clause of the Fourteenth Amendment, protects against compelled testimonial self-incrimination.

Ruth will argue that the subpoena should be quashed on the grounds that she will be compelled to give incriminating evidence if she is forced to testify about her attendance at the dog fight. Her argument will succeed if there is a genuine possibility that her testimony might incriminate her.

Self-Incriminating Testimony

State law makes it a felony to either promote or knowingly attend a dog fight where admission is charged.

Ruth paid an admission fee posing as a patron, which shows she knowingly attended. She then observed a staged dog fight. She also took photographs with a concealed camera, and later published an article along with two photos. There is little doubt that a prosecutor can prove that Ruth knowingly attended the dog fight, and the state prosecutor has commenced a grand jury investigation of illegal dog fighting in City.

Because Ruth's testimony would definitely tend to convict her of the state law, she cannot be compelled to testify against herself under the Fifth

Amendment. However, the general procedure is that she must appear before the grand jury, be sworn in and actually assert her rights. Thus, while she may not be compelled to testify, it is unlikely that the subpoena will be set aside (quashed).

Fifth Amendment Challenge to the Photographs

Defined *supra*, the Fifth Amendment applies only to testimonial communications.

Ruth will argue that by producing the photographs she will in effect be testifying against herself because if she took the photographs, she attended the illegal dog fight and would thus tend to incriminate herself.

The prosecution will counter that she is merely being asked to produce physical evidence, such as blood samples or voice exemplars, all of which have been found to be nontestimonial and for which there is no reasonable expectation of privacy. However, in Ruth's case the act of producing the photos is itself communicative because she then tacitly admits that as the photographer, she was present at an illegal dog fight. Thus, production of the photos is arguably testimonial.

Conclusion: Ruth will have to appear before the grand jury and assert her First and Fifth Amendment rights. She will not have to testify under the Fifth Amendment and may not have to produce the photos because the act of production may be ruled to be testimonial in and of itself.

CALL 2: Dispatch's Constitutional Claims

First Amendment Claims

Dispatch can challenge the ordinance under the First Amendment, which was defined above. To exercise their claim, Dispatch must first show standing and state action.

Standing

Standing requires that the plaintiff show injury in fact, causation, and redressability.

The ordinance bans all coin-operated news racks from City's public sidewalks, from which Dispatch sells about half of its daily editions. Thus, Dispatch's circulation and profits are imminently threatened. Dispatch has an injury in fact.

The injury is traceable to City's ban. But for the ban, there would be no injury. The injury can be redressed by invalidating the law. Dispatch has standing.

State Action

The Constitution applies only to government action. City Council passed the law under their authority as public officials. There is state action.

First Amendment Challenge #1 – Law to Punish Newspaper

Laws to punish newspapers are per se invalid.

City's ordinance was made after Ruth's refusal came to the attention of City Council. Several Council members publicly stated that Dispatch was guilty of "bad citizenship." They then passed an ordinance that affected only Dispatch, because Dispatch is City's only newspaper and the ordinance left unaffected several kinds of free publications.

Dispatch will have a convincing argument for invalidating the law because the purpose of the ordinance was to punish them.

First Amendment Challenge #2 – Content Restriction

Dispatch can also argue that ordinance is a content-based restriction of free speech because the ban relates to the dog fighting story. As a ban on content the ordinance would be subject to a strict scrutiny test (defined below).

Dispatch will fail on this claim because free papers are left unaffected, and these can publish any type of story, including illegal dog fights. Therefore, the ban is content neutral.

First Amendment Challenge #3: Illegal Time, Place & Manner Restriction

The government has a legitimate interest to regulate time, place and manner (TPM) of speech as long as standards are specifically defined and unrelated to content of expression. The test depends on the forum.

Public Forum

Public fora are government properties that the government is required to make available for speech. Such fora include public sidewalks, from which City has banned Dispatch from selling papers in coin-operated machines.

Test for Public Forum

TPM restrictions in a public forum must be (1) content neutral, (2) narrowly tailored, (3) serve an important government interest, and (4) leave open alternate channels.

(1) Content Neutral

As discussed above, the ordinance is content neutral.

(2) Narrowly Tailored

The ordinance is not narrowly tailored. City could have tried a less restrictive regulation, such as requiring that all racks be a certain number of feet back from the street and/or away from door to business establishments, and limiting sales to hours when children are less likely to be exploited. Further, the ordinance bans all coin-operated racks but leaves unaffected non-coin-operated racks, which might contain materials more potentially damaging to public safety.

(3) Important Government Interest

Even if City succeeds in convincing the court that the ban is narrowly tailored, they will fail in showing an important government interest. The court will easily see that City's stated purpose to improve public safety is not their purpose at all. As discussed above, the real purpose of the ordinance is to punish Dispatch.

(4) Alternate Means

Although Dispatch can sell its papers in other ways through direct marketing or on the street solicitation, City will lose because it cannot meet all the elements of its case.

Equal Protection Involving a Fundamental Right

Under the Fourteenth Amendment the government cannot discriminate. The amendment applies to individuals as well as to business entities and newspapers such as Dispatch.

Here, City is discriminating between Dispatch and all those other publishers with free news racks on public property. Thus, the Fourteenth Amendment applies.

When a fundamental right such as free speech is involved, the court will use a strict scrutiny test. The law must be necessary to promote a compelling state interest where there is no less burdensome alternative means and the law is narrowly tailored.

As discussed above, City will fail under a strict scrutiny test. The state interest of punishing Dispatch is hardly compelling. Even if the interest is public safety, the law, as discussed above, is not narrowly tailored because it restricts more speech than necessary to achieve public safety.

Equal Protection Involving an Economic Right

When the government is merely regulating an economic activity, the court will apply a rational basis test, which means the law must be rationally related to a legitimate government objective.

Even if City convinces the court that its ordinance is merely an economic regulation, it will be struck down as arbitrary and capricious because, as discussed, its intent is to punish.

Conclusion: Dispatch will succeed in having the ordinance invalidated.

JULY 1997 CALIFORNIA BAR EXAM -- QUESTION 2

CONSTITUTIONAL LAW

A City ordinance enacted several years ago requires payment of an annual tax of $500 by each household in City with two or more children. The tax applies only to people who have become residents of City since the effective date of the ordinance. Its stated purpose is to reimburse City in part for the additional public school expenses and costs of recreational facilities attributable to the new residents.

Paul and Pat, husband and wife, became residents of City since the effective date of the tax ordinance and live alone with no children. They have filed suit against City in federal court for a judgment declaring that the ordinance violates their rights under the U.S. Constitution to familial privacy, to due process, and to equal protection.

During discovery, Paul and Pat revealed that they are medically unable to conceive a child and have applied to adopt twins. Although the court had ordered that this information remain confidential and all references to it were ordered sealed, City's attorney has disclosed the information in a press release. Paul and Pat have amended their complaint to allege a third claim against City: i.e., that the disclosure by City's attorney violated their privacy rights under the U.S. Constitution, entitling plaintiffs to an injunction prohibiting further disclosures and allowing the court to impose sanctions for violation of its confidentiality order.

City has moved to dismiss the entire complaint on the following grounds: (1) the plaintiffs lack standing to challenge the tax ordinance, and (2) that, in any event, none of the alleged constitutional rights claimed by Paul and Pat are violated by City.

How should the court decide City's motion to dismiss? Discuss.

City's Motion that Plaintiffs Lack Standing

To have standing, a plaintiff must have a personal stake in the outcome under the outcome under the Constitution. She must show injury in fact, causation, and redressability.

Injury in Fact

The court requires a concrete, particularized injury. Here, City ordinance requires payment of an annual tax on households with two or more children. Pat and Paul have challenged the tax. Currently, they live alone and have no children. However, they have applied to adopt two children. The court will find injury in fact where the injury is imminent. If the adoption is imminent, Pat and Paul will meet the injury requirement.

Causation

But for the City ordinance, there would be no tax and hence no injury. Therefore Pat and Paul can show causation.

Redressability

If the ordinance is found unconstitutional, there will be no tax and no injury. Therefore this element is met.

Conclusion: Plaintiffs have standing.

Ripeness: Courts will not hear the case if it is not ready to be heard. The standard applied is the hardship to the parties.

City will argue that the case is not ripe because plaintiffs have not yet been taxed. Plaintiffs will have to convince the court that their hardship will be great. For example, if the law will dissuade or prevent them from adopting, then the hardship will be great and the court will hear the case.

Constitutional Right Violations

Requirement of State Action

To make a claim under a due process, equal protection, or 1st Amendment protection, there must be state action. The Constitution applies only to government action.

The ordinance has been passed by a city acting in its governmental capacity. Therefore there is state action and plaintiffs can assert their rights.

Claim # 1: Familial Privacy – Fundamental Right (Substantive Due Process)

Privacy is a fundamental right under the Constitution. Recognized fundamental rights include the right to purchase contraceptives, the right to abortion, the right to marry, the right to procreation, and the right to family relations.

Pat and Paul's first obstacle will be to establish that the Ordinance affects a fundamental right. They will argue that the tax impacts their right to have children (procreation) as well as their right to live as a family (family relations). City will argue that Ordinance is a mere economic regulation and therefore subject to only a rational basis test, which merely requires that Ordinance be rationally related to a legitimate government interest.

Strict Scrutiny Analysis

Pat and Paul have the better argument because City is literally putting a tax on having two or more children, much like a population growth measure. The rule is that if a government regulation infringes on a fundamental right, it will be subjected to a strict scrutiny test. It must be necessary to a compelling government interest when there is no less burdensome alternative means to accomplish the interest.

The government's purpose is to reimburse City in part for the additional public school expenses and costs of recreational facilities attributable to new residents. While schools may be necessary, costs for recreational facilities are hardly compelling. Nor are taxes on two or more children necessary for City to run its schools. Moreover, there appear to be many less burdensome alternatives, such as an increase in property tax or a use tax for the facilities. Finally, the ordinance is under-inclusive in that it does not include families with one child.

Conclusion: Ordinance will fail a strict scrutiny test.

City's Argument – Rational Basis Test

If the Court finds that plaintiffs do not have a fundamental right at stake, the court will apply a rational basis test because the tax is an economic regulation.

Defined above, under a rational basis test City will prevail because their purpose of funding additional expenses is legitimate and rationally related to taxing new residents with two or more children who probably use these facilities the most.

Conclusion: In the unlikely event a rational basis test is applied, City will prevail.

Claim # 2: Procedural Due Process

Procedural due process protects against deprivation of life, liberty, or property interests without notice and opportunity to be heard.

The issue is whether plaintiffs have a legitimate interest at stake. No property is at stake and no entitlement is being threatened. City is merely imposing a tax. Therefore, plaintiffs have no procedural due process rights.

Claim # 3: Equal Protection

Government regulations cannot discriminate. Here City is discriminating based on number of children (two or more versus one or none) and duration of residence (Ordinance applies only to people who have been residents since the effective date of Ordinance).

For matters other than race, national origin, gender, and non-marital children, the courts will apply the rational basis test discussed above.

City will easily argue that a tax on new residents, or those with two children, is rationally related to their goal of funding additional public schools and recreational expenses because these are the groups most likely responsible for such increased cost.

Conclusion: Plaintiffs will fail on an equal protection claim.

Claim Against City Attorney's Disclosure – First Amendment/Free Speech

Prior Restraints on Speech

Prior restraints on speech are generally invalid. The government must show special societal harm and the restraints will be subjected to the strict scrutiny test discussed above.

The court has ordered that private information about plaintiffs remain confidential. Although plaintiffs may find their inability to have children embarrassing, and may want to remain private about their interest in adopting, the release of this information would hardly lead to a special societal harm. Therefore, the restraint is invalid and plaintiffs will be unable to obtain an injunction barring further disclosure.

Request for Injunction: Collateral Bar Rule

An injunction must be obeyed however erroneous the action of the court. Unconstitutionality of a court order is not a defense to prosecution for contempt.

The court had ordered that the information remain confidential and ordered that all references to it be sealed. City Attorney was wrong to disobey the court order and is subject to sanctions which the court probably and justifiably will impose.

JULY 1996 CALIFORNIA BAR EXAM -- QUESTION 2

1-HOUR ESSAY

To lessen the exposure of children to lead poisoning, Congress passed the Lead Poisoning Prevention Act ("LPPA"), to be administered by the federal Housing and Urban Development Agency ("HUD"). LPPA requires owners of residential housing, including all state and municipal owners of public housing, built before 1965, when lead-based paint was banned, to test all such dwellings for the presence of lead-based paint. The owner must then record the results of the test with the county recorder. If the presence of lead-based paint is found, LPPA requires the owner at the owner's expense to take remedial steps within 18 months to remove all traces of lead.

LPPA requires each state to designate a state agency to enforce LPPA within that state. LPPA also authorizes private enforcement by a suit in a federal district or state court, including: (a) injunctive actions by lawful residents of affected dwellings, and (b) compensatory damage actions by anyone proximately injured by a failure to comply with LPPA.

After passage of LPPA, State X, through its attorney general, filed suit in federal court in State X against HUD contesting the validity of LPPA under the U.S. Constitution. The suit alleges that Congress lacks authority: (a) to enact such regulatory legislation; (b) in any event, to require individual states to enforce the LPPA; and (c) to regulate through such legislation state or municipally-owned housing.

Ida is a wealthy investor living in State X who owns no residential buildings, but claims to be planning to buy several apartment buildings built before 1965. Ida claims that LPPA imposes such extraordinary liability risks on owners of affected residential properties as to constitute an unlawful confiscation. Ida has filed a motion to intervene as an additional plaintiff in the State X attorney general's pending suit to contest the constitutionality of LPPA as applied to her. HUD opposes Ida's motion to intervene, claiming that she lacks standing.

1. How should the federal court rule on the following arguments of the State X attorney general?

    General welfare, hogen safety

    a. That Congress lacks authority to enact such regulatory legislation. Discuss.

    b. That Congress lacks authority to require the individual states to enforce the LPPA. Discuss.

    c. That Congress lacks authority to regulate state and municipally-owned housing through such legislation. Discuss.

2. How should Ida's motion to intervene be decided? Discuss.

Model Answer Written by Professor Dennis P. Saccuzzo

CALL 1 – How should the Federal Court Rule?

(a) Congress lacks authority – regulatory legislation

The issue is whether the exercise of Congressional power is constitutional.

Commerce Clause – Interstate Regulation

Article 1, Section 8 gives Congress broad powers to regulate commerce among the several states. Congress has plenary power to regulate the channels (roads, mails, rivers, etc.) and instrumentalities (persons or things) of interstate commerce, which means it can regulate for any rational reason.

Here, LPPA requires owners of residential housing, including states and municipal owners of public housing, to test for the presence of lead-based paint. The Act does not affect either the channels or the instrumentalities of ISC. The effect is all in-state, so the rules pertaining to intrastate regulation will apply.

Intrastate Regulation of ISC – Commercial versus Non-Commercial

For a commercial activity, Congress has the authority to enact legislation when it is rational for Congress to believe that the regulated activity could have a substantial effect on ISC.

The purpose of LPPA is to lessen exposure of children to lead poisoning. Owners must test for the presence of lead paint and if it is found, take remedial steps at their own expense. Although expenses are involved, this is hardly a traditional commercial activity because it does not involve profit making, trade, sales, marketing, etc. Moreover, no facts indicate that Congress is regulating a commercial activity. The court will therefore apply the more stringent test for non-commercial activities.

Intrastate Regulation of ISC – Non-Commercial

Under the modern rule in *U.S. v. Lopez*, Congress will lack authority under the commerce clause unless it has an articulated rational basis to believe that the regulated activity has a substantial economic effect on ISC.

Articulated Rational Basis

Under *Lopez*, the courts require legislative findings or facts to show that Congress has a basis to believe the regulated activity would affect ISC. Here, no such facts are presented.

Substantial Economic Effect

Although, as discussed, money is involved, the link between inspecting for lead paint and interstate commerce is highly attenuated.

Conclusion: The United States will be unable to meet its burden of showing Congress had authority to enact LPPA.

(b) Congress Lacks Authority – Requires States

Congress may not compel the states to legislate in a prescribed fashion; nor may they order the states to assume uncertain liabilities (*N.Y. v. U.S.*).

LPPA requires the states to designate an agency to enforce LPPA within the state. This would force the state to regulate in a manner dictated by Congress. Under the rule in *N.Y. v. U.S.*, this is unconstitutional. Congress may not commandeer the legislative processes of the states.

Also unconstitutional is the LPPA provision authorizing compensatory damages, for it might subject the states to uncertain liabilities. Even if it did not, both private remedies would be doubtful.

The court has held that the commerce power did not authorize Congress to enact a civil remedy provision where the causal chain between the regulated activity and interstate commerce was too attenuated, which is the case here (as previously discussed).

Conclusion: Congress lacks authority to require the states to enforce LPPA.

(c) Congress Lacks Authority – Municipally Owned Housing
Under the property clause Congress has the power to regulate federal property. There is no express power to regulate state- or municipally-owned property. However, the real issue is whether there is a 10th Amendment limit on the commerce power.

10th Amendment
The 10th Amendment gives states general police powers to regulate the health, safety, and welfare of their private citizens. The control of lead-based paint and lead poisoning of children is a traditional state function that relates to its 10th Amendment police power. The state will argue that Congress has exceeded its power in its regulation of municipally owned housing because such a regulation infringes on state 10th Amendment powers.

Modern Rule: No Limit on Commerce Power
Modernly, the 10th Amendment cannot be used by the states to limit Congressional laws equally applicable to private citizens and states. Under *Garcia*, the 10th Amendment does not pose a limit on Congress' power to apply an otherwise valid commercial regulation to state and local government.

Here, the law applies to owners of residential housing, including state and municipal owners of public housing. Under modern law, state and municipal owners have no special protection under the 10th Amendment. Therefore, assuming the federal law was found valid, Congress would have as much authority to regulate state and municipal owners as it does to regulate private citizens.

Conclusion: Congress has authority to regulate state- and municipally-owned housing under a valid exercise of its commerce power. Under present facts Congress has not validly exercised its power so the law will be struck down.

CALL 2 – Ida's Motion

Standing

HUD claims that Ida lacks standing. To have standing, a plaintiff must have a personal stake in the outcome. She must show injury in fact, causation, and redressability.

Ida lives in State X, but owns no residential buildings. Although she claims to be "planning" to buy affected buildings, she has not suffered any harm. Nor is she in imminent danger of harm. Such danger might exist if she had made a down payment or offer. However, the court will require a concrete, particularized harm, which Ida has not suffered. Thus, she will lack standing.

Ripeness

Ida's case will also fail under this doctrine because it is not ready to be heard. She has not yet suffered an injury.

July 1995 California Bar Exam -- Question 2

1-Hour Essay

Because teenage pregnancies have increased the number of school dropouts, the Board of Education of City (Board) adopted an "Alternative Education Program" (AEP) for unmarried students under age eighteen who become pregnant. All such students must participate. AEP offers a special core educational curriculum supplemented with personal counseling and instruction on prenatal and infant care designed to alleviate the educational, emotional, social, and health problems confronting unmarried teenage mothers. Once placed in AEP, the student remains a participant through the term of her pregnancy and until the end of the school year in which her pregnancy terminates.

Pam, an unmarried sixteen year old eleventh grader at City High School, is pregnant. She wants to remain in her regular classes at City High School but has been assigned to AEP. She has sued the Board in federal district court for declaratory and injunctive relief, seeking return to her regular classes. Pam's complaint alleges that being assigned to AEP violates her right to equal protection of the law guaranteed by the United States Constitution and penalizes her for exercising a fundamental right protected by the substantive due process provision of the Constitution.

Shortly after Pam's suit was filed, the school year ended and during the summer Pam suffered a miscarriage. The Board has transferred Pam back to her regular high school classes and has moved to dismiss her complaint on the grounds that: (1) the action is moot; and (2) the complaint fails to state a claim for relief under the Constitution.

How should the court rule on the issues raised by the Board's motion? Discuss.

Is the Action Moot?

Pam is challenging a school program (AEP) that requires unmarried students under the age of 18 who become pregnant to participate in a program that would remove them from the regular classroom and provide an alternative curriculum and counseling.

Standing

The first issue is whether Pam originally had standing to challenge the program. To have standing, a plaintiff must have a personal stake in the outcome under the Constitution. She must show injury in fact, causation, and redressability.

Pam is an unmarried 16-year-old in the 11th grade who became pregnant. She therefore fell squarely within the bounds of AEP. She suffered injury in fact because she was removed from her regular classroom. Her injury was the direct result of Board's policy and is redressable by her request for declaratory and injunctive relief because such relief would allow her to return to regular classes as she desires. Thus, she had standing to bring the claim.

Mootness

The next issue is whether Pam's case has become moot. A real case or controversy must exist at all stages, and a federal court will not hear a case that has become moot.

Pam suffered a miscarriage. Because she is no longer pregnant, she has been transferred to her regular classes. Thus, she apparently does not have an ongoing stake in the controversy. Absent an exception, Pam's case is moot and will be dismissed.

Exception to Mootness

An exception to mootness occurs when the case is capable of repetition yet evading review. To qualify under this exception the plaintiff must show a reasonable expectation that the same controversy will recur involving the same party.

Pam is only 16 and about to begin the 12th grade. There is a reasonable expectation that Pam can get pregnant again before she finishes high school, and the case would probably evade review because of the relatively short time frame in which she would be pregnant and excluded from her regular classes. Therefore Pam's case falls within the exception and the Court will hear her case even though she is not currently pregnant.

Conclusion: The court should rule against City's motion to dismiss based on mootness.

Pam's Constitutional Claims

Pam is claiming violation of her rights to equal protection and her fundamental rights protected by substantive due process. To make such claims she must first show state action.

State Action

The Constitution applies only to government actors. Private conduct need not comply with the Constitution. State action will also be found under the public function doctrine in which private actors exercise traditional state functions.

Here, the Board action is under the auspices of the City High School. Because the action is based on City power, the court will find state action. Even if City power is not being used, education is a traditional state function, so state action will be found in any case.

Equal Protection (EP)

The Fourteenth Amendment prohibits states from depriving anyone of equal protections under the law. This means that government regulations cannot discriminate. Similarly situated people must be treated the same.

Pam has at least three claims that she is being discriminated against: gender, age, and marital status.

Equal Protection Claim Based on Gender

Pam has an EP claim based on gender. Only students who become pregnant must attend AEP. The action applies only to women, and is arguably facially discriminatory (discriminatory on its face).

Where a regulation involves gender discrimination, the Supreme Court has held the government to a very high standard of intermediate scrutiny. Under U.S. v Virginia (VMI), the justification must be exceedingly persuasive and rests entirely on the government. Further, the government must not rely on overbroad generalizations about differences between males and females in arguing that the regulation is substantially related to an important government purpose.

Intermediate Scrutiny Analysis

The Board will argue that it has an important interest to alleviate the educational, emotional, social, and health problems confronting unmarried teenage mothers. They will assert that the AEP is substantially related to these objectives because single unmarried pregnant women will continue their schooling and receive special help.

Pam will counter that the government's argument is not exceedingly persuasive because no facts have been presented to show that Pam will drop out of school or that she is in need of special help. Further, there are less restrictive alternatives to deal with the problems of teenage pregnancy, such as after-school classes.

Under the modern test for gender discrimination, the Board will probably fall short; Pam will likely prevail.

Equal Protection Claim Based on Age and Marital Status

Pam also has a claim of discrimination based on age because only those under 18 are affected, whereas those over 18 are not. Similarly, she has a claim based on marital status because only unmarried pregnant girls are sent to the program.

Where the government discriminates based on age or marital status, a rational basis test will be applied. The regulation must be rationally related to a legitimate government purpose, and the burden of proof will be on Pam.

Pam will be unable to meet her burden of showing the regulation arbitrary and capricious. Just about any rational purpose will satisfy this test, and selecting women under 18 and single is rationally related to the legitimate purpose of protecting the health and safety of the most vulnerable young mothers and their children.

The Board will prevail on the age and marital status EP claims.

Substantive Due Process

If a government regulation infringes on a fundamental right it is subjected to the strict scrutiny test. The regulation must be necessary to promote a compelling state interest where there is no less burdensome alternative means to accomplish the state interest. The burden is on the government.

Privacy is a fundamental right. Included in the right to privacy is the right to purchase and use contraception, marriage, education, and family relations. The right to marry includes freedom to make choice in matters relating to one's personal life, including the right to freedom of choice in child bearing and child rearing.

The Board's arguments in favor of AEP are essentially the same as those discussed above under gender. However, they will have to meet the higher burden of necessary for a compelling state interest. They will fail.

Pam will successfully argue that the forced counseling alone infringes on her right to choose how she will bring up her child. Further, while the need to prevent dropouts is strong, it is hardly compelling. Moreover, if preventing dropouts and providing education for unwed mothers is the problem, Board action is under-inclusive because it leaves out married pregnant girls and all the fathers of their children who might drop out. As discussed above, there are less restrictive (*i.e.*, less burdensome) means to accomplish Board's goals.

Conclusion: Pam will prevail on her substantive due process claim and probably on her gender discrimination claim as well. She will succeed in her quest for declaratory and injunctive relief.

FEBRUARY 1991 CALIFORNIA BAR EXAM -- QUESTION 2

1-HOUR EXAM

City, a municipality in State X, owns and operates a landfill site for household and commercial non-hazardous waste disposal. City finances this operation by charging fees based on a rate formula involving the weight and volume of waste delivered at the site. City's landfill is relatively new and therefore has substantial unused capacity.

Outko, an out-of-state trucking firm engaged in hauling non-hazardous waste, has entered into contracts with various out-of-state municipalities to transport their non-hazardous wastes for disposal to City's landfill. Inko, a State X trucking firm with its offices in City, has been hauling non-hazardous waste from sources within city, from elsewhere in State X, and from outside of State X, to City's landfill for disposal.

City has recently enacted an ordinance banning disposal of out-of-state waste in City's landfill and imposing a new rate fee for waste from sources anywhere outside of City, but within State X. This new rate fee is twice that charged for waste of identical weight and volume from sources within City.

The National Association of Waste Truckers (NAWT) is an organization representing waste haulers. Both Outko and Inko are members of NAWT. On behalf of all of its members, NAWT plans to bring an action against City in federal district court in State X, challenging the constitutionality of the landfill ordinance.

1. What challenges, if any, under the U.S. Constitution, may be brought against City's landfill ordinance, and how should each be decided? Discuss.

2. May NAWT properly assert those challenges? Discuss.

Model Answer Written by Professor Dennis P. Saccuzzo

CALL 1 – What challenges may be brought?

Preemption Doctrine

Federal law preempts state law where (1) federal and state law are mutually exclusive, (2) state law impedes a federal objective, or (3) Congress has a clear intent to occupy the field.

Interstate commerce is ordinarily regulated by Congress. City's attempt to enact an ordinance banning disposal of out-of-state waste in City's landfill and imposing a new rate fee for waste from sources anywhere outside of City but within State X affects interstate commerce and would be preempted under any of the three condition stated above. However, because no mutually exclusive laws, federal objectives, or facts indicating an intent by Congress to occupy the field are given, City's ordinance will not be preempted.

Dormant Commerce Clause

In general, state and local laws are unconstitutional if they (1) discriminate against or (2) unduly burden interstate commerce.

City's law is facially discriminatory in that it bans out-of-state waste entirely and charges a new rate fee from in-state sources outside the city. The court will apply a strict scrutiny test, which means the law must be narrowly tailored to a compelling state interest and there cannot be a less burdensome alternative means to accomplish the state interest.

Undue Burden – Strict Scrutiny Test

City will argue that its ban on out-of-state waste and increased fees for out-of-city waste is a valid exercise of their police power under the 10th Amendment. Their interest in the ban is protecting the health and safety of City by restricting the amount of garbage that comes in. However, the city landfill has substantial unused capacity, and plaintiff will successfully argue that City can use less discriminatory means such as using its capacity to burn and bury garbage.

Conclusion: City's ordinance constitutes an undue burden under a strict scrutiny test and plaintiff will prevail absent an exception.

Exception: Market Participant Doctrine

According to this doctrine, City will be excepted if it is a market participant, that is a buyer or seller in the market.

City owns and operates the landfill site. As an owner and operator, it qualifies as a market participant and will be exempted under the Dormant Commerce Clause.

Privileges and Immunities Clause (P & I Clause)

Under Article IV, states may not deprive citizens of other states the privileges and immunities it accords its own citizens unless there are substantial reasons other than that the person is a citizen of another state. Such privileges apply only to economic interests or civil rights. However, the right is specific to individuals; aliens, corporations, and trusts are not protected because they are not recognized as citizens under this clause.

Outko and Inko both have a financial interest in hauling waste. Outko has contracts and Inko has been hauling from various sites. Therefore, an economic interest is at stake. However, if Outko and Inko are corporations, then Article IV would not apply. The facts are unclear, and state that both are "firms." If they are not corporations, then the law will be valid only if it is necessary to achieve an important government purpose and there are no less restrictive alternative means. As discussed, the law does not meet this strict scrutiny test and absent an exception, will be struck down.

It is noteworthy that the market participant doctrine exception does not apply to the P & I Clause. As discussed, City prevails under a Dormant Commerce Clause challenge under the market participant doctrine. However, under the P & I clause, there is no such exception. Thus, if Outko and Inko are not corporations, they can prevail under this clause.

Contracts Clause

Under the contracts clause states may not enact laws that retroactively impair existing contract rights. The impairment must be substantial. Where substantial impairment is found, the state law will still be held valid if it serves an important and legitimate public interest and is narrowly tailored to promote that interest. Generally, the test for private contracts is less stringent than that for public contracts.

Prior to City's ordinance Outko had entered into contracts with various out-of-state municipalities to transport their nonhazardous waste for disposal to City's landfill. Thus, the contracts clause applies. However, it is arguable whether City's ordinance constitutes a substantial impairment. Although the ban is total, Outko is free to use other landfills to meet its contractual objectives, even if they had to pay more. City's interest in protecting its citizens against excess garbage is certainly legitimate, and although the ordinance may fail the narrowly tailored prong under a strict scrutiny test, as indicated the courts are less stringent on this prong for private contracts. On the balance, City has the better argument and will probably prevail. It is more likely than not that City will prevail. If City does not prevail, Outko may be entitled to damages.

Equal Protection

The rule is government regulations cannot discriminate. Where an economic interest is at issue, the courts will apply a rational basis test.

The ordinance bans out-of-state waste and charges twice the fee for out-of-city waste in the state. Therefore it discriminates. The interests affected are economic, so City will prevail if it can show its regulations are rationally related to a legitimate interest. Because cutting back on garbage is rationally related to protecting the health of citizens, City will prevail.

CALL 2 – NAWT Standing

Associations have standing if (1) the members have standing, (2) the interest asserted is germane to association purposes, and (3) individual membership in the lawsuit is not required.

(1) Members Have Standing

To have standing, one must (1) suffer injury in fact, (2) caused by the government, that (3) can be redressed by the requested relief.

Both Outko and Inko have suffered injury. Outko is banned from hauling outside waste and will have difficulty fulfilling its contracts. As discussed, it may be entitled to damages. Inko will be charged double for hauling out-of-city waste from the state. But for the ordinance, they would not have suffered these injuries, and if the ordinance is rescinded or enjoined, the injuries will be redressed. Thus, Outko and Inko have standing and they are members of NAWT. Other similarly situated members of NAWT will also have standing if their Privileges and Immunities or contract rights have been impaired.

(2) Purpose Germane

NAWT represents waste haulers. The ordinance has an adverse effect on waste haulers. Therefore, the purpose is germane.

(3) Individual Membership Not Required

In general, an association can sue for declaratory or injunctive relief that would benefit all its members, but it cannot sue for damages for specific members because that would require individualized proof.

Because NAWT is asking to have the ordinance invalidated and is not asking for legal damages, no individualized proof is required. Therefore NAWT may bring most claims.

However, meeting this element for the Privileges and Immunities Clause claim will be problematic. First, it should be noted that as an association NAWT would probably not be recognized as a citizen under the Privileges and Immunities Clause, just as corporations are not. Second, if Outko and Inko are corporations, then they are not protected under the clause and the court may reject a claim by NAWT because to allow such a claim would be allowing an end run around the rule that corporations are not covered.

CRIMES

JULY 2004 CALIFORNIA BAR EXAM -- QUESTION 1

1-Hour Essay

handwritten: 1. Assault 2. Battery 3. Murder 4. Conspiracy Robbery

On August 1, 2002, Dan, Art, and Bert entered Vince's Convenience Store. Dan and Art pointed guns at Vince as Bert removed $750 from the cash register. As Dan, Art, and Bert were running toward Bert's car, Vince came out of the store with a gun, called to them to stop, and when they did not do so, fired one shot at them. The shot hit and killed Art. Dan and Bert got into Bert's car and fled. *handwritten: Self-Defense*

Dan and Bert drove to Chuck's house where they decided to divide the $750. When Chuck said he would tell the police about the robbery if they did not give him part of the money, Bert gave him $150. Dan asked Bert for $300 of the remaining $600, but Bert claimed he, Bert, should get $500 because his car had been used in the robbery. Dan became enraged and shot and killed Bert. He then decided to take all of the remaining $600 for himself and removed the money from Bert's pocket. *handwritten: Heop*

On August 2, 2002, Dan was arrested, formally charged with murder and robbery, arraigned, and denied bail. Subsequently, the court denied Dan's request that trial be set for October 15, 2002, and scheduled the trial to begin on January 5, 2003. On January 3, 2003, the court granted, over Dan's objection, the prosecutor's request to continue the trial to September 1, 2003, because the prosecutor had scheduled a vacation cruise, a statewide meeting of prosecuting attorneys, and several legal education courses. On September 2, 2003, Dan moved to dismiss the charges for violation of his right to a speedy trial under the United States Constitution. *handwritten: Procedural Due Process*

1. May Dan properly be convicted of either first degree or second degree murder, and, if so, on what theory or theories, for:

   a. The death of Art? Discuss.
   b. The death of Bert? Discuss.

2. May Chuck properly be convicted of any crimes, and, if so, of what crime or crimes? Discuss. *handwritten: Conspiracy*

3. How should the court rule on Dan's motion to dismiss? Discuss.

Nancy E. Johnson & Dennis P. Saccuzzo

Call 1. May Dan be Convicted?

(a) Art's death

Homicide

Homicide is the killing of a human being by another. Art was shot and killed following a robbery in which the victim, Vince, shot him. Thus there was a homicide. For murder, there must be the mens rea of malice.

Murder
Causation
Actual Cause

Dan did not shoot Art: Vince did. However, but for Dan and Art robbing Vince, Vince would not have shot and killed Art. Therefore, the actual cause of Art's death is the felony robbery.

Proximate Cause

It is foreseeable that if one commits a robbery a victim will use self-defense measures and shoot and kill one of the co-felons.

Malice

There are four types of malice under the common law: intent to kill, intent to do serious bodily harm, wanton/depraved heart (reckless indifference for the quality of life), and felony murder. The issue is whether any of these apply to Dan.

Intent to kill/Intent to do serious bodily harm

Vince shot Art. No facts indicate Dan intended for Art to be killed or seriously injured.

Wanton/Depraved Heart (Reckless Indifference for the Quality of Life)

Arguably Dan showed wanton/depraved heart when he and Art robbed the store and pointed guns at Vince, the store owner. Pointing guns at another person shows reckless indifference to life. However, Dan did not shoot Art. Therefore, to find malice it is necessary to impute the malice from the underlying robbery using the felony murder rule.

Felony Murder

Felony murder is a death caused in the commission or attempt of an inherently dangerous felony. Robbery (a trespassory taking and carrying away of the personal property of another from the other person by force with the specific intent to permanently deprive the victim of his interest) is an inherently dangerous felony. Dan and Art took $750 away from Vince by pointing guns at him and later divided the money among themselves. Therefore, they committed a robbery. During the robbery,

Art's death was caused. Malice for the death will be implied from the intent to commit the underlying felony. Therefore, Dan can be held liable for the killing of Art, absent an exception.

Exception to the Felony Murder Rule

Under the *Redline* rule, a defendant is not liable for the killing of a co-felon by a police officer or victim. Dan and Art robbed the store together. They were co-felons. Art was shot by Vince, the victim. Under the *Redline* rule Dan will not be liable for felony murder.

Because none of the 4 forms of malice apply to Dan, Dan cannot be convicted for first or second degree murder of Art.

(b) Bert's death

Causation

Actual Cause

But for Dan shooting Bert, Bert would not have been killed, so Dan is the actual cause of Bert's death.

Proximate Cause

It is foreseeable that if one shoots someone, that person will die, so Dan is also the proximate cause of Bert's death.

Malice

Intent to Kill

Dan became enraged, shot Bert, and killed him. This provides strong evidence of Dan's intent to kill Bert.

Intent to Cause Serious Bodily Harm

Even if Dan did not intend to kill Bert, the fact that he shot Bert at close range demonstrates at least intent to cause serious bodily harm.

Wanton/Depraved Heart

Even if Dan did not intend to kill or cause serious harm, pointing a gun at someone and shooting demonstrates a reckless indifference for life. At a minimum, this type of malice will apply.

Felony Murder

Dan, Art, and Bert conspired to commit and did commit robbery, an inherently dangerous felony. However, when Dan and Bert reached Chuck's house they had reached a point of temporary safety and the robbery was complete. Therefore felony murder predicated on the convenience store robbery will not apply. Furthermore, Dan did not decide to take the money from Bert until after he had killed him. Felony murder predicated on robbery of Bert will therefore also not apply.

Conclusion: Dan showed malice (intent to kill, intent to do serious bodily harm, and wanton/depraved heart) and may be convicted for 1st or 2nd degree murder, depending on the nature of the killing.

1st Degree Murder

First degree murder is found where there is a felony murder, premeditation, or poison/bomb/torture/ambush.

Dan shot Bert after he became enraged. This suggests a spontaneous, non-premeditated murder, and there was no poison, bomb, torture or ambush. Dan will not be convicted of 1st degree murder.

2nd Degree Murder

All murders (killing with malice) that are not 1st degree murder are 2nd degree murder. Dan will be convicted of 2nd degree murder based on intent to kill, intent to do serious bodily injury, and wanton/depraved heart, absent a defense.

Defense: Heat of Passion

To succeed on this defense, one must show (1) adequate provocation (2) gave rise to heat of passion (3) with no adequate cooling-off period, and (4) defendant did not cool off.

(1) Provocation. Because his car had been used in the robbery, Bert demanded $500, well over half the $750 that resulted from the robbery and killing of a co-felon. This demand reasonably provoked Dan.

(2) Heat of Passion. Facts stipulate Dan became enraged.

(3) No Cooling Off Period. Dan apparently shot Bert immediately, indicating he did not have time to cool off.

(4) Did not Cool Off. Dan shot Bert while he was enraged and did not cool off.

Voluntary Manslaughter

Where a criminal defendant can prove the heat of passion defense, the offense will be mitigated down to voluntary manslaughter. In some jurisdictions, the defense fails where the defendant caused the situation that provoked him, as is the case here. Unless Dan is tried in such a jurisdiction, he has a good argument for heat of passion. He will not be convicted of 1st or 2nd degree murder, but will be convicted of voluntary manslaughter.

Call 2. Chuck's Crimes

Chuck may be convicted of several crimes.

Extortion

Obtaining property of another by means of threats or future threats is extortion.

Chuck obtained $150 from Bert by threatening to tell the police about the robbery. Chuck committed extortion.

Accessory After the Fact

Accessory after the fact requires (1) a completed crime, (2) knowledge that the crime has been perpetrated, and (3) aid to the felon personally to hinder his apprehension or punishment.

Dan, Art, and Bert committed robbery. Chuck demanded a share of the stolen money in return for his silence, so he knew they had committed the robbery. Moreover, he promised Dan and Bert that he would not turn them in, thus aiding them to avoid capture and punishment. Chuck can be convicted of being an accessory after the fact.

Receipt of Stolen Property

Conviction for receipt of stolen property requires proof of the following 4 elements:

(1) <u>Receiving possession of stolen property</u>. Chuck received $150 from money that had been stolen at a convenience store.

(2) <u>Known to have been obtained in a manner constituting a criminal offense.</u> Chuck threatened to report the robbery, so he knew the source of the $150 to have been the crime of convenience store robbery.

(3) <u>By another person</u>. The money was stolen by Dan and Bert.

(4) <u>With the intent to permanently deprive the victim (owner)</u>. Bert extorted the money. No facts indicated he intended to return it to the convenience store, so this element is met.

Chuck may be convicted of all three crimes.

Call 3. Dan's Motion – Right to Speedy Trial

6th Amendment

The 6th Amendment, applicable to the states via the 14th Amendment, guarantees a defendant the right to a speedy trial. Dan was arrested, formally charged with murder and robbery, arraigned, and denied bail on August 2, 2002. The trial was continued through September 1, 2003, more than a year later, implicating Dan's 6th Amendment right to a speedy trial.

Speedy Trial

In considering whether a defendant's right to speedy trial has been violated, the court will look to the following factors: (1) the length of the delay, (2) the reason for the delay, (3) defendant's assertion of the right, and (4) prejudice to the defendant.

(1) Length of delay

The delay ran from August 2, 2002 to September 2, 2003, or 13 months. Generally, 6 months is the per se length for triggering a claim, and 13 months qualifies as excessive.

(2) Reason for the delay

Dan had requested a trial date of Oct. 15, 2002. Over his objection and at the prosecutor's request, the trial was scheduled to begin on Jan. 15, 2003, more than 6 months after Dan had been formally charged and denied bail. No reasons are given for this delay. For such a delay, compelling reasons should have been provided.

Then, the trial was delayed again over Dan's objections. This time the reasons given were that the prosecutor had a scheduled vacation cruise, a meeting of prosecutors, and continuing education to attend. All of these reasons are personal to the prosecutor, and have no bearing on the case, the need to assemble evidence, or any conduct by Dan that would justify the delay. The delay was therefore frivolous.

(3) Defendant's assertion of the right

Dan requested a speedy trial date of Oct. 15, 2002, two months after he was charged, imprisoned, and denied bail. He therefore asserted his right. He asserted it again on Jan. 3 when he objected to a continuation, and asserted it yet one more time on Sept. 2 when he requested a dismissal. Dan unquestionably asserted his right to a speedy trial on multiple occasions.

(4) Prejudice to the defendant

The longer the delay, the more memories fade and the more time the prosecutor has to amass evidence. Dan is also prejudiced by being imprisoned for an undue length of time without the chance to exercise his right to defend himself. Arguably, Dan is guilty of robbery and voluntary manslaughter. However, he faces charges of first and second degree murder, and has a good case. Thus, he is prejudiced.

Conclusion: Dan was denied his right to speedy trial under the U. S. Constitution. His case should be dismissed.

FEB 2004 CALIFORNIA BAR EXAM, QUESTION 1

1-Hour Essay

Bank was robbed at 1 p.m. by a man who brandished a shotgun and spoke with a distinctive accent. The teller gave the robber packets of marked currency, which the robber put into a briefcase. At 3:30 p.m., the police received a telephone call from an anonymous caller who described a man standing at a particular corner in the downtown business district and said the man was carrying a sawed-off shotgun in a briefcase. Within minutes, a police officer who had been informed about the robbery and the telephone call observed Dave holding a briefcase at that location. Dave fit the description given by the anonymous caller.

The officer approached Dave with his service revolver drawn but pointed at the ground. He explained the reason for his approach, handcuffed Dave, and opened the briefcase. The briefcase contained only the marked currency taken in the bank robbery. The officer said to Dave: "I know you're the one who robbed the bank. Where's the shotgun?" Dave then pointed to a nearby trash container in which he had concealed the shotgun, saying: "I knew all along that I'd be caught." *[handwritten: Admission]*

[handwritten margin notes: Miranda? interrogation]

Dave was charged with robbery. He has chosen not to testify at trial. He has, however, moved to be allowed to read aloud a newspaper article, to be selected by the judge, without being sworn as a witness or subjected to cross-examination, in order to demonstrate that he has no accent. He has also moved to exclude from evidence the money found in the briefcase, his statement to the officer, and the shotgun.

How should the court rule on Dave's motions regarding the following items, and on what theory or theories should it rest:

1. Dave's reading aloud of a newspaper article? Discuss.

2. The currency? Discuss.

3. Dave's statement to the officer? Discuss.

4. The shotgun? Discuss.

Written by Dennis P. Saccuzzo & Nancy E. Johnson

Commentary

This question had 4 structured calls. Call 1 was an evidence issue. Call 3 was a criminal procedure/evidence cross-over, and calls 2 and 4 were criminal procedure (4th and 5th Amendment) questions. The issue in call 1 concerned whether a potential witness could read a newspaper article in court as evidence that he did not have an accent, without being sworn in. This call seemed to confuse many Bar candidates because they failed to recognize it as an evidence call as opposed to a criminal procedure call. The Federal Rules of Evidence expressly require every testifying witness to take an oath, therefore the underlying issue was whether by reading the article Dan would be providing testimonial evidence.

First, as the following model indicates, Dan's reading of the article is logically relevant because it would tend to prove or disprove his innocence. Therefore he is attempting to present evidence. Next, the newspaper reading identifies or absolves Dan. It is therefore equivalent to Dan saying "I am not the robber because I don't have an accent." As such, it is testimonial. Therefore an oath would be required.

Model Answer

1. Dave's Reading Aloud
Logical Relevance

Evidence is logically relevant if it has a tendency to make any fact of consequence more or less probable.

Dan is charged with robbery. Facts in evidence indicate the robber spoke with an accent. Whether Dan has an accent would be relevant as evidence to support or disprove that he was the robber. Dan's offer to read a newspaper to "demonstrate that he has no accent" is thus logically relevant evidence.

Oath or Affirmation

The Federal Rules of Evidence (FRE) require every witness, before testifying, to declare that he or she will testify truthfully by an oath or affirmation administered in a form calculated to awaken the witness' conscience and impress the witness' mind with the duty to do so. Witnesses are subject to cross-examination so that opposing counsel may show bias and challenge the witness' credibility and truthfulness.

Dan proposes to read a newspaper out loud without being sworn in as a witness or subjected to cross-examination. He is attempting to offer highly relevant evidence of his innocence without following the rules that require an oath and permit cross-examination. This motion is out of order and should be denied. It is possible that Dan was the robber and merely faked an accent at the crime scene. He must be required to take an oath as mandated by the FRE in order to awaken his conscience of the duty to be truthful. Moreover, it would be out of order to allow a witness to offer evidence without an opportunity for opposing counsel to show bias or lack of credibility through cross-examination.

The argument that Dan is offering non-testimonial evidence misses the point. The 5th Amendment protects criminal defendants from having to provide self-incriminating testimonial evidence but does not protect them from having to provide non-testimonial evidence. It is illogical to use the 5th Amendment in the converse to argue that as non-testimonial evidence, the newspaper reading can be offered without an oath. A better analysis is that the proffered newspaper reading is, in fact, testimonial because it presumably identifies (or absolves) Dan; it is tantamount to saying "I am not (or am) the robber."

2. The Currency

The 4th Amendment, applicable to the states via the 14th, protects against unreasonable searches, seizures, and arrests.

The currency was seized by Officer (O) from a briefcase that O opened after approaching D at gunpoint and handcuffing D, implicating the 4the Amendment.

For the 4th Amendment to apply there must be government action. Officer is a government actor, meeting this requirement.

To have standing to challenge a seizure under the 4th Amendment, the D must have a <u>reasonable expectation of privacy</u> in the item searched or seized. Dan's briefcase was closed so he has a reasonable expectation of privacy and thus has <u>standing</u> to challenge the search of the briefcase and seizure of the currency hidden inside.

Warrantless searches are per se unreasonable, absent an exception. No facts indicate O had a warrant. Unless there is a valid exception, the currency will be suppressed. One such exception would be search incident to a lawful arrest.

Search Incident to Lawful Arrest (SILA)

Public Arrest

An O can arrest a suspect in public without a warrant if the O has probable cause to believe a felony or a misdemeanor is being committed in O's presence.

The only thing O observed was D holding a briefcase in a downtown business district more than 90 minutes after an armed robbery. O's argument for probable cause rests on the reliability of an anonymous caller who described a man standing at a particular corner carrying a briefcase with a shotgun inside. D did in fact fit the description, but arguably many men carrying briefcases downtown would fit that description. O would have 48 hours to present the case to a judge and for the judge to establish probable cause. A detached magistrate will view the evidence as a whole and determine whether a substantial basis exists to find probable cause. The outcome would be a close call.

Assuming a lawful arrest, the search of the briefcase and seizure of the currency could fall under the search incident to a lawful arrest exception to the warrant requirement. This would require a lawful arrest and a contemporaneous search within the "wingspan" of the suspect.

Arguably, D was under arrest when the officer approached him with his service revolver drawn and explained the reason for the approach. When O handcuffed D, D was clearly in police custody. O opened the briefcase after handcuffing D, so the search was contemporaneous, and the briefcase was in D's possession and thus within the wingspan. O had reason to believe the briefcase contained a shotgun. Under this exception, the Supreme Court has held that it is reasonable to search the person for weapons and to search for and seize any evidence on the arrestee's person in order to prevent its concealment or destruction. O had reason to believe that the briefcase might contain a weapon or currency, either of which would be evidence of the crime. Therefore, O was justified in seizing the currency under this exception if the arrest was lawful. In addition, assuming D had not been arrested, the Supreme Court has held that a seizure prior to arrest is lawful as long as the fruits of the search were not necessary to support probable cause to arrest. In either case, the validity of the seizure of the currency hinges on whether O had probable cause to arrest. As indicated, this would be a close call.

Stop and Frisk

Even if the arrest is not found lawful, the currency may come in under the stop and frisk exception. This exception gives officers the right to detain and question suspects based on reasonable suspicion that criminal activity is afoot.

Even if the anonymous tip does not rise to the level of probable cause, it certainly provided sufficient reasonable suspicion because Dave fit the description given by the caller, had a briefcase, and was at the designated location within a relatively brief time after the robbery.

When an officer has reasonable suspicion, the officer may conduct a pat-down to search for weapons. Again, the policy is to protect the officer. Here, O did not conduct a pat-down. O opened a briefcase. This was hardly necessary for O's protection, given that D was cuffed, and in any case it exceeds the scope of the stop-and-frisk doctrine.

Conclusion: Unless within 48 hours of seizure of the currency a judge determined that there had been probable cause for an arrest independent of the currency, the currency will be suppressed.

3. Dave's Statement to O
The 5th Amendment, applicable to the states via the 14th Amendment, protects against compelled testimonial self-incrimination by government action.

Was Dave in Custody?
When O approached D with his service revolver drawn, D was in custody because D would not feel free to leave under these circumstances. When O handcuffed D, D was probably incapable of leaving. Thus, he was in custody.

Interrogation
The courts define interrogation as any conduct where the police knew or should have known they might elicit a damaging statement.

Officer, the government actor who placed D in custody, said to D, "I know you're the one who robbed the bank. Where is the shotgun?" O's statement, designed to elicit a statement about the whereabouts of the shotgun, qualifies as interrogation because it is designed to elicit a damaging statement. D, in fact, pointed to the shotgun, but did not say anything about the shotgun. Instead, D said "I knew all along that I'd be caught."

The prosecutor has two colorable arguments that O's conduct did not violate D's 5th Amendment rights.

Spontaneous Statement
O asked D where the gun was, not whether D committed the robbery or knew he would be caught. The prosecution may try to argue that because D's statement was not a direct reply to O's question about the shotgun, it was spontaneous and therefore not the result of custodial interrogation. This argument will fail, however, because at the point that O asked about the shotgun's whereabouts, any statement immediately made by D would be the result of O's statements to D.

Exception: Public Safety Doctrine
Assuming custodial interrogation, O had strong reason to believe that a dangerous weapon could be in close proximity, which would represent a risk to the public. O's

question about the gun was thus a matter of public safety because even with D handcuffed, a shotgun in the downtown area represents a danger to the public. Where the public safety is at issue, the Supreme Court has held that such interrogations do not violate a suspect's rights under *Miranda*.

Conclusion: D's statement would not be excluded under the 5th Amendment because of the public safety doctrine.

Right to Confrontation & Hearsay

The 6th Amendment guarantees a defendant the right to confront adverse testimony and provides the basis for excluding most out-of-court statements being offered for their truth against a defendant.

Hearsay

Hearsay is out-of-court statement offered for the truth of the matter asserted. Absent an exemption or exception, such statements are inadmissible.

Dave's statement was made in the downtown business district, and thus was out of court. Arguably, it is not being offered for its truth, that is that Dave knew he would be caught, but rather as evidence of D's belief that he committed the crime. If the out-of-court statement is not being offered for its truth, it is not considered hearsay and would be admissible.

Party Admission

Assuming the statement is being offered for its truth, it could come in as a party admission. A party's own admission, offered against a party, is exempted from the hearsay rule and is non-hearsay.

Here, D made the statement that "I knew I'd get caught," and it is being used against him, so it should be exempted as non-hearsay because it qualifies as a party admission.

Testimonial Hearsay

Recently (March 2004), the Supreme Court has held that testimonial hearsay is inadmissible in criminal trials unless D gets the right to confrontation (*Crawford*). At a minimum, testimonial hearsay includes prior testimony, grand jury testimony, and police interrogation.

Pursuant to his 5th Amendment right not to be compelled to incriminate himself, D has elected not to testify. Consequently, he is unavailable as a witness. Further, his statement most likely will be seen as the product of police interrogation, which is testimonial. However, because the statement is a party admission it is non-hearsay and would not be considered inadmissible under a *Crawford* analysis.

Conclusion: D's statement may be admissible as non-hearsay because it is a party admission.

4. The Shotgun

5th Amendment

The 5th Amendment, applicable to the states via the 14th Amendment, protects citizens from compelled testimonial self-incrimination. D may try a number of legal theories to exclude the shotgun. However, he pointed to the gun, and the 5th Amendment protects only against testimonial communications. Pointing is non-testimonial and would therefore not be covered by the 5th Amendment.

Inevitable Discovery

Further, even if the discovery was the result of unlawful police conduct, it would likely come in anyway under the <u>inevitable discovery doctrine</u>. Given that the shotgun was in a nearby trash container in a heavily populated area, it most certainly would have been found.

D Lacks Standing

D's biggest problem is that he lacks <u>standing</u> to challenge the shotgun. One does not have a reasonable expectation of privacy in a public trash can. In fact, the Supreme Court has specifically held that there is no reasonable expectation of privacy in garbage. Therefore, D lacks standing, and the shotgun is inadmissible.

FEBRUARY 2003 CALIFORNIA BAR EXAM -- QUESTION 3

1-HOUR ESSAY

Don was a passenger in Vic's car. While driving in a desolate mountain area, Vic stopped and offered Don an hallucinogenic drug. Don refused, but Vic said if Don wished to stay in the car, he would have to join Vic in using the drug. Fearing that he would be abandoned in freezing temperatures many miles from the nearest town, Don ingested the drug.

[handwritten: Duress]

While under the influence of the drug, Don killed Vic, left the body beside the road, and drove Vic's car to town. Later he was arrested by police officers who had discovered Vic's body. Don has no recall of the events between the time he ingested the drug and his arrest.

[handwritten: Intent — Involuntary Intoxication]

After Don was arraigned on a charge of first degree murder, the police learned that Wes had witnessed the killing. Aware that Don had been arraigned and was scheduled for a preliminary hearing at the courthouse on that day, police officers took Wes to the courthouse for the express purpose of having him attempt to identify the killer from photographs of several suspects. As Wes walked into the courthouse with one of the officers, he encountered Don and his lawyer. Without any request by the officer, Wes told the officer he recognized Don as the killer. Don's attorney was advised of Wes's statement to the officer, of the circumstances in which it was made, and of the officer's expected testimony at trial that Wes had identified Don in this manner.

[handwritten margin: Identification Photo]

Don moved to exclude evidence of the courthouse identification by Wes on grounds that the identification procedure violated Don's federal constitutional rights to counsel and due process of law and that the officer's testimony about the identification would be inadmissible hearsay. The court denied the motion.

At trial, Don testified about the events preceding Vic's death and his total lack of recall of the killing.

1. Did the court err in denying Don's motion? Discuss.

2. If the jury believes Don's testimony, can it properly convict Don of:
   (a) First degree murder? Discuss.
   (b) Second degree murder? Discuss.

FEBRUARY 2003, QUESTION 3
CRIMES

-- Written by Dennis P. Saccuzzo & Nancy E. Johnson

Commentary:

The following question called for an analysis of criminal procedure (6th amendment and due process), hearsay, homicide, and the defenses of duress and involuntary intoxication. The sheer breadth of issues made this question particularly challenging. To complicate matters, there was a complex interaction between the two defenses of duress and intoxication. Whereas duress is not a defense to homicide, involuntary intoxication is. However, to prove involuntary intoxication in this case, one had to prove duress. As a result, there were numerous possible answers depending on which way you came down on each issue. This is typical of Bar essay fact patterns.

It is not unusual that the fact pattern confronts the candidate with murky or unsettled law. The point is that Bar examiners are not so much interested in any particular conclusion. Instead, they are examining your ability to write in a lawyer-like manner, which means you reason logically and confidently from a premise to a conclusion using the stipulated facts.

There were a few points of law and some issues of approach (form) that caused candidates to lose points on this fact pattern. First, it is important to remember that before the 6th Amendment right to counsel applies, there must be a felony or proceeding resulting in actual loss of liberty. In this case, Don was charged with a felony. Next, the right then <u>attaches</u> at critical stages, as enumerated in the model answer.

Regarding hearsay, it is always necessary to first show that the statement was in fact made out of court by expressly stating in your answer where or when the out-of-court statement was made. More importantly, it is essential to search for exemptions, exceptions, and/or exclusions. An interesting point regarding the prior identification exemption is that the California Bar has consistently included in their selected answers those that do not point out that a third party can testify as to a declarant's prior identification only if the declarant is available and subject to cross-examination. Indeed, although the federal rules themselves are silent on the matter, several hornbooks state that the declarant must testify at trial and be subject to cross on the identification in order for the exemption to apply to a third party witness (usually a police officer).

Many Bar candidates showed considerable confusion concerning homicide. Remember, as the following model illustrates, that the first step in determining whether there has been a first or second degree murder is to establish the common law elements of murder (actus reus, causation, and mens rea). Each of the four types of mens rea – malice – must be analyzed. First degree murder is created by statute: all other forms of murder are then second degree.

Call 1. Don's Motion to Exclude Evidence of the Courthouse Identification by Wes

Constitutional Right to Counsel

The 6th Amendment right to counsel is guaranteed and therefore applies in all felonies and in any action resulting in an actual loss of liberty. When these circumstances exist, the right to counsel attaches at critical stages including adversarial preliminary hearings, post-indictment interrogations, post-indictment line-ups (but not at photo showings), arraignment, and pleadings in court. Don is charged with murder, a felony crime, therefore the 6th Amendment right to counsel attaches.

Facts indicate that Don had already been arraigned on a charge of first degree murder and was at the courthouse for a preliminary hearing. Although he was not yet in the hearing when Wes identified him, what occurred was more akin to a line-up in which Don was the only suspect, rather than the scheduled photo showing. Although no right to counsel attaches for a photo showing, the right to counsel does attach in a line-up. Therefore, a critical stage has been reached, Don's right to counsel attaches, and he has a 6th Amendment right to counsel. However, when Wes encountered and identified Don at the courthouse, Don's lawyer was also present. Because Don had representation at the time of the identification, his right to counsel was not violated and the court did not err in denying Don's motion to exclude the evidence of the courthouse identification by Wes on the grounds that the identification violated Don's federal constitutional right to counsel.

Constitutional Due Process

There is a denial of the right to due process when a pre-trial identification is unnecessarily suggestive such that there is a substantial likelihood of misidentification.

When the police took Wes to the courthouse, they knew that Don had been arraigned and was scheduled for a preliminary hearing at the courthouse on that day. The police's express purpose of having Wes identify photographs of several suspects is suspicious. Normally, photo showings are done at the police station, and the police should have known that there was a possibility, if not a strong likelihood, that Wes would encounter Don at the courthouse. The result was similar to what is known as a "show-up" in which the police bring the witness only to the suspect. The underlying circumstances (police awareness), suspicious conditions (in the courthouse) and show-up-like procedure make the identification highly suggestive and thus a violation of Don's due process rights. Therefore, the court erred in denying Don's motion to suppress the courthouse identification on the grounds that it violated Don's due process rights.

Hearsay

Hearsay is an out of court statement offered for the truth of the matter asserted. Wes was in the courthouse entry when he told the officer he recognized Don as the killer. The statement was therefore made out of court. It is being offered for its truth, namely that Don was in fact the killer. Therefore, the statement is hearsay and absent an exception or exclusion, it will be inadmissible.

Exemption: Prior Identification

A prior identification of a person after perceiving the person is exempted from the hearsay rule. The in-court witness need not be the declarant as long as the declarant is available and subject to cross examination concerning the identification.

Wes' statement to Officer that Don was the killer was an identification of Don and, as such, Officer's expected testimony qualifies as a prior identification. If Wes is available and subject to cross examination concerning his identification, the officer's statement would be exempted from the hearsay rule and therefore admissible.

Exception: Present Sense Impression

A statement describing or explaining an event while perceiving the event or immediately thereafter is an exception to the hearsay rule. Here, the event at issue was the recognition of Don as the murderer by Wes. Facts indicate that without any request by the officer, Wes spontaneously told the officer he recognized Don as the killer. Wes therefore described the event of his recognition while he was perceiving Don. Therefore, the statement also comes in as a present sense impression.

Exception: Excited Utterance

This exception to the hearsay rule requires a startling event. The statement in question must be made under the stress of the event and related to the event.

Arguably, when Wes encountered Don in the courthouse, he was startled. First, no facts indicate that Wes expected to see Don. Second, most people would be startled to come face to face with a killer: Wes would be especially startled because it was Wes who actually witnessed the killing, and he walked into the courthouse expecting to see only a set of photographs. Moreover, Wes' statement that Don was the killer was made spontaneously, without any request by the officer. Assuming the statement was made in close proximity to the identification, Wes would have still been under the stress of the event. Finally, the statement of identification was related to the event. In fact, the statement was the event. The statement would, therefore, also be admissible as an excited utterance.

Call 2. Convicting Don

Homicide

A homicide is the killing of a human being by another. Facts stipulate that Don killed Vic, left the body beside the road, and drove Vic's car to town, and that Wes witnessed the killing. Because there was a killing of Vic by Don, there was a homicide. The issue is whether Don can be convicted of first or second degree murder. The prosecution must show causation and mens rea and meet the criteria for first or second degree murder, and Don must have no defenses.

Causation

Don's conduct must be both the actual and proximate cause of Vic's death. To show actual cause the courts use a "but for" test: but for Don's actions, Vic would not have died. To show proximate cause, courts use a foreseeability test to determine whether it is foreseeable that Don's conduct would cause Vic's death.

No facts go to the method of the homicide. However, because it is stipulated that Don killed Vic, it would appear that Don's conduct was the "but for" cause and that the death was foreseeable. Further, it can be argued that but for Don's taking an hallucinogenic drug, he would not have killed Don, and that it is foreseeable that if one takes such a drug, a killing might result. Therefore, the prosecution should have no trouble showing that Don was both the actual and proximate cause of Vic's death.

Mens Rea (Malice)

For a finding of first or second degree murder there must be a finding of at least one of four types of malice: (1) intent to kill; (2) intent to do serious bodily injury; (3) wanton/depraved heart, and (4) felony murder, which is a death caused in the commission or attempt of an inherently dangerous felony. Once one of the forms of malice is found, then the distinction between first and second degree murder depends on whether the specific criteria for first degree murder are met. If they are not, then the killing would be considered a second degree murder.

Intent to Kill

No facts indicate intent to kill. In fact, Don has no recall of the event. Even if such intent might be raised by Wes' testimony, it may, as discussed below, be excused by Don's intoxication.

Intent to do Serious Bodily Injury

Again, because Don has no memory and Wes' testimony is unknown, no facts support this mens rea.

Wanton/Depraved Heart

While Don was a passenger in Vic's car, Vic stopped and offered Don an hallucinogenic drug. Don refused. Had Don accepted the drug voluntarily and then killed Vic, his act of taking a dangerous drug when the possible consequences of such conduct are so well known would have been consistent with this form of malice. However, Don did not take the drug until Vic said that Don would have to take it if he wished to stay in the car and Don feared he would be abandoned in freezing temperatures many miles from the nearest town.

As discussed below, at this point Don was faced with a choice of evils. He decided to take the drug and later killed Vic. It is possible that a jury could find that Don should have refused the drug and that his conduct reflects wanton/depraved heart.

Felony Murder

The inherently dangerous felonies that form the predicate mens rea for first degree felony murder are burglary, arson, rape, robbery, mayhem, kidnapping, sodomy, and sexual molest. Even if Don's taking of the drug had been a felony without defenses, the conduct is not among the enumerated felonies. Therefore first degree felony murder will not apply.

If taking the drug had been a felony without defenses, then second degree felony murder would apply because the underlying felony was not an enumerated one.

However, Don has a valid defense (duress) to the underlying felony, as discussed below. A defense to the underlying felony is a complete defense to felony murder.

First Degree Murder

To qualify for first degree murder, the killing must occur in the context of a felony murder, involve poison, bomb, torture, or ambush, or be premeditated. No facts indicate any of the above conduct. In the unlikely event that premeditation could be shown, the specific intent to kill Vic could be negated by Don's intoxication. Thus, it is extremely unlikely that Don could be convicted of first degree murder.

Second Degree Murder

Second degree murder is the intentional killing of another with malice aforethought. All homicides in which one of the four types of malice is found and which are not first degree murder are second degree murder. As indicated, a jury could find wanton/depraved heart. If so, then absent a defense, Don would be found guilty of second degree murder.

Defenses:

Duress

Under the common law, the defense of duress was shown when there was an imminent threat that would cause a reasonable person justifiable apprehension of death or serious bodily injury. The threat can be directed at the defendant or his family and the situation creating the coercion cannot be the defendant's fault. Duress is a defense to all crimes except homicide.

Don's duress defense goes to his ingestion of the drug and would be a complete defense to felony violation of drug laws. However, he is being charged with murder, not violation of drug laws. The real issue is whether the duress was sufficient such that Don can claim that his intoxication was involuntary.

Don's fear that induced him to take the drug was that he would be abandoned in freezing temperature many miles from the nearest town. Such abandonment would create a justifiable apprehension of death or serious bodily injury because Don could have frozen to death or suffered serious frostbite resulting in loss of extremities. Therefore, Don took the drug under duress.

Intoxication

Intoxication is <u>involuntary</u> if a defendant is unaware he has taken an intoxicating substance, takes the substance under medical advice without knowing its intoxicating effects, or takes the substance under duress. As discussed above, Don took the hallucinogenic drug under duress. Involuntary intoxication is a defense to all crimes, including homicide.

For <u>voluntary</u> intoxication to be a defense, it must negate an element of a crime, such as premeditation. For <u>involuntary</u> intoxication, the intoxication need not necessarily negate an element of a crime. Instead, the intoxication must produce a state of insanity such that the individual did not know the wrongfulness of his actions or could not conform his conduct to the law, depending on the jurisdiction. An hallucinogenic drug, by definition, causes people to see or hear things that do not exist, thereby greatly impairing the user. In this case, Don does not even have a recall of the events between the time he ingested the drug and his arrest, and the jury believes him. Therefore, the jury must believe that Don was seriously impaired and probably met the requirements of the insanity test. As such, Don will have a complete defense.

Conclusion: Don cannot be convicted of first or second degree murder. First, he ingested the drug under duress, which would negate a theory of wanton/depraved heart and support his involuntary intoxication defense. Second, Don has a strong involuntary intoxication defense, given the seriously impairing effects of hallucinogenic drugs.

FEBRUARY 2000 CALIFORNIA BAR EXAM -- QUESTION 6

1-HOUR ESSAY

A Picasso sketch was taken from Town museum by a burglar. The sketch was recovered three weeks later when an art dealer in Switzerland read about the theft. The dealer recognized the sketch described in the article as the sketch he had purchased from a young woman with an American accent.

Police had been unable to identify the burglar or match fingerprints found at the scene of the theft. Sally is a petty thief with convictions for burglary. Tec, a Town police investigator, believed Sally had knowledge of the theft. He decided to trick Sally into providing information. Tec went to Sally's home, told her he was arresting her for _False Arrest_ the museum burglary and theft and handcuffed her. After Tec advised Sally of her _Miranda_ rights, Sally immediately replied: "Hey, come on. I didn't do the museum job. Donna did. She told me she broke in and took a drawing. She said she sold it in _Fruits of the poisonous tree_ Switzerland." _Hearsay_

Based on Sally's information, the grand jury issued a subpoena ordering Donna to appear, submit to fingerprinting, and produce her passport. After the court denied Donna's motion to quash the subpoena and ordered her to comply, she submitted to fingerprinting and turned over her passport. Her fingerprints were found to match those in the museum. Her passport bore a date stamp showing that the holder had entered Switzerland two days after the museum burglary.

Sally has left town and cannot be located. Donna has been charged with burglary and theft. _Unavailable_

Donna moved to exclude the following evidence:

(1) Sally's statement to Tec, which Donna claims: (a) is hearsay, the admission of which would violate her rights under the Sixth Amendment, and (b) was obtained in violation of Sally's rights under the Fourth Amendment;

(2) The fingerprints she provided, which Donna claims were obtained in violation of her rights under the Fifth Amendment and are the "fruits" of an unlawful search and seizure; and

(3) Donna's passport, which she claims was obtained in violation of her rights under the Fifth Amendment.

What should the prosecutor argue in opposition to Donna's motions, and how should the court rule on each? Discuss.

Written by Professor Dennis P. Saccuzzo

Call 1 – Sally's Statement to Tec

A. Hearsay and Sixth Amendment Rights

The Sixth Amendment protects the rights of a criminal defendant to confront adverse witnesses. Here, Sally's statement to Tec is being used against Donna, and Sally is unavailable because she left town and cannot be located.

Hearsay

Hearsay is an out of court statement offered to prove the truth of the matter asserted. Sally's statement to Tec was made out of court in Sally's home. It is being offered for its truth, that is, to show it was Donna who took the drawings. Therefore it is hearsay and absent an exception or exemption it will be inadmissible.

Sally's statement to Tec is actually hearsay within hearsay. Sally is repeating what Donna told her, but the issue is what Sally said to Tec. To be admissible it will be necessary to find an exception or exemption for each level of hearsay.

1. Donna to Sally – Admission by a Party Opponent. A party's own admission, if offered against her is exempted from the hearsay rule under the FRE. Here, Donna's statement to Sally is being used against Donna. Sally claims that Donna told her that Donna broke in and took the drawing. Donna admitted to the crime and her statement to Sally qualifies as a party admission and therefore is admissible.

2. Sally's Statement to Tec. Sally's statement to Tec will be more problematic for the prosecution. The prosecutor might try declaration against interest. This exception to hearsay requires (1) that the witness be unavailable, (2) a statement against financial or penal interest; (3) against interest when made and (4) a reasonable person would not make unless she believed it to be true.

Although Sally is unavailable (as discussed above) it would be a stretch to say that Sally's statement that Donna did it was against Sally's interest. While it can be argued that the statement did show Sally's knowledge of the crime and possible criminal liability as an accessory, Sally was in fact trying to exonerate herself. The court is unlikely to accept the prosecutor's argument.

The prosecutor might also try the excited utterance exception. This requires a statement made following a startling event. The statement must be made under the stress of the event and related to it.

Although Sally may have been startled by Tec's arrest and handcuffing, it would be a stretch to say her accusations against Donna meet the spirit of "related to the event." The court is unlikely to accept the prosecutor's argument.

Conclusion: Sally's statement to Tec is most likely to be ruled hearsay without an exception. Because it does not fall within a reliable exception to the hearsay rule, its admission into evidence would violate Donna's Sixth Amendment right to confrontation.

B. Sally's Fourth Amendment Rights

The Fourth Amendment applies to the states via the 14th Amendment and protects against unreasonable searches and seizures. It requires government conduct and a reasonable expectation of privacy.

1. Government Conduct and Warrant Requirement. Here there is government conduct because Tec is a police investigator. Further, a home arrest requires a warrant or an exception to the warrant requirement. Facts indicate that Tec did not have a warrant. In fact, he did not even have probable cause. Instead, facts stipulate that Tec decided to trick Sally into providing information. This is a clear violation of Sally's Fourth Amendment rights.

2. Reasonable Expectation of Privacy and Standing. The prosecutor will successfully argue that Donna did not have a reasonable expectation of privacy in Sally's house. To assert one's Fourth Amendment rights one must have standing, which requires a reasonable expectation of privacy in the thing seized or area searched. Tec was in Sally's home; Sally must assert the right. Because Donna lacks standing, she will be unable to assert a Fourth Amendment right.

Call 2 – The Fingerprints

A. Fifth Amendment Rights

The Fifth Amendment applies to the states via the 14th Amendment and protects against compelled self-incrimination. However, this right applies only to testimonial communications. Physical evidence is excluded.

Here, the issue is whether Donna's fingerprints violate her Fifth Amendment rights. They do not, because fingerprints are not testimonial; they are physical evidence. The Supreme Court has held that even blood samples are physical evidence, the taking of which does not violate the Fifth Amendment. Indeed, the police routinely take fingerprints of suspects. Thus, Sally's Fifth Amendment rights were not violated.

B. Fruits of an Unlawful Search

As discussed above, the subpoena ordering Donna to appear was based in larger part on Tec's illegal false arrest of Sally. Nevertheless, Donna's claim of a Fourth Amendment violation will fail.

First, one of the limitations of the exclusionary rule is grand jury proceedings. The Supreme Court has held that grand juries can make use of illegally obtained evidence. Second, as indicated, Donna has a problem asserting a Fourth Amendment right because of her lack of standing. Finally, Donna has no reasonable expectation of privacy in her fingerprints. Her claim will therefore fail.

Call 3 – The Passport

Donna will argue that requiring her to turn over her passport also violates her Fifth Amendment right against compelled self-incrimination. This claim will be a bit more difficult for the prosecutor because of the argument that the act of producing the passport itself is communicative. Donna will argue that producing the passport will cause Donna to admit tacitly to the crime. This argument will fail. First, the passport is physical; it is not a testimonial statement. Second, although the passport is strong circumstantial evidence against Donna, it itself is not direct evidence that Donna had committed a crime. The passport merely shows Donna had the opportunity to commit the crime because she entered Switzerland two days after the burglary.

Conclusion: The court should admit the passport.

JULY 1999 CALIFORNIA BAR EXAM -- QUESTION 1

1-HOUR ESSAY

Conspiracy

Al, Bob, and Charlie planned to bring 50 cases of whiskey ashore from a ship anchored in the harbor near their town and sell it to a local bar owner. They believed the whiskey had been produced abroad and was subject to a federal import duty. They also knew that smuggling items into this country without paying duty required by the Tariff Act is a crime. In fact, however, the whiskey in this shipment had been produced in the United States.

The three met at Al's house on Monday and agreed to bring the whiskey ashore by row-boat on Friday night. On Wednesday, however, Bob called Al to say that he and his wife were going to visit relatives that weekend and Bob would not be able to help bring the whiskey ashore. Al said that was all right, that he and Charlie could handle the boat and the whiskey, but that Bob would naturally be cut out of the profits on this job.

Broke-off

When Charlie learned from Al that there would be just the two of them he became apprehensive, but was afraid of what Al might do to him if he tried to back out. Therefore, on Thursday, Charlie informed the police of Al's plan and did not show up on Friday night. Al was arrested on Friday night as he came ashore, alone, with the whiskey and was loading it into a truck he had stolen from a nearby Coast Guard parking lot.

Duress

Al, Bob, and Charlie have been charged with theft of the truck and conspiracy to import dutiable goods without payment of duty.

Al has been charged with attempt to import dutiable goods without payment of duty. He has told Len, his attorney, that he plans to testify that he knew all along that the whiskey was produced in the United States.

Based on the above facts:

1. Should Al, Bob or Charlie be convicted of:
    (a) Conspiracy to violate the Tariff Act? Discuss.
    (b) Theft of the truck? Discuss

2. Should Al be convicted of attempt to import dutiable goods without payment of duty in violation of the Tariff Act? Discuss.

3. If Al insists on testifying that he knew the whiskey was produced in the United States, what, if anything, should Len do? Discuss.

P.R.

CRIMINAL LAW/PROFESSIONAL RESPONSIBILITY

July 1999 California Bar – Question 1

Model Answer Written by Professor Dennis P. Saccuzzo

CALL 1 – Should Al, Bob, or Charlie be convicted of

(a) Conspiracy

Conspiracy is an agreement between 2 or more people to commit an unlawful act. At common law it required (1) an agreement; (2) intent to agree; and (3) intent to achieve the unlawful purpose. Today, the Federal Courts and a majority of states require an <u>overt act</u> in furtherance of the conspiracy. However, the law is unsettled because there is wide variation among the jurisdictions about what constitutes an overt act, and in some states forming the agreement qualifies as an act.

The facts indicate that Al, Bob, and Charlie met at Al's house and <u>agreed</u> to bring whiskey ashore. They believed the whiskey had been produced abroad and knew smuggling such items without paying the duty was a crime. Thus all three agreed to commit an unlawful purpose and had the specific intent to commit the crime. That they intended to agree is shown by their plan to bring the whiskey ashore by boat on Friday. Their knowledge that the planned act was illegal and goal to profit reveals their intent to commit the unlawful purpose. Thus, under the common law all three are guilty of conspiracy. Individual liability for the three may vary, however, depending on whether they are being tried in a jurisdiction requiring an overt act and whether they effectively withdrew from the conspiracy.

Withdrawal and Overt Act Requirement

In the majority of states, withdrawal requires an affirmative act inconsistent with the objectives of the conspiracy that is communicated to the other co-conspirators in time for them to effectively abandon the conspiracy. In states requiring an over act, to withdraw generally requires that the defendant neutralize the crime, such as by informing the police. The withdrawal defense generally does not apply to criminal liability for the conspiracy, but does relieve the defendant of liability for future crimes by co-conspirators.

Al

Al's liability for conspiracy depends upon whether there was an overt act and when both Bob and Charlie effectively withdrew. If there was an overt act and either Bob or Charlie did not effectively withdraw, Al is liable for conspiracy. As discussed below, Al would be found liable for conspiracy.

Bob

On Wednesday, Bob called Al to say he would not be able to help bring the whiskey ashore. Bob will argue that he withdrew before there was any overt act, and therefore is not guilty of conspiracy. This argument will fail.

First, it can be argued that meeting at Al's house was a sufficient act in furtherance, or that calling to tell Al he wouldn't be able to help was also an act. In the majority of states, just about any act that furthers the conspiracy will do, and by informing his co-conspirator that he wouldn't be there, Bob gave Al time to prepare for Bob's absence. Further, arguably Bob's act was <u>not</u> inconsistent with the object of the conspiracy. Bob did not repudiate the conspiracy. He merely said he wouldn't be able to help bring whiskey ashore. As a result, Al said he would not be entitled to profits <u>on this job</u>. Finally, Bob never informed Charlie.

Impossibility

Discussed in greater detail below, Al, Bob, and Charlie will argue that what they were conspiring to do was not a crime. This defense will fail because impossibility is not a defense to conspiracy.

Conclusion: The evidence indicates a sufficient overt act took place before Bob's purported withdrawal, and even if there wasn't, Bob's withdrawal was not sufficient to constitute a valid defense. Bob will be found guilty of conspiracy along with Al.

Charlie

Charlie withdrew by telling the police. However, the same arguments concerning overt act discussed above apply to Charlie. The alleged co-conspirators "met" at Al's house and there was a phone call by Bob to Al that arguably assisted Al's planning. Moreover, Charlie did not inform his companions of his withdrawal. However, Charlie did take affirmative steps to repudiate the conspiracy and neutralize it by going to the police on Thursday, a day before the planned crime. Unfortunately for Charlie, in the majority of jurisdictions he still will be liable for conspiracy, but will not be liable for future crimes that occurred after he went to the police. Under the minority Model Penal Code, Charlie's going to the police and neutralizing the crime would relieve him from liability for conspiracy.

A <u>duress</u> defense will not work. Duress requires a threat of death or serious bodily harm as well as coercion and the situation creating coercion must not be D's fault. Here, Charlie was merely apprehensive, afraid of what Al might do. While he may have feared for his life, no facts indicate coercion, and this situation was as much Charlie's fault as anybody's because he met and agreed to commit the unlawful purpose.

(b) Theft of the Truck

Co-conspirators are liable for all crimes of other conspirators if the crime is foreseeable and in furtherance of the conspiracy.

Al

Facts stipulate that Al stole the truck from a nearby Coast Guard parking lot and loaded the whiskey on the truck. Al is guilty as the principal, and his crime was in furtherance of the conspiracy because he used the truck to perpetrate the crime.

Bob

As discussed, Bob did not effectively withdraw. He is a co-conspirator. It is foreseeable that Al would steal a truck to transport the whiskey, and, as indicated, the theft was in furtherance of the conspiracy. Thus, Bob will also be guilty of the theft.

Charlie

Charlie's liability for the theft will depend on when Al stole the truck. Charlie withdrew on Thursday. If Al stole the truck before Charlie withdrew, he will be liable for theft of the truck. Circumstantial evidence suggests the truck was stolen on Friday night, and if so, Charlie will not be liable for the theft.

CALL 2. Should Al be Convicted of Attempt?

Attempt

Attempt is a substantial act toward the perpetration of an intended crime. It requires specific intent to commit the crime and a substantial step beyond mere preparation.

Specific Intent

The facts stipulate that Al planned to bring 50 cases of the whiskey ashore believing the whiskey had been produced abroad and therefore subject to a federal import duty. His intent is demonstrated by his knowledge of the illegality, plan, and purpose, which was to profit by avoiding the tax. Therefore Al had the specific intent to smuggle items into the country without paying a duty in violation of the Tariff Act.

Substantial Step

Al followed his plan. On Friday night he came ashore with the whiskey. In furtherance of this plan he stole a truck from a nearby Coast Guard parking lot and loaded the whiskey into the truck.

Absent a defense, Al should be convicted of attempt.

Legal versus Factual Impossibility

Factual impossibility is a mistake concerning an issue of fact that makes commission of the crime impossible. The crime could have occurred only had the facts been as the defendant thought.

Legal impossibility is a mistake about how a crime is defined. This defense arises when a defendant engages in conduct he believes is illegal but which is not.

Legal impossibility is a defense to attempt; factual impossibility is not. It is frequently difficult to distinguish the two, and Al will no doubt argue legal impossibility. His argument will fail.

The facts stipulate that Al knew that smuggling items into this country without paying a duty is a violation of the Tariff Act. Further, he believed the whiskey that he smuggled ashore on Friday was subject to an import duty. Therefore he had the specific intent to violate the Tariff Act. This is a factual impossibility. Had the facts been as Al had assumed, his action would have been a crime. Thus, this is a case of factual impossibility and is no defense.

Conclusion: Al should be convicted of attempt.

<u>Merger</u>

Al can be convicted of conspiracy, attempt, and theft. Conspiracy does not merge with attempt, and the theft of the truck was a separate crime in furtherance of the conspiracy.

CALL 3. What Should Len Do?

Competence

Len has a duty to be reasonably competent. Assuming Len knows that Al's testimony is perjury, relevant law and rules of professional responsibility will guide Len's conduct in this conflict.

Conflict of Duties

Len has a duty of loyalty to his client to be a zealous advocate. However, rules of professional responsibility state that while an attorney abides with a client's objectives and consults on the means, an attorney owes a duty of candor to the tribunal and cannot engage in conduct that would violate a law or a rule of professional responsibility.

Candor to the Tribunal

An attorney may not make a false statement or omit a material fact in interactions with the tribunal. Under the ABA rules, when a client plans to perjure himself, a lawyer should take the following steps:

(a) Counsel the client not to testify; for example, Len could advise Al of his 5th Amendment right not to incriminate himself as well as the penalties of perjury.

(b) <u>Try to withdraw</u>. According to the rules of professional responsibility, withdrawal is mandatory where the lawyer will violate a model rule or law. Allowing Al to perjure himself is tantamount to suborning perjury as well as a violation of several rules including <u>misconduct</u> (that is, lawyer will not engage in conduct involving dishonesty, fraud, deceit, or misrepresentation). Unfortunately for Len, the judge is unlikely to allow Len to withdraw if the representation has gone too far or Al's trial is in progress.

(c) Under the ABA rules, the lawyer would then be advised to breach confidentiality and tell the judge. Authority for this rule is the case in *Nix*, in which an attorney threatened to breach confidentiality if the defendant perjured himself. However, the rules in California are contra.

(d) California Rules.

In California, if the defendant insists on testifying and the lawyer cannot withdraw, the lawyer is advised

(1) To do nothing to further the deception.

(2) Not to ask questions or assist; for example, Len would allow Al to take the stand but would not use the usual direct exam. Instead, he would allow Al to give his testimony as a narrative.

(3) Omit references to the perjured testimony (as if stricken).

In the remainder of the trial, and in his closing statements, Len must not make any references to the perjured testimony.

Information gained from a constitutionally proper wiretap gave law enforcement agents a reasonable suspicion that Deft was a cash courier in a money laundering scheme associated with distribution of narcotics. To obtain probable cause to arrest Deft and to build their case against other participants, the agents placed Deft under surveillance. They saw her drive into an office park complex and legally park the car. She left a male companion in the car and walked into the complex carrying a soft cloth briefcase. As she walked, Deft engaged in evasive actions the agents recognized as moves designed either to reveal or lose any potential surveillance.

Deft walked into a building where the agents lost sight of her for a few moments. When she emerged and approached the car, it became apparent to the agents that she was aware of the surveillance. The agents approached Deft and asked her questions about the money laundering scheme. During this conversation, agent Able seized and squeezed the briefcase held by Deft. When he felt a lump he could not identify, Able reached into the briefcase and felt a heavily taped bound object about three inches in diameter which he removed from the briefcase. Able will testify that he has seen such objects in the past, and they frequently contained drugs. Able cut the package open and discovered a substance that a field test indicated was cocaine. He arrested Deft.

Without *Miranda* advice and waivers, Able asked Deft if she owned an automobile. She replied that she did and pointed to the car the agents had seen her park. She refused Able's request that she consent to a search of the car. The agents nonetheless searched the car, finding a loaded handgun concealed under the dashboard.

Deft is awaiting trial on charges of possession with intent to distribute cocaine and unlawful possession of a handgun.

On what grounds under the United States Constitution might Deft move to suppress:

1. The narcotics? Discuss.

2. Deft's statement that she owned the car? Discuss.

3. The handgun? Discuss.

February 1999 – Question 2

Written by Professor Dennis P. Saccuzzo

Call 1 – The Narcotics

Fourth Amendment

The Fourth Amendment applies to the states via the 14th Amendment and protects against unreasonable searches, seizures and arrests. For the Fourth Amendment to apply there must be government conduct and a reasonable expectation of privacy.

Government Conduct and Expectation of Privacy

Here Deft was approached by law enforcement officers. The officers asked her questions and seized and squeezed her briefcase. Without a warrant they subsequently reached into the briefcase and removed an object. Because the law enforcement officers are agents of the government, there was government conduct.

The issue is did Deft have a reasonable expectation of privacy in her briefcase. Normally, briefcases are closed, as was the case here, so its contents are not openly accessible to public view. Therefore Deft had a reasonable expectation of privacy.

Conclusion: The Fourth Amendment Applies

Warrantless Search

The Supreme Court has held that under the Fourth Amendment warrantless searches are per se unreasonable, absent an exception.

Under the facts the government agents did not have a warrant. Warrants require probable cause, and the facts stipulate that the agents had only reasonable suspicion based on a legal wiretap, and had observed Deft take evasive action while she was under surveillance.

Because the search was warrantless, absent an exception it will not be legal under the Fourth Amendment and the evidence derived from the search will be excluded.

Exception to Warrantless Search: Stop and Frisk

A well established exception to the warrant requirement is the stop and frisk exception. This exception, known as a Terry Stop, allows the police the right to detain and question an individual based on articulable reasonable suspicion that criminal activity is afoot.

Articulable Reasonable Suspicion

The agents already had reasonable suspicion that Deft was a cash courier in a money laundering scheme associated with narcotics based on a constitutionally proper wiretap. This suspicion was confirmed and enhanced when Deft engaged in evasive actions that the agents recognized as moves designed either to reveal or lose any potential surveillance.

Because the police had ample articulable facts to form a reasonable suspicion, they were within their authority to stop her and ask her questions.

Seizure of the Object

The next issue is whether the seizure of the 3 inch object was proper. Under the stop and frisk exception, the police may conduct a pat down of the individual if they suspect that she is armed or carrying contraband. Brief property seizures are also valid if the police have suspicion that they contain evidence or contraband.

The issue is whether Able had reasonable suspicion that Deft's briefcase contained a firearm, evidence, or contraband. When Able seized and squeezed the briefcase he reasonably could have believed the briefcase contained a gun because money laundering involving narcotics is dangerous and criminals involved in these activities may carry guns for protection. Further, he may have believed the briefcase contained money or narcotics.

The problem here is that Able could not identify the lump he felt. Therefore, he lacked articulable reasonable suspicion to proceed further and his actions exceeded the present constitutional limits of the stop and frisk doctrine.

However, if the court finds Able had the right to continue, then the fact that he had seen such objects before in the past and that they frequently contained drugs would have provided the additional suspicion he needed to proceed with the search that ultimately led to the discovery of the drugs.

Conclusion: Under the present limits of the stop and frisk doctrine, Able exceeded his constitutional authority and the narcotics must be suppressed.

Call 2 – Deft's Statement That She Owned the Car

Fifth Amendment: Miranda

The Fifth Amendment applies to the states via the 14th Amendment and protects against compelled testimonial incrimination. Under the rule in Miranda, the police may not conduct a custodial interrogation without first advising the suspect of her rights. Here, Deft was asked if she owned an automobile without a Miranda warning.

Custody

The standard for custody is that the suspect does not feel free to leave. Facts stipulate that Deft's statement was made after she was arrested. Because one would not feel free to leave after being arrested, Deft was in custody.

Interrogation

Interrogation refers to any conduct where the police knew or should have known they might elicit a damaging statement. The issue is whether asking someone if they owned an automobile might elicit an incriminating statement. The prosecution will argue that it is legal to own an automobile and that an affirmative or negative answer to this question would not per se tend to incriminate a suspect. Because the mere fact of ownership of an automobile is not incriminating, the prosecution will prevail.

Conclusion: Miranda does not apply because although Deft was in custody, the question asked of her does not rise to the level of an interrogation because it was unlikely to elicit an incriminating statement.

Call 3 – The Handgun

The government agents searched Deft's car without her consent and without a warrant. As indicated, warrantless searches are per se unreasonable absent an exception. The issue is whether the agents had a valid exception for the search.

Exception: Search Incident to Lawful Arrest (SILA)

The police are allowed to conduct limited searches if they are incident to a lawful arrest. As indicated above, Able's reaching into the briefcase probably exceeded the limits of the search and frisk exception. If so, the discovery of the cocaine was illegal. Because the cocaine was the basis for the arrest, under this scenario the arrest was not lawful and this exception will not apply.

Even assuming it did apply, such searches must be contemporaneous with the arrest and within the wingspan of the police. The purpose of the wingspan requirement is to allow the police to discover weapons that might be used against them. Under the rule in Belton, police can also search anything in a car including containers (but not the trunk) under the SILA exception.

Here, the police appear to be exceeding the constitutional limits allowed by the Supreme Court under the Belton case. Deft was not in her car when she was arrested, and the police had nothing to fear from the possible contents of her car. In fact, the car was parked away from the arrest scene. The agents may argue that there was a man in the car, and that they had probable cause to suspect drugs or contraband. This could have created an <u>exigent</u> circumstance. However, the police had no basis at all to suspect the man in the car, and Deft was in custody. They should have requested a search warrant.

Conclusion: Even if the arrest was lawful, the police exceeded the constitutional limits of the SILA exception when they searched the car. Further, it is doubtful that an argument based on exigent circumstances will work.

Exception: Automobile Exception

Under this exception, if the police have probable cause, they can search a car including the trunk. They can also open any package that can reasonably contain the suspected item for which probable cause exists.

The issue is did the police have probable cause based on lawfully obtained evidence not considering the drugs, which as indicated, may have been unlawfully obtained. The agents here had reasonable suspicion from a constitutional wiretap. Their surveillance added to this suspicion because Deft engaged in evasive action. It was also apparent that Deft was aware of the surveillance, which further added to their suspicion because an innocent citizen is unlikely to be alert to or aware of professional surveillance. Under these facts, it is likely that a detached magistrate would have found probable cause to issue a warrant to search for narcotics, weapons, and large amounts of cash. Therefore, the agents had sufficient probable cause to search under the dashboard and the evidence of a loaded gun was legally obtained.

Conclusion: The handgun is admissible under the automobile exception.

JULY 1997 CALIFORNIA BAR EXAM -- QUESTION 6

1-HOUR ESSAY

Don arrived home at night and found Vic assaulting Don's wife. Vic escaped before Don could apprehend him. Convinced that the legal system would never bring Vic to justice, Don spent three months searching for Vic so that he could take care of the matter himself.

Alex, whom Don did not know, had his own reasons for wanting Vic dead. Alex heard of Don's desire to locate and retaliate against Vic. Hoping that Don would kill Vic, Alex sent Don an anonymous note giving Vic's location. Don, taking a pistol with him, found Vic where the note said he would be. After a heated argument in which Don accused Vic of attempting to rape his wife and Vic denied the accusation, Don shot Vic in the head.

Vic was rushed to a hospital where he was preliminarily diagnosed as "brain dead" and placed on life support systems for three days during which follow-up studies confirmed the permanent cessation of all brain function. A hospital physician then disconnected the life support systems which had kept Vic's heart and respiratory systems functioning, and Vic was pronounced dead.

Don and Alex were both charged with murder. Evidence of the above facts was admitted at trial. The prosecutor argued that the murder was willful, deliberate, and premeditated and that it was committed during the commission of felonies of assault with a deadly weapon and burglary. Alex was alleged to have aided and abetted Don. The court instructed the jury on aiding and abetting and on premeditated murder, felony murder, burglary, and assault with a deadly weapon, but ruled that there was no evidence to warrant instructions on manslaughter. The jury convicted both Don and Alex of first degree murder. Both have appealed.

1. How should the appellate court rule on Don's arguments that:

   a. The uncontradicted evidence established that the hospital physician, not Don, killed Vic? Discuss. *Incorrect*

   b. The court erred in instructing on murder in the commission of a felony? Discuss. *Incorrect*

   c. The court should have instructed on manslaughter? Discuss. *Correct*

2. How should the appellate court rule on Alex's arguments that:

   a. The evidence is insufficient to support his conviction as an aider and abettor? Discuss. *Letter*

   b. The evidence is insufficient to support his conviction of first degree murder even if it does support a finding that he aided and abetted Don? Discuss.

Question 6 -- JULY 1997 California Bar Exam
Written by Jennifer Saccuzzo, Esq. & Professor Dennis P. Saccuzzo

I.   **DON'S ARGUMENTS:**

A. Vic's Death

Don (D), who was convicted of the first degree murder of Vic (V), is now arguing on appeal that the hospital physician, not he, killed V. D's argument is based upon uncontradicted evidence that a hospital physician disconnected life support systems which had kept V's heart and respiratory systems functioning after V had been admitted to the hospital and diagnosed as "brain dead." V was admitted to the hospital because D shot V in the head.

A **homicide** is defined as the killing of a human being by another. Vic has been killed. Don shot him, causing him to become brain dead. The physician then disconnected his life support system. Thus, whether caused by Don or the physician, a homicide has occurred. To prove a murder requires the mens rea of malice. **Malice** may be shown by the 1) defendant's intent to kill, 2) the defendant's intent to inflict serious bodily harm upon another, 3) reckless indifference for human life, or 4) can be proven through the felony murder rule. Furthermore, a defendant must be both the **actual and proximate (legal) cause** of another's death in order to be convicted of murder.

Here D was both the actual and proximate cause of V's death as follows: But for D shooting V in the head, V would not have been admitted to the hospital, later diagnosed as being "brain dead," and then have life support systems disconnected by the treating physician. Additionally, it is forseeable that a physician would disconnect life support systems of an individual diagnosed as "brain dead." By shooting V in the head, D was the <u>substantial factor</u> in V's death. In fact, had the physician been negligent in treating V's injuries, later resulting in V's death, D would still be liable for V's murder.

Moreover, while at common law "death" was considered the cessation of heart and respiratory functions, modern courts define "death" as the permanent cessation of brain activity. As such, because V was diagnosed as "brain dead" upon admission to the hospital, the physician's actions of cutting of life support equipment had no true bearing upon V's death since V was already legally dead prior to the physician's actions. Thus, for the foregoing reasons the appellate court should rule against D if malice can be found.

Don appears to have the intent to kill Vic. He searched for Vic for 3 months to "take care of the matter himself." Once Don became aware of Vic's location, he took a pistol with him to that location. Don subsequently shot Vic in the head. Even if a jury does not believe that Don had intent to kill, Don at least had intent to do serious bodily injury because shooting someone in the head with a gun is substantially certain to cause such injury. Further, in bringing a gun to Vic's house, Don acted with reckless disregard for the consequences of his actions. Thus, Don demonstrated at least three types of malice. The next issue is whether malice can also be found under the felony murder rule.

B. Felony Murder

D is also arguing on appeal that the court erred in instructing the jury on murder in the commission of a felony. The felony murder rule dictates that a defendant may be convicted of first degree murder if a homicide results during the defendant's commission or attempted commission of an inherently dangerous felony. Inherently dangerous felonies include burglary, arson, rape, robbery, mayhem, kidnapping, sodomy, and sexual molestation.

Here the prosecutor argued that D committed murder during the commission of the felonies of assault with a deadly weapon and burglary. However, the underlying felony used for conviction under the felony murder rule must be independent of the actual killing. Therefore, D's felony of assault with a deadly weapon prior to shooting V in the head could not be used as the felony to convict D under the felony murder rule. To do so would frustrate the purpose of the felony murder rule since the assault was essentially a lesser included offense of D's actions of shooting V.

As for the prosecution's argument that D committed murder during the commission of burglary, such a felony would be an appropriate predicate for felony murder. However, the facts give no indication that a burglary by D actually took place. Common law **burglary** is defined as the breaking and entering of a dwelling of another at nighttime with the intent to commit a felony therein. Many modern courts have eliminated the nighttime element of the crime. Nonetheless, there is no evidence in the facts of D unlawfully breaking and entering into a dwelling or any other structure. If the defendant cannot be found guilty for the underlying felony, then felony murder rule cannot be used to convict the defendant. As such, the lower court's instruction on the felony murder rule should be ruled as an error by the appellate court if there are no facts to support a conviction for burglary.

C. Manslaughter

Finally, D is appealing his first degree murder conviction because the lower court ruled that there was no evidence to warrant jury instructions on manslaughter. Murder may be mitigated to **voluntary manslaughter** if the defendant can prove one of the following: 1) the homicide was committed during the heat of passion, 2) the defendant has an imperfect defense of self, 3) the defendant was mistaken in his/her justification for the homicide, or 4) the defendant has diminished capacity. **Involuntary manslaughter** won't work here because as discussed above, malice can be shown. Involuntary manslaughter applies only where no malice is found.

In D's case, the only facts which allude to a possible manslaughter charge over a murder charge are those facts raising the issue of **heat of passion**. In order for a defendant to claim that a homicide was committed in the heat of passion, the defendant must prove that he/she was **provoked** to commit the homicide, that a reasonable person would likewise have been provoked, that there was insufficient time for a reasonable person's passions to cool prior to committing the homicide, and that the defendant did not actually cool off prior to committing the homicide. Words alone do not rise to the level of reasonable provocation and therefore by itself D's heated argument with V would fail to satisfy the provocation element.

D may also attempt to argue that he was provoked to kill V because he had found V assaulting D's wife. However, D witnessed this action three months prior to killing V and such time would be a sufficient **cooling off period** for a reasonable person. Thus, the court properly ruled that there was no evidence to warrant instructions on manslaughter.

II.   ALEX'S ARGUMENTS:

A. Aider and Abettor

Alex (A) was also charged and convicted with the murder of V for aiding and abetting D. On appeal A is arguing that the evidence is insufficient to support his conviction as an aider and abettor.

Aiding and abetting is a crime in which the aider and abettor aids or encourages another to commit the crime with the intent that the crime be committed. Liability for aiding and abetting is found in accomplice liability. **Accomplice liability** requires active aiding and intent. Mere knowledge of the crime and/or mere presence at the crime scene is not enough to be convicted as an accomplice. Accomplices are liable for the crime itself as well as all forseeable crimes.

According to the facts, A wanted V dead. Although A did not know D, A had heard of D's desire to locate and retaliate against V, so A sent D an anonymous note providing D with V's location in hopes that D would kill V. Such an action demonstrates A's desire and intent to help D carry out a crime. Moreover, D had been searching for three months for V, so A's information actively aided and encouraged D to kill V by readily providing V's location.

Because D did in fact kill V after D located V where A's note said V would be, A was properly convicted as an accomplice to murder and the appellate court should rule against A.

B. First Degree Murder

Finally, A is arguing that even if the evidence supports a finding that he aided and abetted D, the evidence is insufficient to support his conviction of first degree murder. As discussed above, **accomplices to a crime are liable for the crime itself as well as all forseeable crimes**. The issue is whether D committed first degree murder.

As indicated, first degree murder cannot be found through the felony murder rule. To find D guilty of first degree murder the prosecution must show that the murder was premeditated, or that it involved poison, bomb, torture, or ambush.

Other than felony murder, the only theory that would apply is premeditation. As indicated, facts showed that Don searched for Vic for three months. When he located Don with the help of Alex, he brought a gun. Voluntary manslaughter does not apply, despite the heated argument (as discussed above). Don had a motive (that Vic had assaulted his wife), was seeking revenge, and shot Vic in the head. As indicated, he was both the actual and proximate cause of Vic's death. Therefore, there were sufficient facts to show premeditation.

Because Alex can be held liable only for the crime Don committed with his aid, Alex cannot be held liable for first degree murder unless there was a finding that Don's killing of Vic was premeditated. Although this certainly seems to be the case, the facts do not explicitly state that the first degree murder conviction was based on a finding of premeditation rather than felony murder. If it was not, Alex's conviction will probably have to be lowered to second degree murder. Don's malice easily supports second degree murder.

1-HOUR ESSAY

Dan owns and operates a service which uses bicycle messengers to deliver small packages. Dan also deals in heroin. Some packages delivered by his service contain heroin that Dan has sold to the recipients.

Dan currently employs three messengers, Al, Bill and Craig.

Al has worked for Dan for several months. He has never discussed the heroin sales with Dan, but has covertly inspected some packages and knows that many of them contain heroin. Dan suspects that Al is aware of the heroin and to keep him loyal pays him substantially more than standard messenger wages.

Bill does not know that the packages contain heroin. He suspects that they do, but is indifferent to the content of the packages he delivers. Dan pays Bill standard messenger wages.

Craig is newly hired and does not suspect any illegality. He is also paid the standard messenger wages.

Eventually, worried about his involvement, Bill took a suspicious package to Lex, his family lawyer. Bill did not examine the contents. Instead, he gave the package to Lex and asked Lex to do so. Lex found heroin in the package and resealed it. Without telling Bill what was in the package, Lex gave it back to Bill stating only: "What you don't know can't hurt you."

Dan's scheme was discovered when Craig had an accident and a package containing heroin broke open. Dan, Al, Bill and Craig have been charged with sales and transportation of heroin and conspiracy to transport heroin.

1. As to which, if any, of the defendants would the above facts support conviction of the charged offenses, and on what theory or theories? Discuss.

2. Has Lex violated any rules of professional conduct? Discuss.

CRIMINAL LAW/PROFESSIONAL RESPONSIBILITY

July 1996 California Bar – Question 3

Model Answer Written by Professor Dennis P. Saccuzzo

CALL 1 – Dan, Al, Bill, and Craig have been charged with sales and transportation of heroin and conspiracy to transport heroin. The issue is whether the facts support a conviction of the charged offenses for any of the defendants.

Sale and Transportation of Heroin

This is not a common law crime. However, all crimes require a voluntary act or omission (actus reus), a mental state (mens rea), and concurrence of the actus reus and mens rea. Arguably, all four defendants committed the actus reus of the crime (sales and transportation of heroin). Dan deals in heroin and causes packages of heroin to be delivered by his three messengers. Al, Bob, and Craig deliver packages of heroin that presumably are sold to Dan's customers. The real issue is what is the mens rea required for conviction and whether any of the defendants had that mens rea in concurrence with their voluntary acts that constituted the crime.

Dan – Transportation and Sales

Dan willfully, purposefully and intentionally engaged in the actus reus of the crime. He dealt in heroin. He sold heroin through packages delivered by 3 men who he hired, supervised, and paid. His mens rea is specific intent, meaning that he intended to do the prohibited action of the crime. Under the Model Penal Code his mens rea was acting purposefully, that is purposefully doing the act. There was a concurrence between Dan's transportation and sales of heroin and his mental state. Dan would be guilty as charged regardless of the mental state required of this crime.

Dan – Conspiracy

Conspiracy is an agreement between 2 or more people to commit an unlawful act. The agreement need not be expressed; it can be implied. At common law conspiracy required (1) an agreement; (2) intent to agree; and (3) intent to achieve the unlawful purpose. Today, the federal courts and a majority of states require an <u>overt act</u> in furtherance of the conspiracy by one of the co-conspirators.

As discussed, Dan intended to achieve the unlawful purpose of selling and transporting heroin, meeting the third element. He also engaged in many overt acts including hiring 3 messengers and causing heroin to be transported. The issue is whether Dan made an agreement with any of the other 3 defendants. If such an agreement can be found, each of the co-conspirators will be liable for all crimes of the other co-conspirators that are foreseeable and in furtherance of the conspiracy.

Al and Dan – Conspiracy

The issue is whether Al impliedly agreed and intended to agree with Dan. Al covertly inspected some of the packages and knew they contained heroin. Nevertheless, he continued to work for Dan, and has worked for several months. Suspecting that Al is aware that he is more than a messenger, Dan pays Al substantially more than the standard messenger wages. Al accepts the money, apparently without question. Given that Al is fully aware of his actions, and benefits from his activities, he has impliedly agreed with Dan. His intent is shown by his continued work and the extra pay he receives and accepts. Thus, Dan and Al have an implied agreement and both meet the elements of conspiracy.

Al – Transportation and Sales

As indicated, a co-conspirator is liable for all crimes by other co-conspirators that are foreseeable and in furtherance of the conspiracy. Because Al's co-conspirator, Dan, has committed the crime of transportation and sales, liability will attach to Al as well under a conspiracy theory. In addition, Al will probably be held liable as a principal.

General intent is the next level of mens rea. It requires only the intent to commit the actus reus. There is little doubt that Al intended to deliver the heroin, given that he knew the packages contained heroin and yet he continued to deliver them and receive his extra pay. Under the Model Penal Code, Al easily meets the knowing standard, acting with awareness of the nature of his conduct. Unless this is a specific intent crime and the prosecutor cannot convince the jury of Al's specific intent, Al will be convicted as a principal.

Bill – Conspiracy

Bill doesn't know the packages contain heroin. He receives the standard messenger wages. Although he may be reckless or negligent as discussed below, there are no clear facts indicating an agreement or intent to agree. Thus, he will not be liable for conspiracy.

Bill – Transportation and Sales

Recklessness involves a conscious disregard for the nature of one's conduct. Although Bill may not have specific or general intent, his conduct does meet a recklessness standard.

The facts show that bill suspected the packages contained heroin but that he was indifferent to the content of the packages. He consciously disregarded the risk of delivering what was likely heroin.

If Bill cannot be found reckless, he certainly acted negligently, which means he should have been aware of a substantial and unjustified risk. In addition to all of the above facts concerning his suspiciousness and indifference, Bill's lawyer said "what you don't know won't hurt you." A reasonable person in Bill's shoes should certainly have known at this point that something was wrong, despite his unethical and incompetent attorney (discussed below).

Conclusion: Bill is probably liable if the mens rea is reckless and certainly liable under a negligence standard.

Craig – Conspiracy

Craig does not suspect any illegality and is newly hired. There are no facts indicating an agreement. He cannot be convicted of conspiracy under the facts as presented.

Craig – Transportation and Sales

The only possible way liability can be found would be if this were strict liability crime, which means Craig could be found guilty merely for engaging in the actus reus of the crime by unknowingly delivering the packages. It is unlikely that there would be a constitutionally valid law that would convict Craig for his acts. With only a few exceptions such as statutory rape and regulatory actions, the law requires a "guilty mind"or some criminal culpability. There is none here and Craig will not be convicted of a crime.

(2) Has Lex violated any rule of professional conduct?

Competence

An attorney has a duty to be reasonably competent. Lex did not act competently.

When Bill asked Lex to examine a package that Bill suspected was heroin, Lex should have immediately informed Bill that if the package did contain the suspected heroin, Lex himself would be in a conflict. Lex has a duty as an officer of the court to obey the law (and possession of heroin is against the law). Further, as discussed below, Lex may be required to turn the contraband over to the police. In this case, it is possible that the court would find that the evidence is not protected by privilege, and compel Lex to reveal its source.

A competent attorney would have advised Bill of his potential legal liabilities if the package did contain heroin, and would have made sure that Bill was fully informed of his rights and options (such as turning the unopened package over to the police).

In addition, advising Bill that "what you don't know can't hurt you" is not only incompetent, it is gross negligence and probable illegal because Lex is impliedly aiding Dan (and Bill) to violate the law by delivering the heroin to a customer.

Scope

A lawyer shall not assist criminal or fraudulent conduct. By re-sealing the package and not properly advising Bill of his potential criminal liability for transporting heroin, Lex effectively assisted Bill in commission of a crime, as discussed below.

In California, the rules of conduct explicitly state that a lawyer shall not advise the violation of any law. Here Lex tacitly advised Bill to deliver the package in violation of the law.

Communication

Lex has a duty to keep his client reasonably informed. By not properly counseling Bill about his possible criminal liabilities and legal options, Lex failed in this duty.

Confidentiality and Conflict of Duties

With only a few exceptions that do not apply to the present facts, an attorney shall not reveal a matter relating to representation. After he opened the package, Lex had a duty to maintain confidentiality. This duty conflicts directly with Len's duty as an officer of the court to <u>obey the law</u>.

When Lex opened the package, he knowingly was in possession of heroin. Although attorneys certainly have a right and responsibility to investigate physical evidence of a crime, here the knowing possession of such evidence is probably a crime itself. After his investigation, Lex would have to turn the evidence over to the police.

Attorney-Client Privilege

The issue is whether the evidence would be protected by the attorney-client privilege. It is not actually clear from these facts that it would, so Lex may have subjected himself to a situation where he must violate his duty of confidentiality if ordered by a court to reveal the source of the heroin. This is because the California Evidence Code exempts use of an attorney's services to perpetrate a crime from the privilege.

In sum, Lex is in considerable trouble no matter what he does. His first mistake was opening the package. However, to advise his client that what you don't know can't hurt is not only grossly incompetent and highly unprofessional, but it also subjects Lex to prosecution as an accomplice or even as a co-conspirator.

Notes

Notes

Notes

Notes

Notes

Notes

Notes

Notes

Notes